gain, a sense of power, national security, or just plain fun—but the pleasure of the hoax is important.

THE PLEASURES OF DECEPTION chronicles dozens of astonishing and often hilarious hoaxes, many of them little-known or forgotten, and the careers of famous hoaxers—including R. V. Jones, a scientist who turned his pursuit of fun to important practical uses, and Horace de Vere Cole, the "prince of practical jokers," whose true story is told here for the first time. Mr. Moss tells of media hoaxes; he sheds new light on literary hoaxes from Shakespeare frauds to Clifford Irving, and on swindlers and imposters, including the famous "Tichborne Claimant." He ranges over scientific hoaxes like the Piltdown man, and tells for the first time some of the deceptions employed in World War II. It's enlightening, it's funny, and it's all true. No fooling.

Norman Moss is a British writer and journalist who received much of his education in the United States. His articles have appeared in newspapers and magazines on both sides of the Atlantic. He is the author of *Men Who Play God: The Story of the Hydrogen Bomb*, and *What's the Difference?*—a British-American / American-British dictionary. Mr. Moss lives in London with his wife, the actress Hilary Sesta, and two sons.

THE PLEASURES OF DECEPTION

THE PLEASURES OF DECEPTION

By

NORMAN MOSS

'For the deceiving of the senses is
one of the pleasures of the senses.'
FRANCIS BACON
The Advancement of Learning

READER'S DIGEST PRESS
distributed by
Thomas Y. Crowell Company
New York, 1977

Printed in the United States of America.
LC# 77-131

LIBRARY OF CONGRESS CATALOGING IN PUBLICATION DATA

Moss, Norman.
    The pleasures of deception.

    Bibliography: p.
    Includes index.
    1. Impostors and imposture--Biography. I. Ti-
tle.
CT9980.M6   920'.02   77-131

ISBN 0-88349-131-1

10   9   8   7   6   5   4   3   2   1

2818769

Contents

Introduction

A HOAX is a kind of lie, albeit a white and a light-hearted one. It is a lie that is manufactured rather than told. The structure that is manufactured sustains a fiction which could not stand as an unsupported statement. Like: 'I've found a hitherto undiscovered play by William Shakespeare'; 'My friend here is the Emperor of Ethiopia'; 'The D-Day landing was only a feint and not the main attack'; 'Stalin was my Uncle Joe'; 'I represent the Bank of Portugal' (the man who pulled off this one actually *got* a license to print money).

The hoaxer is an artist, in the sense in which Freud used the term when he said that an artist is a dreamer who is in control of his dreams. He invents a world, and persuades other people to live in it. It differs from the real world in that it contains some of the hoaxer's fictitious creations: a chair that will not be there when the person sits down, or a sum of money that will not be in the bank when he goes to collect it.

Francis Bacon thought that deception was fun. But when he said so, in his famous essay 350 years ago, he was not recommending it. In fact, he was issuing a warning against wasting time on what he called 'the arts of pleasure sensual', or at another point, even more alluringly, 'the arts voluptuary'. It was here that he included hoaxing: 'With arts voluptuary, I couple practises jocularly, for the deceiving of the senses is one of the pleasures of the senses.'

Deception tests the means by which we perceive reality, and it reminds us sharply of what these means are. We have our sense organs which receive data, principally ones affixed to our head – eyes, ears, nose. But this data is given shape and meaning by the thing inside our skull, the brain. This has only second-hand evidence of what is real out *there*.

Deception must seem particularly frivolous for the scientist because *per*ception, working out just what is there, is his vocation. It may also tempt him for just this reason. Like the playful punch for the athlete, it makes fun of the faculties that he prizes most. But we are all using these faculties and perceiving things at every waking moment. Anyone who has been involved in a practical joke on either the delivering end or the receiving end knows something of the pleasures.

It is important to note that for the person who is fooled the fun, if any, lies in the process of being fooled, not the consequences. A deceived spouse cannot be relied on to react with a chortle of glee, and the editors of McGraw-Hill did not go around chuckling after they found that Clifford Irving had hoaxed them into parting with most of a million dollars. For deception is not practised only for fun. It is also practised to steal money, fame or the love of women, to win battles and sink ships, to demoralize populations and overthrow governments.

In all these different kinds of deceptions, certain questions arise often.

One is the motivation of the hoaxer. These are usually mixed, and are not only the obvious ones. Persuading other people to enter his world must give the hoaxer a sense of power, although this may be buried in his unconscious. He is making things happen. At its crudest and nastiest, the man who telephones a hoax bomb warning can watch people pouring out of a building and get a certain amount of satisfaction out of knowing that he was responsible. He is likely to be a man with very little power to make things happen in the normal run of things. In a more subtle hoax, and a less anti-social one, the perpetrator has the pleasure of manipulating people and their perceptions, of knowing that they are following his wishes rather than their own, that he knows more about their situation at the moment than they know themselves.

This desire for power over others lies somewhere at the back of most deceptions. Whatever the end in view, the impulse to deceive helps to determine the means chosen. The aim may be just to have some fun, but the practical joker is usually a different kind of humourist from the person who tells jokes. If the aim is to part someone from his money, it is this predilection that will make a person a confidence trickster rather than a burglar. Sometimes, the presence of mixed motives is obvious. Stanley Weyman, a con man of awesome gall, took great risks in using his own name when he carried out his impostures, because he wanted people to know who had conned them so brilliantly.

Professor R. V. Jones switched from fooling his fellow-scientists for fun to fooling the German war machine without breaking his stride, and he enjoyed the one as much as the other. Some of the actor E. A. Sothern's finest and funniest performances were off-stage.

I once met a former confidence trickster who was so proud of his exploits that, now that he was leading a relatively honest life, he wanted me to ghost-write his autobiography for him. I was curious, and talked to him about it a few times. I soon found that I could not believe anything he told me about himself. Apparently, he created fantasies compulsively. When he was a con man, he had put them to work to earn him money. Now that he was no longer constrained by this purpose, he was not putting much effort into making them credible, but was letting his imagination run wild. (Other people were evidently less critical; I saw him later in a television documentary about criminals, re-enacting with professional actors as a true case one of the more improbable stories he had told me. He was having a whale of a time).

Another question that is raised sometimes is the dividing line between the invented world of the hoaxer and the true world. This is sometimes blurred, and cannot be relied upon to stay put. When an imposter plays a role, and continues to play it for years, at what point does he become something of the person he has pretended to be? After all, we all 'put on a face to meet the faces that we meet'. What is one's identity anyway? If a hoaxer dreams up an absurd society and asks people to join it, and they *do* join it, then at what point does the society cease to be a hoax?

A question that is raised constantly is why and how we are fooled. Some of the answers are usually clear when the whole story is told, and they are many.

We can be fooled simply because our perceptions are dulled by habit, and we look at things through half-closed eyes. We see half of a familiar picture, and assume that the rest is there. We accept it just because we read it in the newspaper, or see it on television. Sometimes, we accept a thing as true because it is something we want to be true: that there is a genuine scheme to get rich quick, or to help win the war. We are fooled, sometimes, because we give way to social pressures, rather than trusting our own powers. Professor Stanley Milligram, a Yale University psychologist, conducted some experiments that demonstrate the frequency of this. In one, under the pretext of testing visual perceptions, he showed a card containing three lines to four people, and asked them which they thought was the longest. The first three people were plants, and well-rehearsed; they chose a line that was manifestly the wrong one. Half the time, the fourth person followed the others rather than his own senses and chose the wrong one also. In another experiment, two psychologists, Gardner and Lois Murphy, passed a foreign coin around a class of young teenagers and, an hour later, asked them to draw the coin showing where the hole in it was. The coin had no hole. All but four of them drew a coin with a hole in it somewhere. The Murphys then talked three of these four into agreeing that it did have a hole and their memory was faulty. Only one held out. (The teacher said later that he was the worst-behaved member of the class.)

We are fooled also, very often, because we find it difficult to check back on our own assumptions, and this is because we find it difficult to locate them. Time and time again in looking at hoaxes, we find that people have accepted the most unlikely things because to question them would be to question something they have already accepted as true.

Most people have the experience of being deceived from time to time. Everyday life provides a lot of instances, with people manufacturing evidence and spreading false trails. The wife invents a bogus friend for coffee afternoons so that she can have an affair. The homosexual acts hetero. The businessman maintains the picture of a business that is prosperous and stable, whereas actually it is ailing and precarious.

I am concerned in this book with people deceiving people, and not very much with deceptions that consist only of *things*, whether jewelry or works of art. These add very little to our understanding of the process of deception, though they may shed a lot of light on our values and our criteria of appreciation. Manufacturing an ancient Cretan artifact, a 16th Century painting or a 100-dollar bill is a technical exercise, and is more akin to spoofing a radar scanner with a decoy than to working on someone else's mind to create a false impression.

This book recounts deceptions that are perpetrated for different reasons and by different means. There are here hoaxers who are ingenious schemers, others who are gifted actors, and still others who are gifted authors. There are comedians and swindlers. There are hoaxers of colossal nerve who deceive face to face, and others, perhaps more shy, who do so at vast distances, and even across the years. There is a scientist who carried out practical jokes, and serious deceptions, and then theorized about it. He will come first, because his ideas may illuminate occasionally some of what follows. It is all true. No fooling.

CHAPTER 1

A Hoaxer for all Seasons: R. V. Jones

> But now one Mr. Jones
> Comes forth and depones
> RICHARD BARHAM, *The Ingoldsby Legends*

ONE evening a good many years ago, Gerald Touch, later to become a leading British Government scientist but then a young research student at Oxford University, was visiting an elder colleague in his home when the telephone rang. Touch was alert for the sound, and waited to see what would happen. Earlier in the day, he had been having a discussion with another young research graduate, a physicist, who claimed that it was possible to persuade a highly intelligent scholar to do the most outlandish things simply by talking to him on the telephone. When Touch questioned this, the young man, whose name was Reginald Jones, promised to demonstrate it to him that evening.

Touch's host answered the telephone, looked puzzled for a moment, and then hung up.

'Who was it?' asked Touch.

'Don't know,' was the answer. 'Nobody at the other end.'

It was Jones, who hung up as soon as the telephone was answered. He rang again several times, and each time he hung up. Then, a little while later, he telephoned him again and pretended to be a telephone engineer. He said they had had a report that something was wrong with this telephone. The scholar said something did seem to be wrong, since people had been trying to get through to him without success.

'Hmm, I see,' said engineer Jones. 'We'll send somebody around to look at it in a week or so.'

'A *week*?' repeated the scholar. 'Can't you do better than that?'

'Afraid not. We're short-staffed. People off ill.'

'But can't you do *anything*? I don't want to be without a telephone for a week.'

'Don't see how. . . . I'll tell you what, though. It may just be a leak to earth. In that case, we could fix it from here. It might be possible to find out whether it is, if you'd like to cooperate.'

'Oh yes, please. What can I do?'

'Well first, tap the telephone with something. A fountain pen, say, and let me hear the sound. . . . That's right. . . . Hmm, can't tell. What kind of shoes are you wearing? Rubber heels? Ah yes, well, that's it. You'll have to take your shoes off if you don't mind.'

So the highly intelligent scholar stood in his socks tapping the telephone with a fountain pen, with Touch enjoying the spectacle. Leading him on step by step, Jones had him perform a number of undignified manoeuvres, including standing on one leg and striking the instrument with a rubber ring.

Then Jones said, 'I'm afraid I still can't tell. There's only one thing more to do–well, no, I think we'd better leave it until we can get our own man around.'

The scholar was hooked now. 'Oh no, please!' he said. 'If there's anything else I can do, I'd like to try it.'

'Well, all right then. It's a crude approximation of a test we do with our own equipment. You have to get a bucker of water, and lower the telephone into it, slowly.'

The victim rushed off to get a bucket of water. When he returned, Touch decided that the joke had gone far enough, and that the telephone would be damaged if he went through with the rest. He was almost incoherent with laughter, but he gasped out his objections, and tried to wrest the instrument away.

The other fought him off, and said down the phone, 'I'm terribly sorry, but there's a young friend here who's trying to stop me. I think he's a bit drunk. He says it'll damage the phone if I put it in the water.'

'Who is he?' Jones demanded.

'He's a young physicist.'

'Physicists! They're the bane of our life here in Oxford. They *always* think they know about telephones, and they're *always* wrong.'

So the highly intelligent scholar persevered, and gently lowered the telephone into the bucket. Forty years later, Touch still chuckles with pleasure when he recalls the spectacle.

Professor R. V. Jones, as the prankster now is, went on to play other practical jokes, that earned him a reputation in British scientific circles. But that was only the beginning. Using the same techniques, he hoaxed the Nazi war machine into sending hundreds of bombers to the wrong place night after night at a crucial point in the Battle of Britain, and into dissipating their strength in other ways. Later still, he published a paper, which he first delivered as a lecture to the Institute of Physics in London, called *The Theory of Practical Joking: Its Relevance to Physics.*

The telephone joke that Touch witnessed remains one of his favourites, and it finds an important place in his paper:

'With some hoaxes, the period of induction of the victim may be extended. In this type, which is probably the most interesting philosophically, the object is to build up in the victim's mind a false world-picture which is temporarily consistent by any tests that he can apply to it, so that he ultimately takes action on it with confidence. The falseness of the picture is then starkly revealed by the incongruity which his action precipitates. It has not proved difficult, for example, to persuade a Doctor of Philosophy to lower his telephone carefully into a bucket of water in the belief that he was cooperating with the engineer in the telephone exchange in finding a leak to earth. The prior induction consisted of building up in his mind a picture of something wrong with his telephone.'

Jones is today the Professor of Physics at Aberdeen University, Scotland, and a member of many governmental committees on subjects ranging from the history of science to safety in mines. In recent years, he has performed some considerable feats in experimental physics, and has also lectured at C.I.A. headquarters in Langley, Virginia, on hoaxing and deception, a subject that is very much his own.

He is an entertaining, courteous man, considerate and punctiliously polite in the way of an engagingly well-behaved schoolboy. He has something of a schoolboy's clean looks about him, with pale blue eyes and rosy cheeks above a tall, bulky frame. He has a placid family life, with a wife who travels with him and often attends his lectures, and three grown children. He is the kind of Englishman who rarely talks about women or sex: he unbends only in certain directions. But he is quite capable, in one of the more staid and distinguished London clubs, of whipping from his pocket the tiny harmonica that he always carries and playing a few bars to illustrate a point about bagpipe music, either oblivious to the consternation this causes, or else acknowledging it only with an amused twinkle in his eyes.

Most of the strands that make up his life today began at Oxford in the 1930s. He did not shine as an undergraduate; he seemed to need the confidence that academic success and a Fellow's status brought him before he could open up.

Many of his friendships date back to those graduate years. It was then that he began working on defence projects, and also then that he excelled first in the kind of scientific work that has earned him his high reputation, devising new instruments and new methods of experimentation. It was also then that he first developed his talent for practical jokes. He was one of the group of young scientists at the Clarendon Laboratory when its director was Professor Frederick Lindemann, a formidable figure in the British scientific community who later became famous as Lord Cherwell, Sir Winston Churchill's scientific adviser throughout the Second World War.

While Jones was there, he invented a person called Colonel Musselwhite, who used to write letters to *The Times* with his own scientific theories. These letters usually began: 'Sir, It is a common fallacy among scientists that . . .'.

In one, which caused quite a stir, Col. Musselwhite set out to show that, contrary to the popular view, light colours absorb more heat than dark. He said that he had always found a brown suit the most comfortable thing to wear in the heat of a Bengal summer. He pointed out that nature gave dark skins to most animals that live in hot climates, while polar bears are white.

These were still the great years of the Empire, and the readers of *The Times* had a lot of experience to offer of tropical climates. Letters came in for and against the theory. One writer said that he had refuted it by an experiment. He sat in the sun for an hour, wearing first a black police helmet, and then a white topee. He had cut a hole in each, and put a thermometer inside. The thermometer showed that his head was hotter with the black helmet on.

When there was a correspondence about which stars could be seen with the naked eye, Col. Musselwhite outdid everyone else by saying that he could see the fourteen stars of the Pleiades (there are only seven) and the dark companion of Sirius, a star which is sometimes elusive to the most powerful telescopes.

Then he presented his theory about razors. A razor would give a better shave, he said, if it were kept on a north-south axis, so that it would pick up the earth's magnetic charge. Lindemann, dining with the editor of *The Times*, gave the game away, and no more Colonel Musselwhite letters were printed.

Jones was assigned by the junior scientists at the Clarendon Laboratory the task of organizing a disruption of a biennial seminar being held by the Oxford Junior Scientific Society. They felt some disruption was merited since the Society had shut out the Clarendon Laboratory as an institution from the proceedings because, as they saw it, the Clarendon Laboratory had put on a display at the previous seminar that had stolen the show. So Jones simply telephoned the chairman in the middle of a meeting in the guise of the boiler-room mechanic, and told him in urgent tones that there was a pressure-block in the steam pipes and a number of other serious faults, which he spelled out in detail, and the steam radiators were liable to blow up. The chairman passed the news on to the meeting and they hastily evacuated the building. What tickled the Clarendon people was that this collection of distinguished scientists was stampeded by scientific nonsense (there is no such thing as a pressure-block and the radiators could not blow up) just as easily as any other gathering.

Once, in 1938, when the American nuclear physicist Leo Szilard, who was to help initiate the atomic bomb project, was visiting Oxford, Jones telephoned him and pretended to be the science correspondent of the *Daily Express,* calling from Fleet Street. He said he had a report that Szilard had invented a radioactive death ray. Szilard wanted to know where the report came from and whether he could meet him in London. He got so excited that Jones wondered whether he was on to something.

When a young research graduate called James Tuck arrived at the Clarendon Laboratory, he asked one day whether anyone thought it was possible to supplement his meagre grant by backing horses. Always inventive, Jones told him that the man to see about this was Lindemann. He said Lindemann had worked out a scientific system for backing horses, and spent the first hour of every day studying form and telephoning his bookmaker. He said further that he bet with laboratory funds, and some of the laboratory's current research was financed out of the winnings.

Young Tuck believed this, and Jones sat back with interest to watch Lindemann's reaction when Tuck approached him. But someone else took up the tale and, lacking Jones' sure-footed-ness, over-reached himself. He told him that Lindemann had ploughed some of his winnings back into racing, and had created a race called the Lindemann Stakes. At this point, Tuck realized that he had been fooled.

Then Jones gave him a few other tit-bits of information about his new colleagues. He said that whereas there wasn't really a successful horse-player among them, the brilliant spectroscopist Derek Jackson was a part-time jockey and had once ridden in the Grand National. But this was so patently absurd that Tuck would not swallow it. (It was true. Jackson, at this writing a professor at the *Faculté des Sciences* in Paris, was the son of a wealthy family and a keen and skilful rider. When he was asked once why he took up molecular physics, he said, 'You have to do something in the summer when there's no fox-hunting.')

Jones also told Tuck that, whereas Lindemann may not have made his mark on the turf, he was once, in his wide-ranging career, tennis champion of Sweden. This too was an absurdity, and when Lindemann next came into the common room, Tuck clapped him on the back and said, 'Prof, you know those fools want me to believe that you were the tennis champion of Sweden?'

Lindemann, never the most approachable of men, gave him a frosty look and said, 'As a matter of fact, I was.'

Tuck became a close friend of Jones, though a wary one. It was he who first told Jones that there was a project afoot to build an atomic bomb, at a bus stop in Oxford in 1939. Tuck later went to Los Alamos with the British team that helped to build the bomb, and remained in Los Alamos for the rest of his career.

Jones was, and remains, a staunch patriot, and by 1939 he was already heavily involved in defence work. His involvement began one Saturday morning in 1935.

Jones had recently written a paper on the design and construc-tion of a thermo-pile, a device for detecting small variations in heat, and this had earned him an academic award. On this par-ticular morning he was in bed in his rooms in Oxford suffering miserably from the 'flu; since he is not one to cosset himself, he had tried to cure it with a cold bath, and was now shivering from the effects of this as well. While he was in this state, an American couple appeared at his door. They were Commander Paul McNeil, U.S.N. retired, and his wife. Commander McNeil had invented a device for locating aircraft by the heat of their engines through infrared detection, and he was due to demonstrate it to the R.A.F. the following week. Something had broken down, and he had asked who in England could build him a new thermo-pile. He had been referred to Jones.

Jones said he was in no condition to start work on a new project, but Commander McNeil's enthusiasm was more infectious than Jones's germs, and eventually he stumbled out of bed and agreed to go to work on it. Another factor that may have been prodding him on was that even in 1935, for any intelligent, reasonably alert citizen of the United Kingdom, the subject of how to detect approaching aircraft was not entirely an academic one.

Jones built the device in the Clarendon Laboratory, and then took part in the demonstration. He then wrote a report to the Air Ministry explaining why the device would not be of much use. The Air Ministry were impressed by the report's honesty. Meanwhile, Lindemann, himself involved in defence thinking through his friendship with Winston Churchill, had seen him working on the machine, and was also impressed with his potential value. Between the two, they persuaded Jones that he could serve his country immediately. He went to work for the Air Ministry in the following year, giving up a much-prized travelling fellowship, though he remained at Oxford for a while; he worked on radar, navigational guidance, and other scientific aspects of air warfare.

Scientists were joining defence projects in Britain in those prewar years with a casualness that now seems almost unbelievable, often doing the work in their spare time in open laboratories, and recruiting friends to help them. When Air Ministry Intelligence wanted to know about a new radio transmitter tower in the Harz Mountains in Germany, Jones simply wrote to an old Oxford chum who was at Berlin University, and he took a train to the spot, hiked up to have a look and sent him a report.

Jones found his new colleagues to be congenial spirits. Once, soon after war broke out, a civil servant came down from White-hall to visit the R.A.F.'s experimental station at Farnborough, 30 miles outside London, where many of the scientists worked, and annoyed them by telling them just how they should go about things. They retaliated by pouring a bagful of soot into his rolled-up umbrella. They prayed for rain before he left, but none came. In fact, the first rain came a few days afterwards, when the civil servant was leaving the cabinet office. He had hurt his arm recently, and he stood on the steps struggling to open his umbrella with one hand. The policeman on duty out-side the cabinet office kindly said, 'Excuse me, sir, let me help you with that.' He opened the umbrella and was showered with soot. The civil servant was so appalled at the thought of what might have been the consequences of this prank that he made a special journey to Farnborough to tell the scientists there what had happened. 'You really mustn't do this sort of thing, chaps,' he said. 'It might not have been a policeman under that umbrella, but the Prime Minister himself!' This was greeted with applause and cheers, and the bureaucrat fled back to Whitehall.

But the work was serious, and the issues sometimes critical. Jones's big moment came in 1940, during the Battle of Britain. He decided that the Germans were using pairs of directional radio beams from the Continent to guide their night bombers to targets in Britain. The bombers would fly along one beam, guided by radio signals, until they encountered the signals from the second beam crossing it, which would tell them that they were over the target. Jones reported his conclusions to Linde-mann, who was already installed as Churchill's adviser. Jones was summoned to 10 Downing Street to present his views to Winston Churchill and his military chiefs. (His reputation being what it was, he assumed that the telephone call was a hoax, and it took a second, more urgent call to get him there.) He was then 28.

Churchill describes the scene in his history, *The Second World War*. 'For twenty minutes or more he spoke in quiet tones, un-rolling his chain of circumstantial evidence, the like of which for its convincing fascination was never surpassed by tales of Sherlock Holmes or Monsieur Lecoq. As I listened, the Ingoldsby Legends jingled in my mind:

But now one Mr. Jones
Comes forth and depones
That, fifteen years hence, he had heard certain groans
On his way to Stone Henge to examine the stones. . . .'*

Churchill ordered a plane with detection equipment to be sent up to the point over Derby where Jones said that the beams could best be located. But the chiefs of the Air Force were unconvinced, and that afternoon they called in the Director of Research at the Marconi firm in Britain, who said that radio beams could not be projected over Britain because of the curvature of the earth. The R.A.F. was not going to take young Jones's word over that of the leading expert in the field, and they said it was a waste of time sending any planes up to look for beams.

The struggle for mastery of the air over Britain was critical, and Jones decided that this was the moment to stake his all. 'I know who ordered those planes up,' he said. 'It was Churchill himself. If that order is cancelled. I'll tell him so.'

He knew that if he turned out to be wrong, his duties for the rest of the war would be something like an office boy's. But, as he says, it all went like a dream. The detector planes went up and they found the beams exactly where he had predicted they would be.

This was where the real fun began. The obvious countermeasure would be to jam the beams. But Jones had a more devilish idea: to duplicate them, and misdirect the Germans. He had a transmitter duplicate one of the two beams, so that the enemy planes were guided off-course.

Again, Winston Churchill tells of the results, with evident satisfaction: 'For the next two months, the critical months of September and October, the German bombers wandered around Britain bombing by guesswork, or else being actually led astray. One instance happened to come to my notice. An officer in my Defence Office sent his wife and young children to the country during the London raids. Ten miles from any town they were much astonished to see a series of enormous explosions occurring three fields away. They counted over a hundred heavy bombs.

---

* *The Ingoldsby Legends,* a 19th century set of poems by Richard Barham, was familiar to every English schoolboy of Churchill's generation.

They wondered what the Germans could be aiming at, and thanked God they were spared. The officer mentioned the incident the next day, but so closely was the secret kept, so narrow was the circle, so highly specialized the information, that no satisfactory explanation could be given to him, even in his intimate position. The very few who knew exchanged celestial grins.'

One of the celestial grins belongs to Jones. The incongruity—to use a key word in his analysis of hoaxing—of the high explosive attack on an empty field must have pleased him even more than that of the undignified antics which he induced over the telephone.

Later, the Germans worked out what was happening and developed a new kind of beam, but Jones and his colleagues deflected this one as well. The 'battle of the beams' played a major part in the Battle of Britain and, later, in the Allied air offensive against Germany.

The principle of all the beam deceptions was the same as that of the telephone joke: control the channel of communication, and use it to give someone a false picture of his situation. Later, Jones was involved in another problem of the same kind: spoofing German defensive radar with metal foil and decoys, and then spoofing the counter-spoof measures. This was similar to the beams battle; the problems of deceiving a machine are the same as those of deceiving a human being.

Occasionally, in the battle of the beams, there was a requirement for pure hoaxing, and then Jones was expected to come up with something. The most important of these involved the G beam, a radar navigational device that was to guide British bombers over Germany. A bomber was shot down over Germany carrying the G beam when it was still in its experimental stage. The Air Ministry were horrified that the Germans would now have the device and know its secrets, and would be able to adopt counter-measures even before it was put into use. So Jones was given the task of deceiving them about the nature of the G beam. He was given *carte blanche*, and he rubbed his hands together at the prospect. 'Imagine,' he says, 'being told to play a joke for your country. And being given unlimited resources to do it.'

He decided that part of the answer was flattery, and he would persuade the Germans that the British had copied the method of twin navigational beams that the Germans had used in bombing Britain.

The first thing he did was to give it a new name, the J beam, to confuse German reports of a G beam. He thought that they would probably listen in on the conversation of the crew of the shot-down bomber, and counted on the similarity between 'G' and 'J' in German to cover the difference. Then he had built three J beam stations in Southern England that actually transmitted navigational beams out over Germany. He also invented a conversation describing the new navigational system between two R.A.F. officers, overheard at the Ritz Bar in London, and had this inserted into the report that a double-agent was feeding back to Germany (see chapter 8). He fed back other misleading items of information.

The Germans were fooled, and they jammed the J beams while not realizing that the bombers were using radar guidance. It was six months before they did find out, and started jamming the radar. *Then*, on Jones' advice, R.A.F. bombers began using the J beams to guide them to their targets and back. The Germans, having once established that the J beams were a hoax, did not bother to jam them any more.

A similar situation developed a year later with the H2S, a new and important target-seeking device which worked by short-wave radio. While it was being tested, a plane carrying it crashed in Holland and it was recovered by the Germans at least partially intact. Again, Jones was given the task of persuading the Germans that it was something completely different.

This was like being Colonel Musselwhite again, and Jones rose to the occasion. He went back to his early days in defence, and dreamed up an infrared detector that could seek out submarines. He fabricated some leaks of information about infrared work, which were fed back to Germany through double-agents. He even produced an infrared 'picture' of a ship taken from the air, and made sure that this fell into German hands. It worked perfectly. The R.A.F. was using the H2S for months before the Germans worked out what it was.

Meanwhile, German scientists got busy. They invented an anti-infrared paint, and started coating their submarines with it. Jones is full of admiration for their ingenuity. 'It's a tragedy that it was wasted,' he says. 'Nobody has ever found a use for anti-infrared paint.'*

Jones enjoyed the war, and he admits it. 'Of course I did! I was being stretched. It was something I'd been preparing for for years. Also, there was an exciting tightness about things then, a sense of urgency, a sense that, as Churchill once said, it was more important to be right than to be polite. And there was the feeling of power. You made decisions and things really got done. I once had all the plans for a 1,000-bomber raid cancelled at the last moment.'

But he had no illusions about the nature of war. He was sensitive to the fact that he was a young and healthy civilian taking hard decisions with other men's lives. He recommended the famous commando raid against the heavy-water plant in Norway that was contributing to the primitive German atomic bomb programme, in which all 30 of the attackers were killed, and then a second one, that was successful. After the war, he was an honoured guest at a reunion in Munich of Luftwaffe scientists and Intelligence men who were his direct opponents in the battles of deceptions. He was having such a good time comparing notes about the tricks they played that an English friend in Munich took him on an outing to visit Dachau, the site of the concentration camp, in case he should forget what all the tricks were about. Jones is glad he did.

Unlike many scientists who worked with the services during the war, he takes to military men. He admires the military virtues and enjoys service lore, and is often a guest at squadron and regimental reunions. Both his daughters are married to army officers. He is proud of his prowess with a pistol and rifle.

He was made a Companion of the British Empire for his wartime services, on Churchill's personal recommendation. The American Government awarded him the Legion of Merit in recognition of his service to the U.S. Navy in locating German coastal radar stations in the months before D-Day.

---

* When I told this story in a magazine article, a few people said I was a victim of one more of Prof. Jones's hoaxes, because such a paint is impossible. But the story is true; Jones once explained how the paint works in a lecture to an audience of physicists, and they accepted it. It is complicated, but powdered glass and black paint are ingredients. A submarine coated with it still reflects infrared waves, but does so in precisely the same way as the surrounding water, and so is indistinguishable.

He left Whitehall for Aberdeen University in 1946. He remained friends with Churchill, and when Churchill became Prime Minister again in 1951, he asked Jones to come back to Whitehall for a year to reorganize scientific intelligence, which he did. He had another spell in Whitehall in 1962–63, heading a committee on air defence in the ICBM age. On his last day before leaving, his class stood up and sang together the old Scottish air 'Will ye no' come back again'. Jones decided that he would.

Though he remains English through and through, he has dug roots in Aberdeen and his three children all went to Aberdeen University. As well as his elegant house in the town, he has a cottage in one of the wilder stretches of the Highlands near a good trout stream. He has become an authority on bagpipe music, and is held in esteem and affection in bagpipe circles; there is a pipe tune called 'Professor Jones'.

He is popular with his students, though less universally so than he was because, though he drinks with them and is tolerant of their pranks, he is very unsympathetic to radical student politics, and is the only department head in the university to refuse to have a student/staff committee in his department.

He pulled together his experiences of practical joking and wartime hoaxes to produce *The Theory of Practical Joking: Its Relevance to Physics*. After its first delivery, this was reprinted in the *Physical Society Yearbook*, and he has since written a slightly expanded version.

He explained in this that he was struck by the number of eminent scientists who enjoyed practical jokes. The connection between the two activities that he discovers is in the concept of the model. The scientist constructs a model from evidence that he has. For instance, he seeks evidence of the nature of the atom, which he can never see, and from this he constructs a model of the atom. He then tests it for consistency with what he already knows, and takes action on the assumption that it is accurate.

In a hoax, the evidence upon which a person bases his picture of the world is tampered with, so that he acts with confidence on a false picture; this is the false world-picture. Some incongruity results, hopefully a comical one. He elaborates on this: 'Indeed incongruities mutual to two victims are possible. Each victim is led to believe in a false world-picture which is nevertheless consistent with and complementary to the false world-picture of the other victim. A simple example is the device of privately telling each of two people whom one is about to introduce that the other is a good fellow who has, however, been going through a severe nervous strain, and who is therefore apt to get both irritable and rude if contradicted. It is therefore advisable to humour him by agreeing with all that he says. The two victims then go to great lengths to agree with one another, and separate in the conviction that each has handled the other extremely well.'

One way of giving someone a false world-picture is by controlling the channel of communication by which he is getting his picture. 'The ease of detecting counterfeits is much greater when different channels of examination are used simultaneously. This is why telephonic hoaxes are so easy—there is no accompanying visual appearance to be counterfeited. Metal strips were most effective when only radar, and that of one frequency, was employed.'

So are we hoaxed because we believe the evidence of our senses? It appears from Professor Jones that it is rather because we fail to distinguish the evidence of our senses from the conclusions that we draw from it. A voice on the telephone is only evidence; what is happening at the other end is a conclusion that we draw from the evidence, and the evidence is open to other interpretations. A person's appearance is evidence; his identity is a conclusion. The victim of a hoax has been given manufactured evidence.

Professor Jones has shed some light on the process by practice as well as by precept. The source of his own interest as a scientist is put into focus by a story he tells about James Clerk-Maxwell, one of the fathers of modern physics and also, incidentally, Jones's predecessor by nearly a century in his post at Aberdeen University.

William Kelvin was visiting his laboratory, and Maxwell invited him to look at one of his optical experiments. Kelvin peered through the eyepiece of the instrument and saw, as well as the refractory lines he had expected, a tiny figure of a little man dancing about. This Maxwell had achieved with the addition to the instrument of a zoetrope, a Victorian toy for simulating moving pictures.

Kelvin peered at it, and then said, 'But what is the little man there for?'

'Just for *fun*,' replied Maxwell.

Two Jokers

Let us honour if we can
The merry-making man,
Though we value none
But the money-making one.
JAMES BALDWIN (*unpublished*)

THE most famous practical joker in Britain, in his lifetime or ever, is Horace de Vere Cole, known above all else as the man who hoaxed the British Navy in 1910 by visiting the flagship of the Home Fleet with a group of friends disguised as the Emperor of Ethiopia and his entourage.

An apocrypha has grown up around him. Just as a famous wit is credited with many quips he never made, so Cole has had a lot of hoaxes ascribed to him that were perpetrated by someone else, if at all. Did he really dig up a section of Piccadilly with a group of friends dressed up as labourers, to win a wager that he could break the law and block traffic in broad daylight? Most articles about him say he did, but there is never a date given, nor the names of any confederates. Did he really give a formal party for people he did not know named Winterbotham, Ramsbotham, Higginbotham, and so on, having each bottom announced as the person entered? This is another story told about, a number of people, but it seems doubtful that it ever happened though, perhaps, it should have.

Yet Cole earned his reputation. Here is his friend, the artist Augustus John, writing about his antics in his autobiography *Chiaroscuro*: 'No practical joker myself, I would have preferred to view such activities at a certain distance. It was embarrassing to find myself, without warning, in charge of an epileptic in convulsions on the pavement and foaming at the mouth; or to be involved in a collision between a whooping lunatic and some unknown and choleric gentleman who had been deprived suddenly of his headgear, and who had all my sympathy.'

---

* The reader may recognise this as an adaptation of a quatrain by W. H. Auden.

Cole's hoaxes were not the playful offshoot of an intellectual concern with apprehensions of reality, nor a by-product of his occupation. He had no occupation. He lived the leisured life of a wealthy Edwardian gentleman. His pranks, as he would call them, were aspects of aristocratic playfulness, stemming from prolonged juvenile high spirits.

If his targets were usually the pompous and the proud, this was because the most fun was to be had this way, not because he was a rebel against the social system. Far from it. He was a member of the upper class (his sister, who frequently found him an embarrassment, married Neville Chamberlain) and his politics, in so far as he had any, were high Tory. When he flouted conventions, it was because he considered himself above them; he was denied the place in *Who's Who* to which his birth entitled him because he insisted on putting as his recreation 'f———g' (his spelling). Assisted most of the time by a tall, impressive build and handsome features, and a sizeable independent income, he strode or cavorted through life with the sublime belief that if he chose to play practical jokes, others were placed on Earth to be either his foil or his audience.

His hoaxes were usually simple. His talent was for skill and bravura in performance, not ingenuity in conception.

Once, walking in St. James's with a Conservative member of parliament and old family friend, Oliver Locker-Lampson, he suddenly said, 'I'll race you to Bond Street.' Locker-Lampson, being himself of a sporting nature, agreed. As they ran down Bury Street, Cole allowed Locker-Lampson to pull ahead, then shouted out: 'Stop thief! That man's stolen my watch!'

Others gave chase and caught Locker-Lampson, a policeman was summoned, and when Cole's gold watch was found in Locker-Lampson's pocket, he arrested him. Then Cole explained that he had planted the watch and the whole thing was a joke. The policeman was not amused, and he arrested him too.

They were charged with 'using insulting words and behaviour whereby a breach of the peace might have been occasioned'. Cole was kept in the cells overnight, and the next day in court, he was fined five pounds. A question was asked in Parliament about Locker-Lampson's involvement in a felony. The then Home Secretary, Winston Churchill, had to exonerate him, and he remarked sourly that Cole was 'a dangerous man for his friends'.

Cole seems to have originated the joke of having two men hold opposite ends of a piece of string. He accosted a gentleman on the street, said he was a surveyor, and wondered whether the man would be kind enough to hold the end of a piece of string for him for just a few moments – 'It's important to keep it taut,' he explained. Then he went around the corner and persuaded someone else to hold the other end, telling him the same story. Then he disappeared into the crowd chuckling, leaving the two men each holding one end of the string, each believing that he was on the other end.

He would do the unexpected thing on the spur of the moment just because it was unexpected. His god-daughter, later Mrs. Jane de Vere Madden, recalled an alarming encounter with him when she was a small girl. He was visiting their home at tea-time, and at her mother's suggestion, she showed him some little coloured paper boxes she had been making. He held them in his huge hand for a moment looking at them, then put them into his mouth and ate them. Little Jane dissolved into tears.

He took time off from his honeymoon in Venice with his first wife in 1919, to practise a joke on the whole Venetian population. Noticing that the date was March 31st, he felt he could not let the following day pass without marking the occasion. So he boated out to the edge of the canal city, then went to a nearby riding stable. He surprised the owner of this establishment by negotiating to buy a quantity of horse manure. He went to collect his purchase in the middle of the night, when Venice was asleep, and loaded it aboard a gondola. Then he took it along the canals to the Piazza San Marco, and using a shovel, he deposited it in little mounds following a line around the square. Waking on the morning of April 1st, the Venetians were astonished to see what Venetians had not seen since their extraordinary city was built: malodorous evidence that a number of horses had magically crossed the canals, and trotted in procession around the Piazza San Marco before departing across the water in the same mysterious way they had come. His bride used to tell this story, with some asperity.

He bore a strong physical resemblance to Ramsay MacDonald, the first Labour Party Prime Minister, and was occasionally mistaken for him. He himself used to tell friends that once, when he was coming out of a restaurant, a group of road workers took him for the Labour Party leader, and came over to shake his hand and ask if he would speak to them. He promptly delivered a short, sharp address on the evils of socialism, which he said he had only recently come to appreciate, then departed with a wave of his hand when their perplexity began to change to angry rumblings. His friends, who knew his capabilities at first-hand, believed the story, so it was probably true.

Recounting Horace de Vere Cole's practical jokes, it sounds as if his life was one long, golden, carefree boyhood. In fact he learned at an early age, and more vividly than most of us, that life can be harsh. When he left Eton the Boer War was on, and he volunteered for the army. He became a lieutenant at 18, fought in South Africa, and was wounded in the shoulder and lung with effects that were to remain with him throughout his life.

Later, he moved in that London world of high bohemia where artists and some of the more raffish of the aristocracy mingled, which centred in successive decades on the Café Royal, the Gargoyle Club and the Cavendish Hotel. He had a thick mane of hair, a bristling, upswept moustache, and a fierce, forward, ebullient way with the world that concealed the fact that he sometimes lacked stamina because of his injured lung, and was partially deaf so that he did not understand a lot of what was said to him.

He spent a lot of time pursuing women, when they were not pursuing him. Women found him attractive; his suggested *Who's Who* entry was no empty boast. He married twice, both times to beautiful women much younger than himself. When he was 36, he married Denise Daly, who was just half his age, and they were divorced after a few years. (Some time later, when she appeared in a bankruptcy court, it was said on her behalf that on her marriage she believed that de Vere Cole had settled a large sum of money on her, but that this was just 'a huge joke' on his part.) At 50, he married Mavis Wright, then 23, after a three-year affair which began when he picked her up in the restaurant where she was working.

He wrote poetry all his life, sometimes reflective, rhetorical poems about life, landscapes, war, sometimes humorous narratives, sometimes missives to girl friends scribbled on the backs of menus or hotel stationery. None was published. One, full of his own *hauteur*, yet also containing in its later lines an appealing idealism, began:

I have not loved the World, nor the world me;
I have not flattered its rank breath, nor bow'd
To its idolatries a patient knee . . .

His penchant for practical joking, and his fame in this field, began when he was an undergraduate at Trinity College, Cambridge, after his return from South Africa. There, he seems to have adopted the characteristic Edwardian attitude that play is the important thing, and any more earnest approach to life is ungentlemanly, not to say vulgar. Perhaps this was a reaction against the violence of the battlefield, perhaps a reversion to his natural temperament.

His first big hoax at Cambridge was one of disguise. It arose out of a conversation in his rooms one languid evening with Adrian Stephen, a fellow-student who was to remain a lifelong friend. A minor frontier incident between France and Germany was then in the news, and Stephen thought it might be a good wheeze to stage another as a spoof. He proposed that the two of them hire the uniforms of German Army officers, go over to some village near the frontier, collect a few German soldiers behind them as the 'Captain from Kopenick' had done a few years earlier, and march them across the French frontier. As he envisaged it, they would be challenged by French troops and would surrender, and there would be an international incident, and other amusing consequences.

Cole was attracted to the idea, but pointed out that it would involve a lot of trouble and expense. He had a suggestion for a cheaper joke: the Sultan of Zanzibar was visiting England. Why not impersonate him and pay a state visit to Cambridge?

They did it, with one small alteration: the Sultan's photograph had appeared in the newspapers, so they made it the Sultan's uncle and his entourage. They collected three friends, got themselves costumed and made up at a theatrical costumers in London (Cole always had plenty of money to spend on his pranks), then sent a telegram to the Mayor of Cambridge supposedly from a senior Colonial Office official saying that the Sultan would be arriving and should be shown the principal points of interest. They had thought of pulling the hoax on their own college, Trinity, but decided that this could result in their being expelled. They were received by the Mayor, entertained at the Guildhall, taken around to some colleges in a hansom cab, and then taken to a charity bazaar where Cole, as the Royal dignitary, spent money grandly. The others said nothing about the hoax, but Cole gave the story to the *Daily Mail*, and it became well-known for a while.

It turned out to be a rehearsal–one might almost say a dress rehearsal–for the hoax visit to the fleet in 1910.

The visiting party consisted of Cole and Adrian Stephen once again; Stephen's sister Virginia, later to be Virginia Woolf; Guy Ridley; Duncan Grant, the artist; and Anthony Buxton, later to be a distinguished author and naturalist.

The most authentic account of the episode, and the only one written by a participant, is the one by Adrian Stephen published 26 years later.* He explodes the myth that they planned every detail meticulously weeks ahead, and worked hard to achieve authenticity in dress and language. In fact, their advance planning was limited to getting some costumes and arranging for a fake telegram to be sent announcing their arrival. From then on, they all flew by the seats of their pants.

The Dreadnought, the flagship of the Home Fleet, was anchored at Weymouth. They arranged their costumes with a theatrical costumer's, Clarkson's, who of course had no idea why they wanted them. The four who were supposedly the Ethiopian party wore robes with black face and beards (Virginia had cut her hair short), robes, turbans and crosses; Anthony Buxton was the Emperor, the others princes. Cole was the Foreign Office official escorting the party; he sported a top hat and tails, and the name of Cholmondley. Stephen was a German interpreter travelling around Europe with them.

They got themselves made up in the morning, then set out in a taxi to Paddington Station at around noon. They had a confederate send a telegram to the Commander-in-Chief, Home Fleet, saying that the Ethiopian Emperor and his suite would be arriving on the 4-20 train from London, and adding: 'Kindly make all arrangements to receive them.' It was signed with the name of the then permanent head of the Foreign Office, Hardinge. This was sent at short notice, so that there would be no time to check on it.

---

* *The Dreadnought Hoax*. It was published as a small book by the Hogarth Press run by Leonard and Virginia Woolf, in 1936.

They invented some names for themselves on the way down, though they never got around to one for Stephen. Cole and Stephen had lunch on the train, but the others stayed in their compartment for fear that eating would spoil their make-up. Cole had armed himself with a Swahili grammar which he had bought from the Society for the Propagation of the Gospel, and over lunch on the train, he tried to teach Stephen a few words of Swahili, in the belief that it is the language spoken in Ethiopia (it is not; Amharic is). They were all nervous when they arrived; would they be met by a party of police, alerted to the imposture and waiting to arrest the imposters? Would they be ignored, and have to slink back to London?

They were certainly not ignored. A naval officer in full ceremonial dress greeted them with a salute as they stepped off the train. A red carpet had been laid out in the station, and a barrier erected to keep back sightseers. They were driven to the harbour and taken by launch out to the ship. Curiously, all nerves seem to have vanished at this point. Their roles and their treatment dictated their behaviour, as so often happens in life. Stephen, recalling their arrival and journey across the harbour wrote: 'By the time we reached the Dreadnought, the expedition had become, for me at any rate, almost an affair of every day. It was hardly a question any longer of a hoax. We were almost acting the truth. Everyone was expecting us to act as the Emperor and his suite, and it would have been extremely difficult not to.'

They were received by the Commander-in-Chief, Home Fleet, Admiral Sir William May. Cole introduced the Ethiopians, and Stephen as 'Herr Kauffmann'—a name Stephen had not heard before. They inspected a marine guard of honour, and Admiral May explained the different uniforms to 'Kauffmann' and suggested that he pass on the explanation to the Emperor. Stephen was very unsure of his ability to speak either Swahili or plausible gibberish. He got out three words of what seemed like Swahili to him, and then he had an inspiration. Drawing on his rigorous classical education, he spoke chunks of Virgil's *Aeneid* to them, mispronouncing it just enough so that it was not immediately recognisable as Latin. Later, when he ran out of Virgil, he spoke some Homer, bringing the same mispronunciation to the Greek. He added plausibility by using the same phrase for a repeated situation: as they had to duck through several doorways, one line from the *Aeneid* came to mean 'Mind your head, your Majesty.'

The princes repeated back to him a few of his words. Virginia Woolf–Prince Mendex–who was worried that her voice would mark her as a female, and pleaded a cold, said only, in a gruff tone, 'Chuck-a-choi, chuck-a-choi'. But the others found a phrase to express their admiration and delight at the things they were shown; again and again, they threw up their hands and exclaimed, 'Bunga bunga!' They bunga-bungad their way around the ship appreciatively. The officers smiled at their simple excitement at seeing an electric light.

Stephen, meanwhile, had other problems besides translating. Standing six feet five inches, he was a conspicuous figure. He knew that his first cousin was a staff officer on the ship, and he found himself standing near him on the deck. His cousin did not recognize him, despite the fact that his only disguise was a small moustache. But then he noticed that the captain of the Dreadnought was a man he knew also, an occasional hiker on some organised country walks in which Stephen participated. But he also failed to recognise him in his new role.

There were one or two other worrying moments. They were invited to come downstairs for tea with the captain, but they could not chance the effect of tea and jam sandwiches on their make-up, so Cole explained regretfully that the Ethiopians' religion forbade them to eat unless the food was prepared in special ways unfamiliar in England. Then a breeze blew up across the harbour and a light rain started to fall. Stephen saw to his horror that Duncan Grant's moustache was beginning to peel off, and he wondered what the rain would do to the others' make-up; so he shielded Grant with an umbrella while Grant repaired his moustache, and then suggested to the captain that as the princes were accustomed to tropical heat, they might be more comfortable below, away from the wind and rain, and the party were taken inside.

When the launch took them ashore, the Emperor whispered to Cole, and he produced a glittering bauble which he said was an Ethiopian order that they wanted to present to the escorting officer. The young man explained that he could not accept a foreign order without permission from his superior officer.

They had spent just 40 minutes on the Dreadnought. Then

they took the train back to London, causing a small stir by insisting that the Emperor and his suite could only eat their tea if the waiters served them with white gloves; one of the staff had to dash off the train when it stopped at Reading and buy some. Back in London, they had a group photograph taken of them in their costumes, and then decided that the hoax was behind them. Exhilarated as they were by their success, they agreed that the naval officers were such nice young men that it was a little shameful to have hoaxed them, and it certainly would not do to carry the joke any further.

But Cole was no hider of lights under bushels. The hoax took place on a Monday. On the following Saturday, the *Daily Express* carried a full column story on its front page, which began:

'Five young men and one young woman, all of them extremely well connected and all of them well-to-do, have perpetrated a most amazing and somewhat reprehensible practical joke on the Admiralty, the British Navy and H.M.S. Dreadnought in particular.' It gave details, but did not name the six. Other papers did this in the following days, and some of the others were appalled when they saw the photograph of them in costume in the *Daily Mirror.*

Some people were furious at the hoax, including an uncle of Stephen's who had been delighted at the Zanzibarians spoof. It was one thing to make fun of a tradesman – the Mayor of Cambridge owned a chemist's shop – but quite another to make fools of the Royal Navy. The *Daily Telegraph* said in a huffy editorial that the Admiral's courtesy had been abused, and pointed out that in sending a telegram under a false name, they had committed an offence for which the punishment was a fine or imprisonment for up to a year.

The First Lord of the Admiralty, T. P. McKenna, as minister responsible for the Navy, had to answer questions in the House of Commons. To Colonel Lockwood, Conservative M.P. for Epping, he said: 'I understand that a number of persons put themselves to considerable trouble and expense in pretending to be a party of Abyssinians, and, in this disguise, visited one of His Majesty's ships. The question is being considered whether any breach of the law has been committed which can be brought home to the offenders.''

Col. Lockwood: 'Am I to understand that the right honourable gentleman agrees that the joke, such as it was, was a direct insult to His Majesty's flag?'

Mr. McKenna: 'I hope that the hon. gentleman will not ask me to go further into the matter. It was obviously the work of foolish persons.'

The Irish Home Rule leader, William Redmond, who would seize any opportunity to embarrass the Government, drew laughter by asking whether the hoaxers had in fact conferred the Royal Abyssinian Order on the Admiral, and whether the Admiral had written to the King asking for permission to wear it. Mr. McKenna told him this was not so.

A few days later, he had to assure another questioner that no flags were hoisted or salutes fired, and no special train was ordered for the party's return to London.

Most of the public took a different view from the furious Colonel Lockwood, and patriotic though they were, they found the hoax a subject for amusement. The phrase 'Bunga bunga!' – the black-faced visitors' exclamation – caught on, and became a catch-phrase for the whole affair. The unfortunate Admiral May could not walk ashore in Weymouth without street urchins chanting 'Bunga bunga!' after him.

A common music hall routine, with many variations, would go something like this:

'I say, I say, what did the Abyssinian prince say to the Admiral?'

'I don't know. What did the Abyssinian prince say to the Admiral?'

'You don't know? Well I'll bet the audience does.' Turning to the audience: 'What did he say?'

And the audience would yell back merrily, 'Bunga bunga!'

At one point, Adrian Stephen and Duncan Grant heard a hint in high social circles that Admiral May was to be reprimanded officially. They did not want this to happen because of their prank, and decided that if they apologised personally to McKenna, it might be avoided. So without waiting for the others, they took a cab down to the Admiralty in Whitehall, told the porter that they wanted to see Mr. McKenna about the Dreadnought affair, and were shown in (Britain in 1910 was a small country and a wide open one for members of certain families). The meeting was not a success. McKenna told them sternly that they had broken the law, and could be prosecuted, and they would all do well to lie low for a while. They told him they didn't care twopence about his warnings of prosecution and had come along only to try to smooth things over for the Navy. McKenna threw them out.

Stephen wrote loftily, in his account of it: 'We had come absolutely gratuitously to make what seemed a generous offer, and I did not see why this politician should treat us 'de haut en bas', not even if he had rowed in the Cambridge boat before he was First Lord of the Admiralty.'

The hoax produced one other episode of what must seem to-day like Edwardian high camp. A group of Naval officers called on Cole and Duncan Grant in turn, to avenge the honour of the service by caning them, prep school style. Cole took the visit in a spirit of levity which they did not share. Waving aside his butler's offer to call the police, he said, truthfully, that he had just been ill, but when he recovered he would be glad to meet one of them with boxing gloves, swords or revolvers. This offer was declined. So he said that he would submit to being caned, if he could cane one of them in turn. To his surprise, this offer was accepted. It was accomplished in a nearby mews; Cole bent over a dustbin and thrust out his bottom with the gesture of a duellist baring his chest to his opponent's pistol; the six blows were administered lightly, but solemnly, and then Cole took his turn with the cane. Honour was satisfied.

It was after the Dreadnought hoax that Cole became known in the Press as the 'prince of practical jokers', and he revelled in the title, though he never tried another hoax that might claim national attention. He seemed content to have it recognized as a private accomplishment rather than a public one, like his poetry.

His last years were not happy. His money, invested in real estate in North America, dwindled during the Depression years. He was unable to adjust to a reduced income, or to contemplate seriously working for a living. He moved to France with his wife Mavis and his daughter by his first marriage, to live cheaply on remittances sent by his brother, a financier. He told friends he was writing his autobiography; he made notes, which were lost later. Mavis returned to England to have an affair with Augustus John, though she and Cole continued to exchange passionate letters. He died in Honfleur, after a heart attack, in 1936, at the age of 53.

*   *   *

Alan Abel's career as a hoaxer recalls the reply of the Hungarian playwright Ferenc Molnar, when he was asked how he became a writer. 'In the same way,' Molnar said, 'that a woman becomes a prostitute. First I did it to please myself, then I did it to please my friends, and finally I did it for money.'

Abel is a professional comedian who has somehow made the public into his straight man. He often plays jokes on the public rather than simply for them, and makes the whole of America, and sometimes the whole world, his stage.

The sequence of his hoaxes is not quite as straightforward as Molnar's reply would indicate. At all times, some of his biggest hoaxes were performed just for fun; they did not earn any money, and were not intended to.

His first, and most famous, joke on the public was his Society for Indecency to Naked Animals, which began on a television talk show. Among his other productions are a topless string quartet, the Yetta Bronstein for President Campaign, and the Sex Olympics.

There is a strong element of social parody in all his hoaxes. That a lot of people take them seriously is something that he never ceases to wonder at, and worry about. But they do. When he delivered a lecture to advertising executives, in the guise of a business consultant and author, on 'The Fallacy of Creative Thinking', the gist of which was that it is inefficient to spend a lot of time thinking up new ideas instead of stealing them from other people, he received repeated requests for his book from the president of one of largest advertising agencies in America.

He has the talents of a good stand-up comic: an inventive sense of humour; a ready wit that never leaves him without a come-back; a glibness that ensures that he is never at a loss for a word, or a thousand; an exhibitionist streak that enables him to behave in the most outlandish way in any company without a twinge of discomfort; and the actor's ability to deliver any line with a straight face. He has a good actor's face, too: a pleasant face with dark hair and a slight chubbiness around the cheeks that says nothing about the owner, and that looks like a lot of other faces.

He comes from Zanesville, Ohio, and at Ohio State University, he was popular as a live-wire, a fun fellow with a lot of nerve and a lot of gags, who would do just about anything. He began his career in show business with a hoax. He had an act in which he played the drums with a comic patter. He went to New York, and found that he could not break in. He also found that television studios will listen intently to anything that an advertising agency has to say. So he would telephone the producer of a likely TV show, announce himself as someone at Young and Rubicam, and say, 'I want to send over a great kid. Does a monologue with a snare drum. He may be just what you're looking for.' This got him ushered into the producer's office, and he started getting jobs. This was probably the last occasion on which he hoaxed only one person at a time.

As he tells it, the seed of his first really big hoax was sown one afternoon when he was driving in Texas, touring with a satirical lecture. He was writing and lecturing more than performing in those days. A bull mounted a cow in the middle of the road, and he observed the strong and mixed reactions this produced in other drivers: a woman rigid with embarrassment, others laughing, others pretending not to see. This inspired him to write a story about one G. Clifford Trout, who left $400,000 to his son to finance a Society for Indecency to Naked Animals (the name is oddly ambiguous), to halt the exposure of the sexual organs of cows, dogs, and cats and prevent all sorts of social evils. He sent the story to several magazines, and it was rejected.

One morning over a year later, in 1959, he was watching the *Today* show on television in a hotel room in Witchita, Kansas, commenting to himself on its parade of uninspiring guests, when the idea somehow came to him to pass off SINA as reality rather than fiction. He wrote to the program on the hotel's stationery under the name of G. Clifford Trout Jr., the president of the society, who was meeting with followers in Kansas, and he mentioned his vice-president, Alan Abel, a former tire salesman. The producers of the show rose to the bait, and asked them both to call in.

He offered the role of G. Clifford Trout Jr. to the actor Buck Henry, whom he had found to be a kindred spirit. Henry, who was mostly unemployed in those days, jumped at the chance to spoof the 'straight' TV shows, and the two went along. Interviewed on the air, Henry looked and sounded desperately earnest: 'Don't let your moral standards go lower and lower due to naked animals. It's a shocking situation, and I am spending every single minute of every day and every last dollar of my father's money to correct this evil.'

From that first appearance, the word spread. Abel got someone to produce leaflets, and claimed 55,000 SINA members. The Press pursued them, and there were more TV interviews and newspaper stories. They both found that they enjoyed keeping up the pretence, so they resorted to stratagems to establish that Trout and the legacy really existed. Because he travelled a lot, Abel had rented a telephone answering and mail service with a Fifth Avenue address, and the occasional use of an office there. He called this office SINA's New York headquarters and when he received interviewers, he hung the walls with art work produced by a sympathetic artist showing farm animals and household pets with their sexual organs privatized by clothing. For a photographic session with *Life* Magazine, other sympathetic friends, who were of course in on the joke, brought along their dogs decently clothed. Others laughed, but Abel and Henry were solemn throughout.

The public responded, letters and telephone calls poured in, mostly abusive but some expressing support. A Californian woman offered the Society 40,000 dollars. Abel saw her, suspicious that this might be a trap, but she came with her lawyer prepared to draw up the papers. Abel told her that the society's rules forbad him to accept money from outsiders, and suggested that she give it to another charity instead. She stamped out furiously, and the lawyer looked at Abel with disdain.

The activities of the society lapsed as Abel and Henry became busy with paying work, then rose again at other times. SINA protested to the Fifth Avenue Association at a 'naked' papier mache horse that was in an airline office window, and received an apology and the horse's removal. When Abel and Henry happened both to be in California, the *San Francisco Chronicle*, after an intensive investigation, ran a two-part series on SINA that included a photograph of Henry trying to put a pair of pants on a fawn at the San Francisco zoo. Newspaper editorials cited SINA as a sign that the country was going crazy. British newspapers carried the story in the same spirit, and the Press in other European countries too.

They were found out, after three happy years; Buck Henry was interviewed as G. Clifford Trout Jr. by Walter Cronkite on his C.B.S. evening program just after he had taken a job as a writer on a C.B.S. show, and someone in the organization recognized him.

By that time, Abel had learned how much the public will swallow, and had found a new way to have fun. He also found that the media will go for anything providing they can be persuaded that *they* are not being taken in, and that, if he is crazy, he is genuinely crazy. This was to be the key to some of Abel's later hoaxes.

Fame of any kind is a saleable commodity, and SINA made Abel famous. Now he was in demand as a comedian, and a guest on TV and radio chat shows. So he started making money. But his next hoax was carried out just for fun, and with the help of his wife Jeanne, an actress. In early 1964, he was doing a live radio phone-in show from the Playboy Club in Chicago. It was election year, so to add some life to the show, he had Jeanne telephone from New York and announce herself as Mrs. Yetta Bronstein, an independent candidate for President. Jeanne could put on a good act, and in a Bronx-Jewish accent, she said that if she was elected she would, among other things, hang a suggestion box on the White House fence, and put a picture of Jane Fonda in the nude on postage stamps, to reduce the Post Office's deficit 'and also to give a little pleasure for six cents to people who can't afford *Playboy*.'

Back in New York, the Abels decided to blow 200 dollars or so and a certain amount of time on promoting the Yetta Bronstein candidature just to see what would happen. A lot of Abel's hoaxes are performed just to see what will happen.

He printed handbills headed 'Vote for Yetta and Watch Things Get Better', and left them in public places, and he sent out occasional Press releases announcing more of Yetta's policies, such as making up her cabinet of people who have failed in life and learned to live with it (a lot of public identification with that one, he thought). He got a telephone line for the Better Party, Yetta's political party, to their apartment. Jeanne either took the calls or left recorded messages in the particular dialect and syntax at which she was now becoming adept: 'So why are you calling me? Isn't there something better that you have to do? I'm sorry I can't be here personally to answer your questions. What would the voters think if I didn't do nothing but sit here on the telephone all the time? . . .' Her stock reply on foreign policy questions was that she did not know anything about the E.E.C. or Indochina, but if elected she would have the Government produce a leaflet that explained it to everyone, including her. Abel and a few similarly uninhibited friends paraded with placards.

Most newspapers, at some point in the long campaign, took time out from serious coverage to say something about Yetta Bronstein. She made good copy, and for radio shows she could be counted on for funny on-the-air quotes. People who wanted to interview her in person had to be content with her campaign manager; there was always some excuse given for Yetta's absence. Jeanne is a svelte, attractive blonde then still in her twenties, not the sagging, middle-aged Bronx mother who was Yetta. At one stage, when Abel was away, reporters somehow tracked Yetta to the Abels' apartment in downtown Manhattan. Jeanne was performing the difficult task of telling people at the door that Yetta wasn't there, while she was answering the telephone as Yetta. It was all such a success that the Abels ran Yetta for Mayor of New York (slogan: 'New York Needs a Mother'), and for President again in 1968.

Was the Press wrong to take her seriously? It depends what one means by seriously. In 1968, there was a Yippie candidate and a vegetarian candidate and a Put-On Party. These candidates were interviewed. They said bizarre things about their policies that got printed. Were they serious? They hardly expected to win the election. The only sense in which Yetta was a hoax and they were not is that Yetta Bronstein did not exist.

In 1967, Abel decided to find out how far he could go in satirizing the contemporary preoccupation with nudity; it was the period of the first topless waitresses in San Francisco, the first topless pictures in *Vogue*, and *Hair*. He sent out Press releases announcing the arrival from France of a four-girl musical ensemble called the Topless String Quartet. They found that playing topless gave them added powers of expression, and they hoped that nudity would be a common area of interest between lovers of pop and classical music. They would play at private concerts and make a recording. This produced a straight report in the *New York Post* headed 'Bach, Beethoven, Brahms and Bosoms'. It also produced a lot of requests for interviews.

So the Abels decided that it was worth a little money to carry the hoax further. They advertised for photographic models to pose bra-less, and chose four. They had them photographed wearing only long, formal white skirts and serious expressions, as they played three violins and a cello. They sent out the photographs to newspapers and several printed one. Now there were a lot of requests for interviews, which usually went unanswered because the group did not exist, and expressions of interest from the big recording companies, which had to be fended off. But the quartet now existed for the media, and hence for the public, and it was cited in a *Life* magazine article about nudity in America.

All this was for fun, but now, Abel was offered fees to do the same thing. He became a professional hoaxer. Organizers of conventions wanted him to put on some kind of an act to liven things up. So he created Bruce Spencer, a business consultant, and developed a series of lectures on 'The Fallacy of Creative Thinking', which he varies depending on his audience. Usually, he purveys zany ideas, like renting the heads of bald men as advertising space, which got one advertising executive quite excited until he learned that it was a hoax. Or else he will recall, to illustrate some point, some tricks he has used to make a fast buck. He will tell how he unloaded a surplus stock of Japanese binoculars at Macy's by getting an acrobat to fake a suicide attempt, hanging from a tall building for an hour, and then selling the binoculars in the crowd.

He also shows the audience charts which were drawn by an artist friend, George Wayne, which demonstrate to his satisfaction just how little audiences keep their eyes open. A chart showing figures for each month will have an extra month, like Distember between September and October. Or a percentage chart will add up to 120 per cent. He has also given a spoof lecture as Julius Bristol, golf pro.

This is Alan Abel the professional funny man, with a prepared comic patter, an unfailingly serious platform manner, and a ready, flip answer to questions. Also, a genial, showbiz smile when the joke is exposed at the end and he is introduced to the audience as Alan Abel. He does not really like to offend the customers.

He came closer to it than he usually does when he was visiting the University of British Columbia, and agreed to address one group of students as a recruiter for a private foundation, following several talks by recruiters from big companies. He said that his foundation was engaged in 'highly secret intramural consultation analysis'. He told them his own job was boring and disagreeable, but he got a good salary, he could pad his expense account, they all got two more coffee breaks than General Motors, and, for every employee that stayed longer than ten years, a private burial plot overlooking the Hudson River. A group of boys were furious at his assumption that this was the kind of career that they should want, and they were planning to throw him into the swimming pool until he disclosed that it was a joke. He was worried at how far he had provoked them. It might have been more worrying if they had applauded.

'People will swallow anything at all,' he says, from the benefit of his experience, 'providing you give it to them with serious demeanor. A serious manner implies serious intent. And it helps if you can get yourself presented in a serious context. For instance, if it's in a newspaper or TV show, then they believe it. They think, "Well of course it's true. If it were meant to be funny, it would be on the comics page."'

If he made fun of nudity in the 1960s, he had a lot more to make fun of in the swinging '70s. He and Jeanne did it with a film they made, *Is There Sex After Death?*, which he exhibits himself. Though not shown on the ordinary movie circuits, it received some excellent reviews from critics. It demonstrates, if demonstration were needed, that the current preoccupation with the myriad aspects of sex is simply impossible to parody. There is no detectable difference in tone or credibility between the spoof interview with Buck Henry as an instructor in breast development, and the genuine one with a blue movie director describing proudly how he organized a sex scene featuring a goose and a donkey, 'one minute of cinema magic'.

But the real hoax, a direct line of descent from SINA, was the 1971 Sex Olympics, or the International Sex Bowl, as he called it. He announced this to the Press as Dr. Harrison Rogers, with a lot of details: teams from several countries were participating, contestants would be judged on imagination, potency and grace, among other things, the panel of judges would include a doctor and a psychologist, and the final event would be screened on close-circuit television.

The result was a lot of requests for tickets, a few inquiries

about film rights, and some interviews. Dr. Rogers, who was
Abel plus a beard, met reporters at the same Fifth Avenue office
that housed SINA, now decorated with male and female nudes,
and answered their questions: 'How are the couples training?
How does anyone train for a contest? They practise.'

Harriet Van Horne, the nationally syndicated columnist,
flayed the organizers as 'diabolical, frustrated, dirty old men'. In
Britain the Sunday newspaper *News of the World*, with a circulation of five million, sent its reporter in New York to interview
Dr. Rogers, and then reported the astounding facts on its front
page, in a breathless story beginning: 'The most shocking sporting event ever to be staged is about to be launched on American
TV screens, in a contest that defies the bounds of credibility. . . .'

Reporters were invited to attend one of the heats (it was actually called that) in New York, and turned up in numbers. Dr.
Rogers introduced them to a contestant, a pretty, well-shaped
blonde wearing a towelling robe, who was actually an actress
friend of Abel's called Iris Brook. She told them she regarded
this as a chance to excel, just like a roller derby, that she was a
schoolteacher and her partner a surgeon, and that yes, she felt
that it's not whether you win or lose but how you play the game.
She showed herself an adept pupil of Abel's when it came to
fielding questions, some of which were tricky.

Someone said, 'In track, it's the legs that go first. What would
you say, er—'

She interrupted him with: 'I don't know. I haven't been competing that long.'

What the reporters saw was an excerpt from *Is There Sex
After Death?*, which was about a spoof sex bowl contest. Abel
took off his beard and explained that they had a publicity
budget of only $500 for the film, and this was the most effective
way to spend it.

Abel also writes the so-called 'crazy ads' that are used in some
cities to fill up blank advertising space on buses. He is never
sure that some people will not take them seriously. People
have answered advertisements for six-month-old loaves of bread
for use as building blocks, for $100-bills for rent to impress your
friends, and a week-long crash course in begging on the streets.
When he advertised a scheme to make money by raising squids
('Will eat anything. Especially fond of children'), the National

Better Business Bureau wrote to say they had received complaints and wanted information about his business.

He makes a living as a funny man these days, writing—he has written several books based on his material—broadcasting and hopefully making more films. He and Jeanne moved from their Manhattan apartment to Westport, Connecticut, when a daughter came to them after fifteen years of marriage, and domesticity made another Yetta Bronstein-type campaign unlikely for a while.

He is ensuring that his fame does not blight his ability to hoax the public by training two young people to front for him in any new campaign he devises. In any future hoaxes of his, these faces will appear before the public. They come equipped with a sense of humour and a spirit of adventure, and they learn at the feet of the master how to improvise, to be fast on their feet, how to lead people on, and the meaning of satirical humour.

Abel does not take his hoaxes too seriously, but he sees himself as a social satirist, and he is. However, he is also near the mainstream of American show business humour, and his bite may be sharp but it is never painful.

He himself worries about how easily people are taken in. When one talks to him about hoaxing, he usually raises at some point episodes of appalling political fraud, such as Hitlerism, and the Joseph McCarthy era in America, not to mention the more recent and more obvious Watergate. It worries him that people can be stampeded as they sometimes are, and if he is pressed for a serious purpose, he will admit that he likes to believe that he is sharpening people's sensibilities, so that they are a little more alert, and less vulnerable.

He receives abusive letters and fan mail, and he is tickled by the fact that a number of admiring letters come from prison. These are usually from people who have read his books in the prison library. 'I think,' he says, 'they're struck by the fact that I've done everything they've done, only they did it for money and I did it for fun. And they're in jail and I'm not. I feel they kind of admire the ability to dance on that thin line that separates hoax from fraud.'

CHAPTER 3

Just for Fun

> As regards making other people comic, the
> principal means is to put them in situations in
> which a person becomes comic as a result of
> human dependence on external events,
> particularly on social factors, without regard
> to the personal characteristics of the individual
> concerned . . . everyone is in fact exposed,
> without any defence, to being made comic.
>
> SIGMUND FREUD,
> *Jokes and their Relation to the Unconscious*

No form of hoax is more controversial, and rouses more argument, than the practical joke. There are people who abominate
it: for instance, Constance Rourke, in her cultural history
American Humor, writes: 'Elaborately prepared practical jokes
consumed time, created enemies and brought into peril life and
limb.' But then, women are notoriously less likely to be responsive to practical jokes than men. Horace de Vere Cole quoted
approvingly an Irish poet who was a friend of his as saying that
he had never known a women to laugh at one of his jokes, but
any man who was not bowled over by them must be a homosexual.

If one is seeking a definition, the term itself is apt. It is a joke,
but one that is practised rather than told. It is funny, if it is
funny, because of what happens rather than because of what is
said. It is intended to create a funny situation, and is likely to be
comic rather than witty. Properly, it should be devoid of
cruelty. (The hot-foot, sometimes dignified with the status of a
practical joke, is just a sneaky and dangerous form of physical
assault, and should be treated with no more indulgence.) Professor R. V. Jones writes in *The Theory of Practical Joking – An
Elaboration*: 'If we follow the career of an individual joker who is
also a man of feeling, we find that his jokes become more refined
and less painful.'

Not every practical joke is elaborately prepared, *pace*

Constance Rourke. Some of the funniest are very simple, and require only a minimum of preparation.

I once met a man, an oil industry consultant, who lives in London and travels abroad often. He has found a way to enliven otherwise dull plane trips.

Airlines usually pass among the passengers during the flight an information sheet which gives the plane's position, speed, expected arrival time, and other relevant flight information. Most passengers just glance at this and pass it on. This man pockets it surreptitiously. Then he passes on the flight information sheet from his last trip. Passengers who have set out for, say, Tel Aviv read that they are 35,000 feet over the North Atlantic and will arrive in Toronto at four o'clock local time. There are cries of alarm and calls for the stewardess. He sits there enjoying it all. And he has another flight sheet in his pocket for the next trip.

Or take this. The poet James Whitcomb Riley and the humorous writer Edgard Nye were on a lecture tour of the Midwest together in the 1890s. On one train journey, Nye, who had been holding the tickets, suddenly said, 'Oh God, I've lost one ticket!' He searched his pockets. The conductor was approaching their car, and they knew that if they got off the train, they would miss their next speaking engagement.

'There's only one thing to do,' said Nye, as the conductor drew near. 'You get down under the seat.'

So James Whitcomb Riley, at some cost to his dignity, crawled under the seat. The conductor arrived, and Nye handed him two tickets.

'Who's the other one for?' asked the conductor.

'My friend,' said Nye, pointing under the seat.

'What's he doing down there?' demanded the conductor.

'He always likes to travel like that,' said Nye.

Alexander Woolcott, the writer, critic and Algonquin Round Table wit, was one of those who affected to despite practical jokes as an inferior form of humour. Yet, as a prolific and stylish letter-writer, he too sometimes found an opportunity irresistible.

Once, he received a letter from his friend Beatrice Kauffmann asking him to recommend her daughter to a socially esteemed boarding school. Within the hour, Woolcott sent off a letter to the school urging: 'I implore you to accept this unfortunate child, and remove her from her shocking environment.'

Another friend, the playwright S. N. Behrman, was unwise enough to give Woolcott as a reference when he planned to rent an apartment in an exclusive block. He found himself described in his prospective landlord as a 'notorious drunkard, bankrupt and moral leper'.

More simply still, when it comes to causing mental disruption by message, the publicist Al Horwitz sent telegrams to several aspiring actors he knew reading 'Disregard my previous telegram Zanuck.'

Sometimes, someone carries out a practical joke on the spur of the moment, seizing an opportunity, James Thurber provides an instance in one of his many family reminiscences. An old school friend of his mother's was coming to visit her, and she arranged to meet her at the station. They had not seen each other for many years, and Mrs. Thurber said she would wear a red rose so that her old friend would recognise her. Waiting for the train, she saw an old woman asleep on a bench. She took off her rose and pinned it to the woman's coat. Then she watched her visitor get off the train, stare for a few moments at the sleeping old woman, and then shake her awake gently and say, 'Why Mame Thurber! You're looking just fine!'

There's also the story that's often told in British show business circles about Bud Flanagan and Chesney Allen, famous as the music hall comic team Flanagan and Allen, genuinely funny people off stage as well as on.

One sunny morning, so the story goes, they were driving to the golf course when they saw two workmen erecting a pillar box, the bright red British mailbox, on a suburban street corner. They decided that this should not be allowed to proceed in an orderly fashion, so they stopped the car, put their golf clubs out of sight, and hurried over.

Allen said to the two men: 'Good Lord. You're putting it on the wrong corner.'

'This is where it's marked on the plan,' said one of them.

'Well it shouldn't be,' retorted Flanagan. 'We're from the plans office, and we've just come down to see how you're getting along.'

'It ought to be over there, of course,' said Allen, pointing to the opposite corner. 'Let's see that plan you've got. Let's see who signed it.' They handed him the document.

'Oh, it's Geoffrey!' He showed it to Flanagan. 'Look here, it's another one of Geoffrey's boobs.'

'So it is. Oh, we'll have him hauled over the coals for this,' Flanagan chuckled.

Then, turning to the workmen, he said, 'Look at it, chaps.' He pointed across the street. 'You can *see* that it belongs over there on that other corner. It's more logical, isn't it?'

'Well, I suppose so,' one of them said, looking doubtful.

'Here, I'll put that paper right,' said Flanagan. He crossed out 'Southeast corner' and wrote in 'Northwest corner', and signed it with his name. Then he and Chesney Allen got back in their car and continued on their way to the golf course, with the satisfying sense of five minutes well spent. The pillar box still stands on the Northwest corner.

There is also the time that the German physicist Carl Bosch, working in his laboratory at Berlin University, found that, being next door to a newspaper office, he could look down from his window on to the news desk. So he telephoned the news editor, and told him that he had just invented, after much labour, a device that could transmit sight over an ordinary telephone line. The telephone was a newer instrument then than it is now and television was in the future, so perhaps it was a little more believable than it would be today, but all the same, the news editor was a little skeptical. 'I'll tell you what,' said Bosch. 'Put your hand up and do something, and I'll tell you what you're doing from this end of the telephone line.' So the news editor performed a number of gestures, and Bosch, looking through the window, described every one. Eventually, he was convinced, and the story appeared the next day. (Professor Bosch later went to the Clarendon Laboratory at Oxford, and compared notes on practical jokes one day with young Reginald Jones, and particularly telephone jokes. It was this conversation that led to the telephone-in-the-bucket hoax.)

Some practical jokes, on the other hand, are planned in advance. This applies to another early telephone joke, which goes back to the 1920s, when telephones were much less familiar instruments. It was played, characteristically, by a prankster in an American small town.

He telephoned three or four of his friends, and announced himself as the telephone engineer. He told them that on Saturday morning the Bell Telephone Company planned to clean the lines. This was done, he explained, by a machine which blew down the line, blowing out the dust and dirt. He was calling to warn them to put their telephone in a stout paper bag on Saturday morning, or a pillowcase, so that the dirt and dust that would be blown out of the receiver would not be scattered all over the room. Then he would drop by at each of their houses on the Saturday morning for a cup of coffee and a chat. He would suddenly notice something and ask what in tarnation they were doing with the telephone stuck in a pillowcase. The host would then explain the reason laboriously, and the prankster would listen, perhaps throwing in a question occasionally, enjoying the spectacle.

Most of us would enjoy it. I suggested earlier that a part of the hoaxer's reward is a feeling of power over others, however subtle, however gentle in expression, however deeply repressed. It is most apparent in a scene like this: the one person giving a laborious explanation for what he has done, the other sitting back, knowing that he is deceived, and is acting like a fool, knowing it and savouring the situation. Something of the prankster's character could, perhaps, be judged by how long he keeps the secret to himself before grabbing the fillip that comes from telling the victim that he has been fooled. The person who never shared the secret, who could enjoy his power over the other all by himself without ever revealing that he had it, would be a strange man, and a formidable one.

Sometimes, of course, the disclosure of a hoax is the whole point of it, the dénouement. A practical joke may be played just to demonstrate someone's gullibility in a certain area, or excess of enthusiasm over judgment.

Thus, in 1914, Paul Birault, a reporter on the Paris newspaper *L'Eclair*, saw a cabinet minister dedicate statues on the same day to a musician and a philosopher with warm words of praise, and invented a historical personage called Hégésippe Simon. He sent printed invitations to all the liberal and radical members of the French National Assembly inviting each one to speak at the unveiling of a monument to the memory of Simon, the 'precursor of modern democracy and martyr to the tyranny of the *ancien regime*', on the 150th anniversary of his death. Fifteen senators and nine deputies accepted the invitation, and many expressed their gratitude at this opportunity to 'pronounce the eulogy on this educator of democracy', as one of them put it. *L'Eclair* printed all the letters, to their intense embarrassment.

The editors of Cornell University's student newspaper, *The Sun*, did not know about the Simon hoax when, in 1930, they invented a historic personage called Hugo N. Frye of Elmira, New York, supposedly the founder of the Republican Party in New York State, and sent out invitations in other names to a banquet to commemorate his 150th birthday. They sent the invitations to Vice-President Charles Curtis, Secretary of Labor James J. Davis, and other members of President Hoover's Republican cabinet, as well as senators, congressmen and state figures. In their letter of invitation, they recalled Frye's historic slogans 'Protection for our prosperity' and 'Freedom in the land of the free'.

Most recipients responded by declining the invitation regretfully while expressing their fulsome approval. The Secretary of Labor, James Davis, wrote: 'It is a pleasure to testify to the career of that sturdy patriot who first planted the ideals of our party in this region of the country. If he were living today, he would be the first to rejoice in evidence everywhere present that our government is still safe in the hands of the people.'

Then the Cornell *Sun* revealed the joke, inviting readers to pronounce out loud the name Hugo N. Frye. A Democratic Senator, Pat Harrison of Mississippi, read out newspaper accounts of the hoax and some of the prize answers in the Senate, while Republican senators listened sheepishly.

*   *   *

Sometimes, the practical joke is virtually a theatrical performance by an individual or a troupe of players, scripted in advance and stage managed, for the benefit of an audience fooled into believing that the performance is the real thing.

A very successful performance was arranged by four Oxford undergraduates in 1922. They conceived this one evening when they were sitting around talking about the faddishness, as they saw it, of the interest in the new Freudian psychology. They decided that they could fool Oxford with a spoof lecture on the subject.

So they booked a lecture hall, and sent out invitations to members of college faculties and others, in the name of the non-existent Home Counties Psychological Federation. The lecturer was to be Dr. Emil Busch, the distinguished German psycho-analyst, a colleague and friend of Sigmund Freud, and his subject was 'Freud and the New Psychology'. They were careful not to charge for tickets: if they had, they would have been liable to prosecution on a charge of obtaining money under false pretences.

The part of Dr. Busch was played by George Edinger, later to become a journalist and author. In writing his lecture, he had the help of another undergraduate who was later to become known for more serious authorship, Christopher Hollis. Edinger donned a thin disguise–a touch of make-up and a false moustache–and mounted the platform with his lecture prepared.The hall was packed.

He delivered his talk in a heavily-accented Teutonic-sounding English, and talked about co-aesthesia, the hidden factor in the psyche which even Freud underrated. It had something to do with levels of consciousness. He cited examples of co-aesthesia from his own clinical practice; one was that of a clergyman who, under the impact of an emotional shock, took to puncturing bicycle tyres compulsively, and eating sugar by the bushel.

The audience swallowed it all like a glass of claret. Edinger was on his own when it came to question time, but he was equal to the occasion.

'Would you dissent from Freud in postulating that co-aesthesia is a more vital explanation of the subconscious than sex?' someone asked.

'From Professor Freud, I would not dissent,' Edinger replied. 'He is my very good friend. But of him I feel sometimes that for the number of trees, the wood he does not see.' The lecture ended with earnest applause.

The foursome gave the story to the *Oxford Mail*. They deposited the text of the lecture in the Bodleian Library, where it rests along with other documents of Oxford University's history.

Universities are natural breeding grounds for practical jokes, since undergraduates tend to seek ways to prove their cleverness.

Some undergraduates at Brasenose College, Oxford, once circularised the fifty-three boys who had come to take the

entrance exam, and asked them to attend interviews in one of
the college rooms to determine their psychological suitability.
Three of them posed as members of the teaching staff, and they
asked each boy a number of personal questions about his attitudes, private opinions and his sex life. They advised a few to
consult the college psychiatrist, if they were admitted (there is
no college psychiatrist). The hoax came out when the boys
talked about their psychological interviews, and some of the
authorities overheard.

Hugh Troy, the American artist and illustrator, began his
career as a practical joker when he was an undergraduate at
Cornell. One winter, he noticed that a friend of his had a waste-
paper basket made out of the foot of a rhinoceros. He borrowed
it, and with a classmate he went out to the snow-covered
campus in the middle of the night, and made rhino footprints
leading down to the shores of Beebee Lake, and out on to the ice.
Fifty feet from the edge, there was a gaping hole in the ice. It
seemed clear that a rhinoceros had wandered out on to the ice
and fallen through and drowned. The local newspaper carried
the story, and despite the fact that a check with all the zoos in
the Northeastern United States turned up no missing rhinoceros,
people could hardly wait until the ice melted so that the lake
could be dredged for the animal's corpse.

This is an example of a common kind of hoax, the manufacture of misleading evidence. There is no end of stories of
manufactured footprints, which have produced rumours of
escaped circus elephants and mysterious monsters, not only on
snow-covered campuses, but also in the sand at resort beaches,
and in the 'big-foot' country of the American Northwest, where
reports of a big-footed monster are pursued.

Still on campuses, my own college, Hamilton College in upstate New York, has one story of manufactured evidence that
has been told and re-told by generations of students. It seems
that some students one year took the body of a spider, the wings
of a dragon fly, the head of something else and the tail of something else, and glued them together. They took the resulting
specimen to a biology professor as a strange bug they had found,
and asked whether he could identify it. The Professor looked at
it closely and said, 'Hmm, this is very interesting. Was it
humming when you saw it?'

'Yes, it was,' they replied.

'In that case,' he said, 'I think it must be a hum bug.'

*   *   *

In most of these hoaxes, one person or a few people fool a lot of others. But there is another kind in which a lot of people fool one, ganging up to deceive him. They put on a performance for an audience of one. This gives the perpetrators such a big advantage that it is almost unfair. It is very difficult for an individual, if he does not know he is being fooled, to resist what is apparently the collective belief of a number of people no matter how improbable. This is what Professor Milligram found with his experiments.

This kind of prank is an American tradition. Frederick Marryat, the Victorian author who followed the example of others by touring the United States and writing a book about his tour, wrote in *A Diary of America,* published in 1839: 'There is no country, perhaps, in which the habit of deceiving for amusement, or what is termed hoaxing, is so common. Indeed this and hyperbole constitute the main part of American humour. If they have the slightest suspicion that a foreigner is about to write a book, nothing appears to give them so much pleasure as to try to mislead him: this has constantly been practised upon me, and for all I know, it may in some instances have been successful.' It may indeed; Marryat has one or two passages that seem today to be far-fetched. In one, describing America's puritan heritage, he says that some people he was with one day were shocked when, after a lady stumbled on a step, he asked her solicitously whether she had hurt her leg. They told him quietly that in America, one does not talk about a respectable lady's 'leg', but her 'limb'.

An early victim of this practise was the French naturalist Jean-Pierre Raffinesque; he was taken in by something that combined the fool-the-visitor hoax *and* hyperbole. Raffinesque visited America in 1818, and went to see the distinguished American naturalist James Audubon, in Kentucky. Audubon told him about some remarkable fish he had observed in the Ohio River. One of these was the Devil Jack Diamond Fish, which grew to a length of ten feet, and had diamond-shaped scales that were so hard that the fish was bullet-proof. When the fish was dead, the scales were used as flints. Audubon gave his visitor a detailed description of these fish, and even made some rough sketches for him from memory. Raffinesque, in his published account of his American travels, described these fish; in fact, he got carried away and said that he had actually *seen* the Devil Jack Diamond Fish. His reputation suffered as a consequence.

The snipe hunt is virtually a tradition in rural America, to be practised upon any visitor from the city. The details vary, but a typical case will go something like this. Some of the men in the community will talk about going on a snipe hunt that night, and eventually someone suggests that the visitor might like to come along. He accepts eagerly. They go out into the woods, and search with torches for the snipe's tunnel. They find one. Then they give him a branch to use as a club, and station him at what they say is one end of the tunnel. They will go to the other end, they say, and shine the light into it. The snipe will be frightened and will run out, and he must be ready to club it. Then they fade away and leave him. Many an urbanite American has stood in the forest in the middle of the night, poised at a rabbit hole with a club on his shoulder, in a long, lonely vigil.

The most elaborate practical joke ever practised on a visitor to America was one of the many perpetrated by the actor E. A. Sothern, a well-known figure on the American stage in the middle of the last century. One day, the British impresario Philip Lee, on his first visit to New York, remarked in Sothern's presence that one heard stories in England about the wild literary bohemia in America, but he had not encountered it, and he did not believe it existed. Sothern assured him that it certainly did exist, and that he had not met the right people. He offered to introduce him to this strata of society, and arranged a dinner in a private room in a hotel, with twelve guests. All the others were in fact actors, and friends of Sothern's, who were determined to give Lee the kind of experience he was seeking. Sothern introduced each one to Lee as a well-known writer or critic.

A friend of Sothern's, T. E. Pemberton, describes what happened next. 'For a time, all went well. But while the soup was being served, one well-known man was seen to take from under his coat a battle axe, and another celebrity drew from beneath his jacket a dirk knife with a blade over a foot long, which he gravely unclasped and placed beside his plate. Then another took a six-shooter from his pocket, while his neighbour drew a scythe and a policeman's staff from under the table, and laid them in the middle of the board.'*

Lee, alarmed at the spectacle, asked Sothern in a whisper what was going on. Sothern replied that he was afraid that some of the company had been drinking, and seemed to have quarrelled about a literary matter.

The conversation at the table was civil enough for a while, but then a quarrel broke out at the far end. Then one man sprang to his feet and announced: 'Whoever says that the history of the French Revolution written by my friend David Weymyss Jobson is not as good a book in every respect as that written by Tom Carlyle on the same subject is a liar and a thief; and if there is any fool present who desires to take it up, I am his man!'

At this, pandemonium broke loose. Everyone leaped up, there were cries and oaths, blades flashed and shots were fired. The room was filled with noise, smoke and struggling figures. Lee was terrified. One of the number thrust a knife into his hand and urged him, 'Defend yourself! This is butchery, sheer butchery.'

Sothern alone remained calm. He advised Lee, 'Keep cool, and *don't get shot.*'

The whole hotel was aroused by the uproar, and the performance was terminated when the police were called.

Sothern was a great practitioner of the hoax that depends on snarling up communications. He would have worked out some marvellous jokes with the telephone if it had existed in his day.

The actor W. J. Florence was incensed by one of Sothern's jokes once, and he sent off a hasty and furious note by messenger saying, 'Your conduct is neither that of an actor nor a gentleman.' Afterwards, he regretted this intemperate outburst. He was surprised when he met Sothern in the street, and Sothern greeted him warmly.

Florence told him that he was delighted that they were still on good terms, and said, 'Ever since I wrote that letter to you, I concluded that it had put an end to our friendship.'

---

* From *A Memoir of Edward Askew Sothern*, published in 1889.

Sothern said: 'Letter? What letter? Oh yes, I remember. Something about being neither an actor nor a gentleman? But there was no name at the top. So I guessed that it was intended for Boucicault, and I re-directed it and sent it on.'

A much more complicated one depending on misdirected letters that went on for weeks arose out of his seizing on a chance situation. He spent some time in Glasgow, and he often used to go to a club there. A fellow-clubman and friend was a professor who was a little absent-minded, and had the disconcerting habit of suddenly getting up and leaving a room without any leave-taking.

One evening, Sothern was sitting in the club in the company of the professor and another man who had not met him before, an army major. The major said that he had been to see a con-juror at a music hall, and the man had been drunk. He was quite vocal in his annoyance. Sothern, deciding to take advan-tage of what he expected would happen, nudged him a few times while he was talking. As he anticipated, the professor suddenly got up and walked out.

Sothern said to the Major: 'This is a very awkward business. I was trying to warn you. Didn't you see the indignant way that man got up and left the room?' He went on to explain that the man had married the conjuror's daughter only a few days earlier, and was obviously upset at this attack on his new father-in-law.

The Major was dismayed. Sothern suggested that he write a letter of apology, perhaps saying that he had had a very jolly supper, and might have been a little under the influence of the wine when he spoke as he did. The Major wrote the letter, and Sothern promised to deliver it for him.

He did not deliver it. Instead, he wrote back a letter purport-ing to come from the Professor. This said that when an officer slanders a gentleman's honoured father-in-law, it is hardly an excuse to say that he was drunk when he did so.

The Major replied in tones both hurt and angry. Sothern wrote in the Professor's name challenging him to a duel. The Major showed this to Sothern and asked for his advice. Sothern said he would give the matter some thought, and invited him to call on him the following evening so that they could talk about it. Then he invited the Professor to dinner.

When the Major arrived, he found his epistolary foe seated there. The Professor rose, shook him by the hand courteously, and recalled their last meeting at the club. The Major could only assume that he was trying to patch up their quarrel, so he embarked on a long explanation of his side of it. The Professor, who of course knew nothing of the story that the drunken conjuror was his father-in-law or about the letters, listened in perplexity. Sothern watched them for a while, and then explained all.

He prized his amateur status as a jester, and resisted any suggestion that his hoaxes were anything but jokes. Thus, after investigating spiritualism and associated phenomena, then very much in vogue, and dismissing it all as a fraud, he and some friends gave demonstrations for invited guests of supposed spiritualist happenings. A British spiritualist magazine reported that he was giving seances. He wrote an angry denial:

'We *did* put pens under the table and get signatures from Shakespeare, Garrick and other valuable autographs; we did produce spirit hands and spirit forms; people did float in the air – at least, we made the audience really believe they did. . . . We got into a larger line of business than any of the professional exhibitors, and we were extensively patronised. The only difference was, *we* did not charge anything. We took no money, directly or indirectly. Our entertainment being free, was liberally supported; and when I add that the evenings invariably wound up with a jolly little supper, given at our own expense, it may be understood that the miracle circle was much favored.'

Sothern could be cruel in his humour, using his wit to make fun of people in a vulnerable position, such as waiters or, on one occasion, an untalented and rather vain young actor. He also violated several times another canon of acceptability in humour by appealing to someone's goodwill. Once, he sent a telegram to somebody saying that a mutual friend had died, and his wife and children were arriving by train, and asking him to give them hospitality and comfort.

This is a good place at which to pause and say that there *are* so-called practical jokes which are mean rather than funny, and should not be countenanced. A joke played on someone whose status or nature makes him particularly vulnerable is just a type of bullying, and hardly reflects on the wit of the person who practises it. Practical joking, like boxing, should be practised only with people of roughly the same size and weight. In fact, as in boxing, there is much credit in toppling a weightier opponent, but none in doing down a smaller one.

Another kind of joke that should not be tolerated is one which involves asking someone a favour and then taking advantage of him, so that the reward for generosity is a metaphorical custard pie in the face. This makes an open-hearted nature a bit more cynical, and slower to rush in to help a neighbour. On the television programme *Candid Camera*, the resident prankster once had some fun with a passer-by by pretending to have a speech defect and getting his help in making a telephone call, then making things difficult for the helper while the cameras recorded his antics. Disappointingly, the helper allowed himself to be jollied into taking this in good spirit when all was revealed, instead of landing his deceiver a telegenic punch.

Another kind is one that abuses a service offered to the public. It is very easy to telephone stores and order in someone else's name several dozen orchids, three grand pianos, a coffin and a ton of cement. This will simply make the stores concerned understandably less willing to accept orders over the telephone.

In America, and only in America, so far as I am aware, you can hire the performing talents of a professional hoaxer.

A famous one of the 1920s and '30s was Luke Barnett. He specialised in playing vaguely disruptive characters, usually with a foreign accent. The industrialist Alfred Corey, entertaining guests at his fishing lodge in Michigan, once hired Barnett to liven up the weekend. He introduced Barnett as his handyman, a bit odd at times but well worth the trouble. Barnett, slovenly and dirty, spent the weekend mumbling resentfully within earshot of one or another of the guests about 'rich pipples who live off the backs of poor, decent pipples', uttering class war slogans, and finally dark threats about bombs. Corey had to let his guests in on the joke to avoid a mass departure.

This way of life had its hazards. Once, Barnett was hired to play a quarrelsome waiter at a dinner attended by James 'Gentleman Jim' Corbett, the heavyweight boxing champion. He picked up some imagined slight and started insulting Corbett every time he passed him, threatening to slap him down. Corbett was not called 'Gentleman Jim' for nothing: he showed well-mannered restraint, and did not rise to Barnett's insults. But Corbett's dinner companion hit him.

Another professional in the field is William Stanley Sims, a New Yorker who switched from accountancy to making a profession of the kind of acts he put on to amuse his friends. Sims specializes in high-speed witty performances at conferences, the kind that Alan Abel is occasionally hired to put on.

Once he gave a talk to the Gourmet Society, and demonstrated the making of an omelette *flambé*, which exploded. Another time, he lectured the National Convention of Undertakers in the guise of an Egyptian authority on ancient Egyptian embalming. He embalmed a corpse as a demonstration and the corpse sat up and waved to the audience.

He was introduced into the list of speakers at a meeting of the American College of Surgeons as Dr. Eric Von Austerlitz, a distinguished Viennese surgeon. He delivered an account of an improbable operation he had performed in a rapid-fire stream of jargon, and concluded: 'In short, I removed the patient's entire alimentary canal, turned it upside down, and stitched it back into position.'

There was a bewildered silence, and eventually someone in the audience asked, 'What was the patient's complaint?'

'Hiccups,' said Sims.

*   *   *

There is a paradox built in to the very idea of a hoax. It is this: the more verissimilitude a hoax has, the more likely it is to be accepted as the truth. Yet the closer in appearance it is to the truth, the closer it becomes to actually being the truth. Sometimes, a hoax goes only a little further than reality. Sometimes it gives reality a slight nudge forward.

Graham Greene and a friend of his, the theatrical 'angel' John Sutro, once wrote a spoof letter to *The Times* in London proposing the creation of an Anglo-Texan Society. The Society is still going strong.

The letter was conceived one day in 1963, in a happy haze brought about by a number of black velvets – Guinness and champagne – consumed on the train from Edinburgh to London. They had just spent an enjoyable evening in the Scottish capital with two Texan girls, and had a few thoughts on

Anglo-Texan relations. They wrote it the next day, in formal terms, expressing the desirability of establishing 'cultural and social links between this country and the state of Texas', and also drawing attention to the special historical relationship between Britain and Texas. They thought it was hilarious. Greene thought that if the letter were published, someone would surely ask what this special relationship could be, but nobody did.

When the letter appeared, only the *New York Times* sniffed something odd. It said in an editorial: 'We feel skepticism, like a calcium deposit, residing right in our bones . . . We wonder whether Mr. Greene doesn't have some insidious plot underfoot?'

Others had purer bones, which lacked the same deposits. Greene, the most peripatetic of novelists, was in Kenya when the letter appeared. He was appalled to receive a cable from Sutro saying: 'Sixty inquiries on first day including Sir Hartley Shawcross Attorney General and Samuel Guinness the banker.'

Sutro decided that if people wanted something as ludicrous as an Anglo-Texan Society, then they should have it, and threw himself into the task with enthusiasm. He called a meeting and officers were elected, including Sir Alfred Bossom, the member of parliament, and Samuel Guinness, both of whom had worked in Texas. Regular meetings started. The high point of the joke so far as Sutro and Greene were concerned, was a giant barbecue held with the help of the U.S. Air Force, attended by 1,500 people, many of them the kind of professional Texans who sport ten-gallon hats and cowboy boots on any occasion. The U.S. ambassador to Britain, Winthrop Aldrich, was empowered by the Governor of Texas to represent him, and he handed a Texan flag to Sutro, who received it with appropriate words of solemn appreciation.

Sutro and Greene resigned after this, but the vehicle which they had started on its way went rolling on, to regular social occasions, including a cocktail party attended by Prince Philip, the placing of a plaque on the site in London once occupied by the legation of the Republic of Texas, and a membership swollen by the North Sea oil boom and the influx of Texan oilmen.

The late Hugh Troy, the artist and illustrator, and the creator of rhinoceros footprints on Cornell's campus, also found out how difficult it is to parody the truth by concocting something still more absurd.

In 1952, the American University in Washington D.C. started a course in ghost-writing (a columnist in the *New Yorker* suggested that to pass an examination in this course, the student should, properly, get someone else to take it). Troy, who lived in Washington, found this amusing. He inserted an advertisement in the Washington *Post* that read: 'Too Busy to Paint? Call on the ghost artists, 1426 33rd Street, N.W. We paint it, you sign it. Primitive (Grandma Moses type), impressionist, modern, cubist, abstract, sculpture . . . Why not give an exhibition?'

When some reporters smelled an amusing story and telephoned, Troy played it straight. He said that they operated out of New York, but were now opening a branch office in Washington because of the demand from Government employees He spoke of the difficulties of getting skilled staff – good cubists were currently in short supply, for instance – and labour troubles.

But the joke was on Troy. Letters arrived at his address. He found to his astonishment that people actually wanted to sign paintings as their own. A few days later, other advertisements appeared that were quite genuine offers by ghost artists soliciting for clients. They may still be in business.

Troy should not have been surprised. He had a somewhat similar experience when he was in the Air Force during the Second World War. He was at an Officers' Training School, and was amazed at the vast amounts of unnecessary paperwork that went on. Myriad details of insignificant operations at the camp were sent to the Pentagon in Washington.* So Troy carried this to what he thought was an ultimate point. He devised a report on fly-paper effectiveness. He wrote out a form and mimeographed a lot of copies, containing questions about the number of flies caught by each strip of fly-paper hanging in the mess hall, along with relevant details such as the positioning of each strip, the weather on that day, and so on. Then he filled in one

---

* Stewart Alsop once wrote that the character of an army is determined by the answer to the crucial question: what do you do with the men when they are not fighting, which is 99 per cent of the time? He compared the British and American armies, having served in both, and said the British answer to the question is parade ground drill, the American is paperwork.

of these forms each day and sent it off to an office in the Penta-gon.

As he used to tell the story afterwards, two other officer-cadets dropped by a week or two later, and said they had been told off because their units had not sent in their fly-paper effectiveness reports. Did he know anything about these reports?

'Sure,' he said, and handed them a sheaf of his mimeo-graphed forms. He left the camp shortly afterwards with his commission, and did not find out when the camp stopped send-ing fly-paper forms, if ever.

Troy acquired a reputation in his lifetime as a practical joker, and no less a judge than Harpo Marx once called him, in an article, 'the most eminent practitioner of the art.' He had a delicate, stylish wit that contrasted with his gargantuan build – he was six-foot-five and barrel-chested. Like Alan Abel, he some-times found his reputation a hindrance when he wanted to spoof someone.

However, one of his happiest spoofs was anonymous. When the Museum of Modern Art in New York held an exhibition of Van Goghs, he found it so crowded that he could hardly see the paintings. He suspected that this was due more to some of the lurid details of Van Gogh's life, recently acted on the screen by Kirk Douglas, than to admiration of his work.

So he carved an ear out of a piece of dried beef, and mounted it in a velvet lined box. Then he typed out a notice explaining that this was Van Gogh's ear, that the artist had cut off and sent to a prostitute. He smuggled this into the museum, and surrep-titiously hung it on a wall. Soon, it became the principal centre of attraction, surrounded by a gawking crowd. The paintings were nearly deserted, and Troy could enjoy them in peace.

Troy pulled off his first spoof on record at home in Ithaca, New York when he was 14 years old, and it could hardly have been more on record since it was in the *New York Times*. It was to get revenge for many a slight from his older sister. Young Hugh announced one day that he had poetic talents, and needled her into scoffing at the idea. He offered to bet her three treats to the movies that if he sent one of his poems to the *New York Times*, the paper would print it. His sister took him up on it.

So he sat down and wrote a letter to the page of the *Times*

Sunday book review section that is devoted to requests from readers for literary information. His letter went:

'Dear Sir, I am anxious to find a piece of poetry by an American, I believe, with some particularly moving stanzas about a gipsy maiden abandoned on the trail by her tribe. – Titus Grisby, Auburn, New York.'

This was published, and young Hugh sat down and wrote his answer:

'T. G. must be referring to the beautiful *Curse of the Gipsy Mandolin*, written in 1870 by the celebrated poet laureate of Syracuse, N.Y., Hugh Troy. – G. Claude Fletcher, Ithaca, N.Y.'

Then G. Claude Fletcher quoted for *Times* readers these memorable lines which appeared in the book review section the following Sunday:

> *So we leave her*
> *So we leave her*
> *So we leave her*
> *Far from where her swarthy kindred roam.*
> *In the scarlet fever*
> *In the scarlet fever*
> *In the scarlet fever*
> *Convalescent home.*

*   *   *

It was said above that it is a rare being who can enjoy a hoax all by himself for a long time, without any need to share with his victim, or someone else, the delicious knowledge that he is fooling him. There is one case of a man who fooled the whole world, and so far as we know, never shared his secret with anyone. This is the Piltdown Man fraud, the fabrication of a fossil that became one of the most famous in the world, a key link in the chain of Man's evolution. Some forty years after the discovery, it was found to be a fake.

We still do not know who perpetrated it, or why. It is a practical joke, albeit a high-toned one, in that it was not done for any material reward. Whoever did it showed skill and expertise, and had the laugh on the scientific world and the general public. If he wanted some accomplishment just so that he could hug it to himself in bed at night, then he achieved it.

The Piltdown skull was discovered in 1912 in a gravel pit near Piltdown Common in Sussex, and it aroused enormous interest immediately. Darwin's Theory of Evolution had trickled down to the whole reading public, and people were very evolution conscious. There were many articles in the popular Press about our simian ancestors, and Stone Age Man.

The principal discoverer was Charles Dawson, a local solicitor and amateur palaeontologist who had already earned the respect of some scientific bodies for his work, in collecting and identifying fossils. A workman repairing a farm road showed him a piece of fossilized human bone which he had found in a nearby gravel pit, and Dawson went to look for more.

He found there the fossilized remains of the skull and jawbone of a creature that exhibited some characteristics of both ape and Man, and appeared to be about 500,000 years old. He had begun to develop a human brain, though he was still thick-headed – the skull bone was twice the thickness of that of modern Man; the forehead was steep, more modern than the low, sloping forehead of the Neanderthal Man. The mandible and the jaw were similar to those of a chimpanzee, while the two teeth found there were human in form, and ground down in a particular way that had been noted before in the teeth of primitive Man.

The exploration of the gravel pit took weeks, and during the latter part, Dawson was accompanied by two colleagues, one of them already distinguished, the other later to become still more so. The first was Dr. Arthur Smith Woodward, head of the Geology Department at the British Museum. The second was a young French palaeontologist and Jesuit novitiate who was to become famous as a philosopher, Teilhard de Chardin.

The discovery was hailed as one of major significance, particularly in Britain. *Nature,* then as now the most authoritative general scientific magazine, said Piltdown Man seemed to be far older than Neanderthal Man, and concluded: 'Dr. Smith Woodward accordingly inclines to the theory that the Neanderthal race was a degenerate offshoot of early Man, while surviving modern Man may have arisen directly from a primitive source of which the Piltdown skull provides the first discovered evidence.'

There was an element of national pride in this enthusiasm.

Charles Darwin and his principal interpreters had all been British, yet the discoveries that shed light on Man's ancestry were all being made elsewhere: in Java, and, more gallingly, closer home, in France and Germany. 'Neanderthal' is actually the name of the valley near Dusseldorf where the first skull of this type was found. Now Neanderthal Man was relegated to the status of a 'degenerate offshoot', which seemed right and proper for a foreigner. Dr. Smith Woodward called his book about Piltdown Man *The Earliest Englishman*.

The Piltdown gravel pit became celebrated. Visiting palaeontologists and geologists were taken there for a token dig, coach parties stopped there, and the local pub was re-named The Piltdown Man.

There were a few skeptics from the start. Not that anyone suspected fraud. But some anthropologists doubted that that skull and that jawbone could have belonged to the same creature. A number of American scholars were among these doubters. The Natural History Museum in New York City always adopted a very cautious approach. It showed a replica of the Piltdown remains in a glass case with a card making no claims for them, but saying simply: 'The brain case represents a very early and human type, the jaw much resembles that of a chimpanzee.'

Most of the skeptics were won over when Dawson found two fossilised pieces of skull and another tooth at a spot two miles away in 1915. It was conceivable that a fossilised human skull and a monkey's jaw had, by coincidence, lain in the same gravel pit. It was hardly possible that the coincidence could be repeated two miles away.

Dawson fell ill and died in 1916, in his late forties, and is commemorated by a memorial stone at the Piltdown site. Piltdown Man became part of our scientific furniture. But as more and more fossils of primitive Man were uncovered, it began to be seen, no longer as the missing piece in the evolutionary jigsaw, but as a piece that did not fit in anywhere in the pattern.

Important fossil finds in the 1930s in several parts of the world built up a fuller picture of the early forms of Man. These showed that the jaw and teeth started evolving towards their human form early on, while the evolution of the skull came later. But Piltdown Man indicated the opposite order: he had a modern forehead and an ape-like jaw. Some anthropologists suggested that there were two separate lines of descent from the apes, and the Piltdown Man was the only specimen so far discovered of one of these lines. By 1948, the Piltdown find had become, as the palaeontologist Sir Arthur Keith called it, 'the Piltdown enigma'. There were a number of speculations about the enigma. No one ever suggested at any stage the possibility of a hoax.

Its exposure came about because new techniques of investigation became available. The most important of these was the fluorine test: fossilised bones acquire fluorine as they lie in the ground, and it is possible to determine roughly the age of a fossil by measuring its fluorine content. In 1949, Dr. Kenneth Page Oakley of the British Museum told the Geological Society in London that he had applied the fluorine test to the Piltdown Man remains and found them to be much less than half a million years old. A dental researcher applied modern techniques of dental analysis to the teeth and came out in the *British Medical Journal* with the startling assertion that the teeth were modern.

In May, 1953, a congress of palaeontologists was held in London. After dinner one evening, Dr. Oakley, who had applied the fluorine test to the remains, was discussing the Piltdown enigma with Dr. J. S. Weiner, also at Oxford University, and Professor S. L. Washburn, of the University of Chicago. Together, they began to add up all the discrepancies in the Piltdown Man that had come to light, including some curious gaps in the record of the way the discoveries were made. They decided that the time was ripe for a concerted attack on the problem using all the modern techniques of analysis. Weiner and Oakley, with a team of assistants, carried out more rigorous fluorine tests than the earlier one, took X-rays, and made other chemical analyses. They were amazed at what they found.

They announced their conclusion in November, 1953. The Piltdown Man was a fake, fabricated with great care and expertise. It was a modern skull made to look like a fossil, and a monkey's jaw, with human teeth artificially ground down. They reported: 'Those who took part in the excavation at Piltdown were the victims of an elaborate and inexplicable deception.'

The reaction was almost one of disbelief. Dr. Weiner reports one man as saying: 'I feel as if something has gone out of my life. I was brought up on Piltdown Man.' For some Britons, the news that the 'earliest Englishman' was a fabrication was the same kind of blow as the announcement by the Vatican a few years later that St. George, the patron saint of England, never existed. But scientists, once they got over the shock, were relieved. With Piltdown Man out of the way, the pattern formed by other fossil discoveries made sense. Sir Mortimer Wheeler said: 'The new Piltdown discovery removes an awkward customer from the line of human evolution.'

But it introduced another awkward customer: the hoaxer. Who could it be, and why did he do it? Palaeontologists knew now that the laugh was on them. But who was laughing? Colleagues and friends of Dawson who were still alive defended him vigorously against suggestions that he had faked the find forty-one years earlier. Teilhard de Chardin told interviewers that neither Dawson nor Smith Woodward could conceivably have been guilty. The author Ronald Millar, in his book *The Piltdown Men*, nominates another scientist, Grafton Elliot Smith as the likely candidate, on the basis of his expertise, his motives, and his personality traits, particularly the assumption of his own superiority and the pleasure in his own wit. Dr. Weiner, in his book *The Piltdown Forgeries*, points the finger of suspicion at Dawson, and cites a number of telling points of evidence, but admits that they are circumstantial.

Dr. Weiner concludes his book on the fraud with the words: 'Though today we are still far from an understanding of many matters concerning Man's origins, we are in no doubt about the reality of the transformation which has brought Man from a simian status to his *sapiens* form and capability.'

We have also learned from the Piltdown fraud some of the curious twists that this *sapiens* quality takes, and also some of the holes in it.

Fit to Print: Hoaxing and the Media

The old saw says, 'Let a sleeping dog lie.'
Right. Still, when there is much at stake, it is
better to get a newspaper to do it.
MARK TWAIN, from
Pudd'nhead Wilson's New Calendar

WITH the creation of the mass media, a whole new area of deception was opened up. This provided the means of fooling the whole public at the same time in the same way. Anything told through the mass media carries credibility. It is more solid than rumour, more respectable than gossip, more believable than hearsay. People who say they never believe what they read in the newspapers in fact absorb what they read as uncritically as any others.

The authority that is usually given to the mass media, regardless of the message, is seen in the lack of discrimination with which unsophisticated readers and viewers talk about them. 'The newspapers say so-and-so.' One wants to ask *which* newspaper. And which part of the newspaper, the editorial columns or the news pages? And whether it was one of the newspaper's own staff or an outside commentator. 'They said on television . . .' But, one wants to ask, *who* said? Was it the news reader, stating it as a fact? Or was he reporting it as someone else's opinion? Or was someone giving it as *his* viewpoint, a politician, a commentator, or a critic? After all, you don't say 'They said on the telephone', you say who told you.

This authority stems partly from the fact that the media, and particularly the news media, deal with public issues that are beyond the experience of most of its audience. (Where they do touch on people's experience, they are given less credence. People are skeptical about newspaper reports of the cost of living.)

Most deliberate deviations from the strict truth consist of

exaggerations or distortions to make a better story. When it comes to sheer invention, the most common kind is the short filler, the brief, unimportant item that gets into the newspaper only because it is unusual or entertaining. Some of these fillers have a long life. I remember reading Arthur Koestler's autobiography *Arrow In The Blue* when it first came out, and reading Koestler's account of his spell as a young reporter in the Paris office of a German newspaper group in the 1920s. A girl in the office specialised in making up these items. He still remembered one: a truck containing butter and milk collided with another loaded with eggs on a road in central France, and one truck caught fire; the result was an omelette eight feet across. Two weeks after I read this, I saw substantially the same story in a London newspaper.

This kind of thing is accepted, if it is, because people read newspapers with uncritical inattention. How many people would accept one, let alone all, of the following stories if they were told person-to-person by an acquaintance:

A hen on a farm in Connecticut laid a red, white and blue egg on July 4th. A cow swallowed a watch; it was recovered after several years and was found to be still going, and only two hours out, because the cow's breathing wound it up constantly. A man painted a spider on his bald head to keep the flies away, and it worked. All these stories were fabrications planted in New York newspapers by a rural correspondent under a Winsted, Connecticut, dateline, and they aroused no murmur of skepticism.

One reason is that the real world usually can be counted on to present the media with news items which are perfectly true and which are no less far-fetched. Stories like these:

Mrs. Marva Drew, a 91-year-old chiropractor of Waterloo, Iowa, has typed out every number from one to a million. 'It was a challenge,' she said. 'One of my patients said that nobody could count up to a million.' – from the *San Francisco Chronicle*, December 10, 1974.

Clive Numbig, an accountant of Pasco, British Columbia, asked Ontario University to return part of the tuition fee he paid for a course on 'Death and Dying'. He refused to continue after he was asked to fill out a death certificate with his own name on it. Professor John Kigo, for the university, said: 'I can't understand Mr. Numbig's attitude. The only other person who objected to filling in the form was found to be illiterate.' – from the *Daily Mirror*, London May 5, 1975.

The Stalybridge, Middlesex, Old People's Club rejected an offer by the local council of a disused mortuary in their neighbourhood as a fun centre. – from the Edmonton, Middlesex *Journal*, April 24, 1975.

The invented filler does harm because it violates the truth and lowers journalistic standards. And it is only fair to say that the tradition of these inventions is dying. News editors today generally look critically at the funny or quaint story that seems far-fetched, particularly if it does not contain names and addresses that can readily be checked.

But other journalistic frauds have, and are intended to have, much more serious consequences than these. The mass media are the windows through which people see national and international events (how else would most people know what is going on in China? Or that China is even *there*?). Distorting the glass can create a life-like but false impression of what is on the other side of it, and help to shape public opinion accordingly. If the deceiver wants to exercise power, then this is power indeed.

There are many examples of politically-motivated media deceptions, varying in degree and importance. The most notorious, unsurpassed in its mendacity and its consequences, was the series of distortions and outright inventions by the Hearst newspaper chain in America in the late 1890s aimed at fomenting war between the United States and Spain. It has often been said that *Uncle Tom's Cabin*, by its effect on public opinion, caused the American Civil War; this is an exaggeration, but it is certainly true that the Hearst newspapers went a long way towards bringing about the Spanish–American War.

The nationalist revolt against Spanish rule in Cuba was nearly played out when William Randolph Hearst, a man with a limitless desire for power over people's minds, took an interest in it. On Hearst's personal instructions his newspapers printed horrendous stories about Spanish repression, concocted by Cuban exiles in New York. 'Feeding Prisoners to the Sharks', was one headline in the *New York Journal*. And of the Spanish military commander in Cuba, General Valeriano Weyler, the *Journal* said: 'There is nothing to prevent his carnal, animal brain from running riot in inventing tortures and infamies of bloody debauchery.' The brains of Hearst journalists did not do badly when it came to this kind of invention.

A few stand out. One, which roused patriotic American feelings, was the battle of Pinar del Rio, reported by Frederick Lawrence, the correspondent the Hearst newspapers finally sent to Cuba after relying for some time on Cuban exiles. In this battle, the town of Pinar del Rio was wrested from Spanish troops by a band of American volunteers fighting for the rebel cause. Only there was no such band and no such battle.

Another was the search of the three Cuban girls. Three Cuban girls, about to sail for the United States, were stripped and searched by a matron of the Cuban customs service on an American ship in Havana harbour, to ensure that they were complying with export regulations. Richard Harding Davis cabled a brief report of the incident. To his dismay, the Hearst newspapers splashed it across their front pages, giving it a lurid hue, and neglecting to mention that the search was carried out by a matron. The *New York World* excelled itself with a half-page drawing of the three girls standing naked before leering Spanish policemen. A resolution was introduced into Congress calling on the Secretary of State to take up this infamy with the Spanish Government, since it had occurred on an American ship. All this happened during the three days that the girls were on the high seas. When they arrived in New York they denied it all, and were furious at the stain on their honour.

A wider campaign was whipped up over Evangeline Cisneros, the beautiful daughter of a Cuban nationalist leader. When her father was captured, she asked bravely that she be allowed to accompany him to prison, and she did. Then Hearst newspapers went to town. They pictured the plight of this girl 'in the clutches of the bestial Spaniards'. Wisely, they left the feverish imagination which this aroused in readers to fill in the details. A world-wide campaign got under way. Appeals were sent to the American Government and the Pope, and women in Britain signed a petition calling for mercy. Hearst newspapers produced Cuban witnesses to the appalling conditions in which she was held, which had reduced her to an emaciated wreck. (This picture of her as an emaciated wreck undoubtedly weakened the libidinous passions aroused by the other image, of the voluptuous Caribbean beauty at the mercy of fiends, but everything has its price.)

In fact, Miss Cisneros was being kept in a fairly comfortable room in a prison building. An enterprising Hearst reporter, Karl Decker, climbed on to an adjacent flat roof, broke the window and helped her out. This was hailed as a feat of gallant daring the like of which had not been seen since Lochinvar put away his riding boots. When she got to America, Hearst newspapers organised a series of receptions around the country, despite the slight embarrassment caused by her glowing health.

After the battleship 'Maine' blew up and sank in Havana harbour, Hearst newspapers left the truth even further behind. Headlines in the following week in the *New York Journal* included these: 'Rush of Soldiers To All Seaside Forts'. 'Recruiting Already Begun. Troops Impatient to March'. 'Citizens Demand That Congress Take Action'. There was no factual basis for any of these. They printed an interview with Theodore Roosevelt, the Assistant Secretary of the Navy, commending the *Journal*'s campaign on Cuba. Though a hawk on the issue, he denounced the report as invention and said the interview never took place. They carried an interview with a prominent senator, John Sherman of Ohio, calling for war with Spain: *he* denounced *that* as an invention. The circulation of Hearst's newspapers continued to rise.

Hearst's own attitude to the truth throughout his life was one of cheerful cynicism. It is shown in the famous cable that he sent to Frederick Remington in Cuba. Remington, an illustrator, was dispatched by Hearst newspapers to sketch scenes of the fighting. He cabled that there was no war, and he wanted to come home. Hearst cabled back: 'Please remain. You furnish the pictures and I will furnish the war.'

Most of his senior executives did not have his boldness, and needed a fig-leaf of hypocrisy. The managing editor of the *Chicago American*, a Hearst newspaper, once instructed his staff to either get or fabricate interviews with prominent Chicagoans supporting one of the newspaper's campaigns. Interviews were invented. Some of the people whose names had been used complained personally to Hearst, and four reporters were fired as a consequence. One of the four, William Salisbury, protested to the managing editor on their behalf. The managing editor reacted with indignation, and told him: 'Anyone who becomes so far lost to a sense of right and justice–to a sense of honor–as to quote a person saying what that person never said deserves no consideration. Mr. Hearst and I will tolerate no deviation from the truth.' This left Salisbury speechless. He slunk out, and accepted his notice without further protest.

One of the foremost fiction-writers in the Cuban non-war was a man who is interesting because his whole career is an inversion of the precepts of journalism, William Mannix. Mannix had a sound journalistic sense of what makes a good story, but no idea that this should relate to something that is actually happening. He served in Havana as a correspondent for the *New York Times* and other papers, and produced stories of Spanish repression which confirmed the picture the Hearst newspapers were giving. He had already lost a job as a local reporter in upstate New York for sending fictitious lists of celebrated guests at Adirondack resorts to big-city newspapers. Deported from Cuba, he went on a lecture tour as a martyr to free reporting. He joined the *Philadelphia Press*, and was fired after inventing a story that involved the paper in an enormous libel suit. Then he got a job on the *Honolulu Advertiser* on a forged recommendation, and six months later was sent to prison for forging cheques.

It was in Honolulu jail that Mannix produced his one enduring work. This was the memoirs of the Chinese statesman Li Hung Chang, a figure well known on the international scene who had just died. It is still found in libraries today. He evidently had access to books on contemporary China because he researched his subject well. An American publisher bought the manuscript after people who had known Li Hung Chang and his role in world politics said it seemed authentic. The book was a big seller, and was serialised in the *Observer* in London.

Released from prison, Mannix started the Pacific Associated Press, with a list of fictitious directors; it syndicated stories and interviews with prominent people in Asia, most of them bogus. When the authenticity of the Li Hung Chang memoirs was called into question and letters on the subject arrived for him, he answered in the names of other directors. Eventually, the Pacific Associated Press carried a story that William Mannix had disappeared in China. Then several newspapers received letters signed with the name of one of the other directors suggesting that they send money to help finance an expedition to go and search for him.

Large-scale and prolonged journalistic fraud on this scale is unlikely today. This is partly because most journalists have a greater sense of responsibility, and partly also because of the multiplicity of Press organs and the facilities available. News media are critical of each other, and it is unlikely that one or two could keep a bogus war going for long without others exposing it.

*   *   *

In all these cases, the people of the media themselves perpetrated the deceptions. But often, others are able to use the power of the Press to carry their own deceptions, either for fun or for profit. Indeed, there are people whose profession it is to use the Press to spread messages which often border on hoax and fraud.

The most famous painting in America is 'September Morn'. Almost certainly it has been seen by more people than any other. It adorns calendars and posters, and has sold more than seven million copies. It was painted by the French artist Paul Chabas in 1902, and it depicts a pretty young girl, winsome and naked, but keeping within the bounds of turn-of-the-century decency by huddling deliciously as she shivers in the mist at the edge of the sea. Its fame is due entirely to a hoax which was designed to rescue it from obscurity, and to the newspaper publicity this gained for it.

The painting arrived in the United States originally as an offering for a brewery calendar, and was rejected. A Brooklyn shop-keeper acquired 2,000 copies, and at ten cents each, which was pretty reasonable even in those days, he could not sell one. Somehow, he came into contact with Harry Reichenbach, who was then just starting to work as a New York Press agent. He offered Reichenbach 45 dollars if he could find a market for these 2,000 pictures. Reichenbach created one.

He turned to Anthony Comstock, a famous anti-vice campaigner of the time, and the President of the vociferous Anti-Vice League. He had the shop-keeper put the picture in the window, then telephoned Comstock to complain that an indecent picture was affronting passers-by on a Brooklyn Street. But Comstock would not rise to this. In his later days, Reichenbach would not even have tried anything so primitive.

He collected a bunch of street urchins, and paid them 50 cents each to do as he said. Then he stormed into the office of the Anti-Vice League, an indignant citizen, and declared to Comstock: 'This picture is an outrage! It's undermining the morals of our city's youth.' He took Comstock by the arm and marched him along to see it. Comstock saw, to his horror, the collection of boys standing in front of the shop window ogling 'September Morn' with precociously salacious expressions. This was too much. He went to the shop-keeper and demanded that he remove the picture. The shop-keeper refused.

Comstock took him to court, described in moving terms the appalling scene of corrupted youth, and demanded an injunction. The court rejected his plea. By this time, every newspaper in New York was carrying the story, and most of them featured photographs of 'September Morn'. Puritan preachers summoned up the spectacle in their sermons, vaudeville comics made jokes about it, and it became a talking point, and rocketed to fame. The original was bought many years later for $70,000 by William Cox Wright of Philadelphia, and in 1975 it was put on display at the Metropolitan Museum of Art in New York.

Reichenbach went on from there to movies. When the fledgling industry was taking its first upright steps, he became the first press agent to play a key role, persuading producers that what people read and heard about a film, and how *much* they read and heard about it, was a bigger factor in deciding whether they bought a ticket than what was in the film. Thus, he became one of those people who use the Press to spread their hoakum across the land.

Once, he hired a group of Turkish waiters in a New York restaurant, garbed them in traditional Turkish costumes, and had them roaming around New York State looking for an American marine who had eloped with their Pasha's beautiful daughter. This received good play in the newspapers. Coincidentally, their quest was similar to the plot of the film 'The Virgin of Stamboul', which was about to be released. But the newspapers were not all that docile, and in Schenectady, a reporter noticed that a label hanging from the silk jacket which one of the Turks was wearing bore the name of a New York theatrical costumers.

Reichenbach ensured publicity for the film 'Trilby', taken from George du Maurier's famous novel about Svengali, by hiring an aspiring actress to fall into a trance while watching it, so that she was taken away to Bellevue Hospital. That she possessed considerable acting talent is indicated by the fact that she had doctors puzzling over her all day; when she eventually awoke she murmured, 'Those eyes! Take them away!' The newspapers were full of interviews with psychologists and doctors about whether someone could be hypnotized by an actor on the screen, and nearly everyone wanted to see 'Trilby'.

Many of Harry Reichenbach's stunts and hoaxes are recounted in his unfinished autobiography, *Phantom Fame: an Anatomy of Ballyhoo*. He seems to have been drawn to the idea of fooling the many from early days. He says that when he was a boy in Frostburg, Maryland, a hypnotist who called himself the Great Griffith arrived in town advertising his ability to cure all sorts of ills. As a demonstration of his powers, he offered to put anyone to sleep for six days. There were no takers of this offer until one young stranger who was visiting his aunt said he had a few days to kill and would not mind. So the Great Griffith hypnotized him, and for six days the man lay in a trance in a store window, where all of Frostburg could see. It was impressive, and a lot of people went to Griffiths to be hypnotized and given a cure for their troubles.

Reichenbach, 'in a spirit of research', he says, visited the store on a quiet morning, slipped behind the curtain to where the man lay in a trance, and whispered, 'The Professor would like to know how you're getting along.'

The prostrate form whispered back: 'Tell the Bozo I'm O.K.'

Reichenbach began his career as a teenager working for a travelling country circus, and then publicizing some acts who travelled on their own. One of these was a psychic medium called the Great Reynard. Travelling through the country towns of Vermont one month and finding business bleak, the youthful Reichenbach bribed a woman in Rutland to take her sleeping infant in its cot to a disused barn in some woodland on the edge of town, and then set up a hysterical hue and cry that the child had been stolen from its home. Reynard offered his psychic powers in the search, and the local chief of police, badgered by the desperate mother and neighbours to try anything, agreed to listen to him. Before a large assemblage, Reynard was blindfolded, then went into a trance, and uttered weird, piercing sounds from his trance that chilled the blood of the onlookers. Then he lurched off along the road, with Reichenbach going alongside, and guiding him by surreptitious signals. He pressed on into the woodlands, with the crowd following, and still guided by Reichenbach, led the way to the barn. The child was found inside, still sleeping. The Great Reynard packed the local theatre for ten nights after that.

Telling this story, Reichenbach makes an observation about the aftermath that will find an echo with anyone who has had much experience of hoaxing. He says he found that Reynard came to believe that he really had psychic powers, and that he had found the missing child in Rutland, Vermont, with their aid. He could not recall Reichenbach guiding him to the place with whispers and signals and, later, denied strenuously that he had done so. Reichenbach writes: 'Reynard's faculty of gradually believing the flattering fictions that I built up around him struck me as rather peculiar. But later on, when I handled famous movie stars like Rudolf Valentino, Wallace Reid, Barbara LaMarr and others, I realised that this was the irony of all publicity. No matter how fantastic the ruse by which an unknown actor is lifted to fame, he'd come to believe it was true, and the poor press agent would be shocked to find that he had never told a lie.'

Others have used the Press as a medium to disseminate their hoaxes just for fun.

Hugh Troy was one of these. His first media hoax shows his essential benevolence. It was when he was still at Cornell, and he used to send in the results of track and field events to local newspapers. He felt sorry for the person who was listed as being last in the race, so he hit upon a way to spare the runner this humiliation. He invented an athlete called Johnny Tsal (try it backwards) who came in last in every event, so that none of the real participants had this indignity. He kept it up for quite a while, until someone noticed.

Others have invented athletic teams, since minor sports results are usually telephoned to newspapers by someone representing the team rather than by a regular correspondent. Morris Newburger, a Wall Street stockbroker, invented a college called Plainfield Teachers, loated in Plainfield, New Jersey, and gave it a football team. Then he telephoned the *New York Times* and *Herald Tribune*, with the results of Plainfield Teachers' games with Winona, Randolph Tech, and other colleges. He invented details, such as coach Ralph Hoblitzel's W formation, with a five-man backfield, a few players, including a valuable tackle called Morris Newburger, and a brilliant Chinese-American quarterback called Johny Chung, a triple-threat who deserved to make all-American.

For a while, Newburger was enchanted to see his creations in print every Sunday, but then he became more ambitious. As publicity agent Jerry Croyden, he started sending out Press releases about Plainfield Teachers, and in particular the winning ways of Johny Chung, who might make all-American and would fortify himself with a bowl of rice between halves. Some of this made the sports pages. But some reporters went looking for Johny Chung, and Newburger was exposed simultaneously in the *Herald Tribune* and *Times*.

Then there were the Chilean octuplets, perpetrated by a group of medical students at Santiago University in 1952, which fooled the world. It involved careful planning. They telephoned newspapers with the story that octuplets had been born in a Santiago hospital. Through a ruse, one of their number was occupying the director's office in the hospital at that moment, and when newspapers telephoned about the story, he confirmed it, in the director's name. Most Chilean newspapers rushed into print with banner headlines while reporters hurried over to get more details. The Associated Press bureau swallowed the story and carried it around the world, and it was printed from Maine to Manila.

Professor Rutherford Aris has the distinction of being the only person ever to get a hoax entry into *Who's Who in America*. He is a professor of chemical engineering at the University of Minnesota, and the author of several books in his field. His hoax entry was not the result of any long-held ambition on his part. Rather, as he sees it, *Who's Who* came to him begging to be taken in, and he finally obliged them.

It happened like this. Rutherford Aris was already listed in

Who's Who in America when a letter arrived from the editors addressed to Aris Rutherford, with a request for biographical data so that he could be listed. He wrote back explaining that they had reversed his first and last names, and that he was already listed.

Unaccountably, this letter was ignored. Instead of a reply, he received the standard letter that goes to people who have not filled in their forms, pointing out the honour of being selected for inclusion, and saying: 'The editors will have no alternative, in the absence of your good assistance, but to compile data from whatever sources are available.'

'So far as I am concerned,' Professor Aris said later, 'the pomposity of these documents was too much, and the undergraduate in me took over.'

His fondness for Scotch whisky and the countryside of Scotland determined Aris Rutherford's wildly unlikely biography. It is replete with names and associations that ring bells in the Scotch whisky world. He had him born in Strath Spey, and educated at the Glenlivet Institution for Distillation Engineering. He also gave him Greek associations (the 'Aris' was presumably short for Aristotle) with a mother whose maiden name was Ephygeneia Aristeides; he was at one time visiting Professor of Distillation Practise at the Technical Institute of the Aegean, in Corinth. He was also a trustee of the Scottish-Greek Friendship Foundation and a member of the Hellenophilic Club in Minneapolis. Aris was tempted to have him born on 1st April, but decided that this would be a give-away; looking at what the editors swallowed, he now thinks he was too cautious. Rutherford was the author of two books on whisky manufacture, and also *American Football: a Guide for Interested Scots.*

All this duly appeared. He sent in an addition for inclusion in the next edition: authorship of a successor to his book about football, *American Baseball: a Guide for Interested Englishmen.*

He had no intention of letting the story out, and only shared the joke with a few friends. He planned to go on adding books in successive years, with one about basketball explained for the Welsh and another about ice hockey for the Irish. But a reporter on the *Minneapolis Star* heard about it from one of his finders, and the newspaper broke the story.

The most famous fake ever foisted on a newspaper had a much more serious purpose than any of these. This was the series of forged Parnell letters which *The Times* printed in 1887, and which caused a political sensation at the time. They were indeed sensational. They were signed with the name of Charles Parnell, the leader of the Irish Home Rule party in the British Parliament. They implicated him in Irish terrorism, specifically, in the assassination of two senior British officials in Dublin five years earlier, the famous Phoenix Park murders. Their appearance in *The Times* was a triumph for the anti-Home Rule forces, though a short-lived one.

Then as now, the Irish question stirred passions, but in those days the feeling was as strong in England as it was in Ireland. Parnell was a man both loved and hated with enthusiasm. The bitter hostility felt towards him by many people who opposed his cause helps to explain the readiness with which these forgeries were accepted as genuine, both by *The Times* and its readers.

They were the work of Richard Pigott, who had operated for years on the fringe of Irish politics, soliciting money from both sides. A Unionist official, Caulfield Houston, asked him whether, through his previous connections, he knew of any documentary evidence that could link Parnell with illegal activities. Piggott never turned away a customer, and he said he did and could find it for a fee. After some searching, he said some renegade Irish terrorists in Paris were prepared to sell it to him. He was given £850 to buy it, as well as his own fee, and he produced the letters.

Houston was delighted at the find, and was in no mood to be critical or to ask searching questions. It was a series of five-year-old letters signed with Parnell's name addressed to people in extremist nationalist circles. One, written before the Phoenix Park murders, demanded: 'What are these fellows waiting for? This inaction is inexcusable, our best men are in prison and nothing is being done. Let there be an end to this hesitancy. Prompt action is called for.' In another, written shortly after the murders, Parnell apologised for having denounced the killings in Parliament but explained that this was politically necessary, and went on to say that Thomas Burke, the Under-Secretary for Ireland and one of the victims, 'got no more than his desserts'.

Houston and some colleagues knew that this was dynamite, that could destroy Parnell politically if it were planted in the right place. The best place was *The Times*, where it would reach the most influential audience and be given the greatest possible credence. They took the letters to the manager of *The Times*, John Cameron Macdonald, and he bought them for £1,780. He did not ask Houston how he obtained the letters. To check their authenticity, he showed them to a handwriting expert, and this was all.

On the strength of this and this alone, *The Times* published the letters, in a series of articles called 'Parnellism and Crime'. It said in an editorial that it was publishing 'documentary evidence which has a most serious bearing on the Parnellite conspiracy, and which, after a most careful and minute scrutiny, is, we are quite satisfied, authentic.' That phrase 'careful and minute scrutiny' was to come back and haunt *The Times*.

The Conservative Government of the day seized immediately upon the letters, which confirmed their darkest suspicions about Parnell. They never doubted that the letters were genuine; after all, they had appeared in *The Times*. A contemporary historian, John Morley, explained: 'They put their trust in the most serious, the most powerful, the most responsible newspaper in the world.'* Two days after the letters appeared, the Conservative Prime Minister, Lord Salisbury, called Parnell 'a man whose advocacy of assassination is well-known'.

Parnell denied authorship of the letters in Parliament, and demanded an official inquiry. He got one, and gradually, the story came out. Piggott fled to Madrid and committed suicide as police came to arrest him. No one else was guilty of anything beyond gross negligence, and a wish to believe the worst about the champion of home rule. Parnell, the hero vindicated, was more popular than ever, and received an ovation when he next rose to speak in the House of Commons.

*   *   *

We have seen before examples of hoaxes that, once exposed, would still not fade away. This is particularly likely to happen to hoax stories that get into print because, once in print, they

---

* *Life of Gladstone* by John Morley.

tend to remain in the files. One of the most durable of these is H. L. Mencken's spoof history of the bathtub in America. In writing the article, Mencken may have taken up the torch from his father. The elder Mencken, without benefit of mass media, used to enjoy starting rumours racing through Baltimore with a few casual remarks in a bar-room. Among the rumours he started were that the Brooklyn Bridge had collapsed, that because of impending floods the Dutch Government was removing the entire population of Holland to the United States, and that Bismarck, then Chancellor of Germany, had resigned and was emigrating to Milwaukee to open a brewery.

Mencken's farrago of nonsense about the bathtub is scarcely more credible than any of these, yet it retains currency to this day. He wrote the article in the *New York Evening Mail* on 28th December, 1917, and called it 'A Neglected Anniversary'. This was the 75th anniversary of the introduction of the bathtub into America, which supposedly took place in 1842 in Cincinnati. The man responsible was one Adam Thompson, who had seen Lord John Russell's bathtub in England, where the bathtub was still a novelty, when he was on a tour of Europe. There had been tubs before in America, it is true, but none connected to the plumbing as his was.

From here on the article, while maintaining its straight delivery, rises further from the grounds of probability, let alone reality. It recounts the attempts to ban the bathtub for all sorts of reasons: that it was dangerous to the health in winter, that it used too much water, and that it 'softens the moral fibre of the republic', quoting from the *Western Medical Repository* of April 23rd, 1843. Boston made taking a bath unlawful except on medical advice. Virginia levied a special tax on bathtubs. But it gradually gained ground. The American Medical Association, at its annual meeting in 1859, polled its members and found that 55 per cent found bathing in a tub harmless and 20 per cent found it beneficial. Finally, President Millard Fillmore introduced a bathtub into the White House, And so on.

One would have thought from his writings that Mencken already had a low enough opinion of human intelligence not to be shocked by any manifestations of people's gullibility. But the reaction to his article evidently surprised him.

He wrote about this nine years later. He said his article about

the anniversary of the bathtub was written 'as a piece of spoofing to relieve the strain of war days', and describes it as 'a tissue
of absurdities, all of them deliberate and most of them obvious'.
He said he was amazed when some people took it seriously, and
still more so when his 'facts' appeared in other people's writings.
He went on:

'As far as I know, I am the first person to actually question
these facts in print. Once more, I suppose, I'll be accused of
taking the wrong side for the mere pleasure of standing in opposition. The Cincinnati boomers, who have made much of the
boast that the bathtub industry, now running to 200 million
dollars a year, was started in their town, will charge me with
spreading lies against them. The chiropractors will damn me for
blowing up their ammunition. The medical gents, having
swallowed my quackery, will denounce me as a quack for exposing them. In the end no doubt, the thing will simmer down
to a general feeling that I have committed some vague and
sinister crime against the United States, and there will be a
renewal of the demand that I be deported to Russia.'

But it would take a heavier swat than this to knock the story
out of the newspaper files and historical 'records'. In his book
Hoaxes, published in 1954, Curtis MacDougall lists fifty-five
references to the history of the bathtub which take Mencken's
article as fact, whether acknowledging the source or not. These
include a reference by a professor at Harvard University's
Medical School, and a speech by President Truman about the
progress of public health, as well as many light-weight newspaper articles of the 'Isn't life funny?' variety; one of these, in
the *Boston Herald*, came only three weeks after another article
in the newspaper which recalled Mencken's spoof under the
heading 'The American People Will Swallow Anything'.

Media men themselves have not always been above using
their authority to spoof the public, sometimes to add zest to the
job. For instance, Jeremy Campbell, at this writing the Washington correspondent of the London *Evening Standard*, began
his career on that paper as one of the reporters producing what
was called the 'London Last Night' page. This page used to report in twittering tones the high life of London the night before,
with particular attention to the debutante set. Campbell soon
became bored with this job, as any intelligent young man would,

and he enlivened it by inventing a debutante called Venetia Crust. He injected into the page such riveting items as the news that green-eyed, stiletto-heeled Venetia asked her father to give her £1,000 to put on horses instead of a party; and that she remarked one night: 'I don't mind the country, I've been to Holland Park twice already, and it's still only May.' His editor, as well as his readers, were unsuspecting. Campbell inserted a paid announcement of a coming-out party for Venetia in *The Times*, among the list of debutante balls for the season. But like most hoaxers, Campbell could not resist talking about his joke. A malicious columnist on the *Daily Mirror* exposed it, and Campbell was fired, to rejoin the paper later in a more suitable capacity.

Tribune, the Socialist weekly that carries the flag for the left wing of the British Labour Party, has its skittish moods. A Christmas issue in 1962 carried a whole page of spoof articles, including one under the name of Chou En-Lai exhorting the British people to revolution and headed 'Death to the Peacemongers!' It set out a European policy which included restoring Calais to Britain after 500 years of French occupation, and, dismissing nuclear war threats, offered the slogan 'Better dead than not red'.

This was the middle of the cultural revolution in China, the intensity of which left little room for a sense of humour. The Chinese Foreign Ministry in Peking issued a statement declaring that *Tribune* had published a forged letter 'in a vain attempt to smear China's policies and defame the leaders of the Chinese nation'. It also protested to the British Government. *Tribune*'s editor, Richard Clements, went along to the Chinese Consulate in London and tried weakly to persuade them that it was only a a joke. *Tribune* never made any jokes about China after this.

Another time, some of the staff decided to have some fun at the expense of *Time and Tide*, a small weekly which had recently been taken over by William J. Brittain, and was becoming an organ of Blimpishly conservative views. They vied with one another in expressing extravagantly conservative attitudes in letters to *Time and Tide* and getting them printed. A typical quote from one went: 'I am of the opinion that the home discipline of daily family prayers on the one hand, and the judicious application of the slipper to that part of the child's anatomy provided by God for the purpose on the other, are the only things likely to, instil a respect for law and order.'

They liked to share their triumphs with others, and after several of the letters had appeared the story was blown on the TV programme *What The Papers Say*, which was then being produced by a former *Tribune* man. Then Richard Clements, who had looked upon these antics by his staff with avuncular tolerance, received a letter over the signature of William J. Brittain, the editor of *Time and Tide*. It expressed 'disgust and dismay' at the deception, and accused the *Tribune* staff of 'a breach of one of the most sacred traditions of British journalism'. Clements worried about this all day. Then he called the staff together and told them that the joke had gone too far, and showed them Brittain's outraged letter. They nudged one another, and then confessed that they had written it.

A newsman with the Armed Forces Network, the U.S. service radio, in Tokyo in 1947 decided to celebrate the fifth anniversary of A.F.N. by broadcasting a story that a 20-foot-long monster had come out of the sea near Tokyo and was terrorising the local population. People who telephoned A.F.N. to ask whether the story was a hoax were told that it was true. He continued interrupting the programme with fresh bulletins for an hour. The army did not find it amusing, particularly a colonel who left a party, rounded up some soldiers, and led three jeeps with mounted machine-guns to the beach. The newsman was fired.

Jean Shepherd, the New York radio disc jockey and a witty writer, used his medium, not to hoax his audience, but to persuade them to join him in a hoax on everyone else. He was a night-time disc jockey on WOR, broadcasting from 1 a.m. to 5-30, and he established a sense of community with his audience. He spoke to them as the 'night people', like himself, who were awake when everyone else was asleep, those who do not go with the herd but have more open minds, sharper wits and a freer, less narrow way of life than the 'day people'. He suggested that they show up the dullness of the day people's mentality with a hoax, by creating a demand for a book that did not exist. He asked them to write in suggesting a title and subject. The result, merging together several suggestions, was *I, Libertine*, by Frederick R. Ewing, a novel based on the life of an 18th century rake. The imaginary Ewing was a former Royal Navy commander known for his scholarly work on 18th century erotica.

It was a great success. Bookshops all over America were flooded with requests for the book. It turned up in the *New York Times* list of books soon to be published. The *Village Voice* in New York ran a news item about Ewing, as did a number of other publications. An undergraduate at Columbia University submitted a term paper on *I, Libertine* and its historical background, and received a respectable mark. People telephoned newspapers and demanded to know why their book pages had not reviewed it. Book review editors joined bookshops in trying to track it down.

As an anti-climax, the book was written and published. Salesmen of Ballantine Books, the big paperback publishers, reported the demand for the apparently non-existent book. So Ian Ballantine, head of the company, when he learned about the hoax, persuaded Shepherd to write the book. He did so in collaboration with Theodore Sturgeon, though the name on the cover was Frederick Ewing. The book was less successful than the hoax.

The B.B.C. once staged a hoax that backfired somewhat. Though it claimed afterwards that it was not a hoax, only an experiment.

It was in 1961. The Third Programme, as Radio 3 was called then, the principal channel for heavyweight arts and cultural programmes, announced a performance of an experimental work by a young Polish composer, Piotr Zak, called 'Mobile for Tapes and Percussions'. The attention of music critics was drawn to this. What they heard was twelve minutes of random sounds made by banging drums, gongs and saucepans, and electronic noises. One can see what some people thought might happen: the discovery by critics of hidden themes and meanings, followed by a puncturing of their pretensions. (This has been achieved in other art forms.)

When the B.B.C. revealed the hoax, a lot of people thought that the laugh was on the critics who reviewed it. Several people wrote to the newspapers about the rubbish that was accepted as 'experimental' music, painting, poetry, and so on. For instance, Rene MacColl, in the *Daily Express*, said: 'Not only did thousands of unsuspecting listeners accept this piece of nonsense with reverence and respect, but two of Britain's most pompous news-papers solemnly reviewed it. For years, people have been duped, often outrageously, by the growing cult of obscurantism.'

MacColl could hardly know how much 'reverence and res-pect' thousands of listeners felt, nor can we, but the critics came out of it rather well. They accepted the piece as a genuine offering, but the *Times* critic said the various sounds had no theme or meaning whatever, which was absolutely correct; the *Daily Telegraph* critic dismissed it as 'wholly unrewarding, and 'non-musical', which was equally accurate; and the critic of *The Listener* called it 'an insult to the intelligence of an adult audience'.

*   *   *

The April 1st newspaper/radio/TV story is a tradition in some parts of the world, though most American newspapers abjure it because they feel that it misuses the authority of the medium. The *Honolulu Star-Bulletin* had a long tradition of April Fool stories that was ended in 1954. This was because of the outrage when citizens found that the report that Congress had passed the Hawaii statehood bill with an amendment enabling them to get income tax refunds was a joke. Other parts of the world are less inhibited. On April 1st, 1959, for instance, the Belgian news-paper, *La Lanterne,* reported the landing of a spaceship in the centre of Brussels, and *La Libre Belgique* reported that a flying saucer had crashed in the Ardennes and the nine-foot-tall being inside was apprehended; a Dutch newspaper reported the in-vention of a helicopter designed to land on church steeples, and another told its readers that a budget surplus was to be shared out among tax-payers.

The B.B.C. is a persistent April 1st jokester, though no April Fool item is allowed to mar the authority of the news bulletins. Most of the April Fool jokes are performed over the radio, the easiest medium for it, but the most famous, and one of the first, was performed on television. This was the famous Panorama report on the Spaghetti harvest festival, in 1957.

It was in the early days of Panorama, the B.B.C.'s major weekly current affairs programme, and the host was Richard Dimbleby, a well-known and widely admired figure on radio even before the coming of postwar television. The first of April

fell on a Panorama night that year. As the last item in the programme, Dimbleby reported from the Italian-speaking Ticino
area of Switzerland about the spaghetti harvest, achieved that
year only after many difficulties.

The viewers saw the strands of spaghetti dangling from the
trees, and women going around with baskets pulling them off.
Dimbleby, with no alteration in his usual genial, mellifluous
tones, and accompanied by violin music in the background,
presented nuggets of information like:

'Spaghetti cultivation here in Switzerland is not of course
carried out on anything like the scale of the Italian industry.
Many of you, I'm sure, will have seen pictures of the vast
spaghetti plantations in the Po Valley. For the Swiss, however, it
tends to be a family affair. Another reason why this may be a
bumper year lies in the virtual disappearance of the spaghetti
weevil, the tiny creatures whose depredations have caused much
concern in the past.

'After picking, the spaghetti is laid out to dry in the warm,
Alpine sun. Many people are often puzzled by the fact that
spaghetti is produced at such uniform lengths. But this is the
result of many years of patient endeavour by plant breeders,
who've succeeded in producing the perfect spaghetti.'

The item closed on the family's harvest banquet, with toasts
drunk to the new crop in the traditional manner, and waiters
bringing in ceremonially the main dish: 'And it is, or course,
spaghetti, picked earlier in the day, dried in the sun, and so
brought from garden to table at the very peak of condition. For
those who love this dish, there's nothing like real, home-grown
spaghetti.'

A few people actually telephoned Panorama to ask where
they could see the spaghetti harvest festival when they went on
holiday. It was a perfect spoof, in that those who saw through it
right away enjoyed it just as much as those who sat there and
swallowed it, truly 'one of the pleasures of the senses'.

It is remembered appreciatively in the American media as
well as elsewhere. On April 1st, 1970, on the National Broadcasting Company's Huntley-Brinkley programme, John Chancellor did an item on that year's pickle crop, with film of a dill
pickle tree. He said he was reporting from the Dimbleby Pickle
Farm.

B.B.C. radio programmes find it easier than TV programmes to drop in hoax items on April 1st. There was a talk explaining that people with red hair can catch Dutch Elm disease, delivered in a meandering manner by a doctor barely recognisable as Spike Milligan. The naturalist David Attenborough told listeners about the Sheba Islands in the Pacific, and local phenomena such as the singing tree mouse and the cream puff bird, and played a tape of the inaudible cricket. On the popular morning programme Today, there was a report of an expedition carried out to mark Edgar Wallace's centennial, to find the Umbopo tribe in central Africa mentioned in his novel *Sanders of the River*, who always have their heads tucked underneath their arms.

One of my own favourites, for intelligent fun, is a spoof production of the Radio 3 arts programme In Parenthesis, put out on April 1, 1972. Here a number of eminent people who contribute to Radio 3 were persuaded to parody themselves. These are the best kinds of parody, in that they contain a great deal of the qualities of the original, and only just slide over, with a clue planted here and there, so gently that only the alert listener will notice it.

The programme included the critic Malcolm Bradbury talking at length about an important new French work of social anthropology, *Fornication Comme Une Acte Culturel*, by Henri Mensonge.* His talk delivered in a tone that was serious while not solemn, and at a fairly rapid pace, is well worth quoting.

'As an insight,' Bradbury said, 'the notion that sexuality is a central social metaphor is not of course new; Freudians and rugby clubs have known as much, and interpreted the perceptions for their appropriate ends. The interesting thing is the way in which, with an extraordinary philosophical lucidity, Mensonge manages to sustain the point that all our notions and presumptions, conscious and unconscious, considered or instinctive, are in fact culturally determined, and occur as part of a coherent and anagogical sequence. Mensonge points out, for example, that the way we enter a room, and our presumptions about what we should do there and find there, are inevitably of a piece with the way in which we enter other places more

* *mensonge* is the French for 'lie'.

physiological and private, and our presumptions and expectations in that instance. . . .

'We live in an age of metaphorical rape, Mensonge tells us: confrontation, assault, intrusion and exposure are becoming validated transactions, the rites of democracy, of mass society. Our public displays of genitalia are confessions that all persons, all flesh are the same: that there is nothing that can be privatized. But equally, of course, it is possible for a society to celebrate the privacy and distinction of personality, to attribute utter scarcity to sexual access, to distinguish the public from the private, and the pubic from both, the classical private sanctum being the chaste female place.'

The programme also featured a discussion, clearly influenced by modern linguistic philosophy, of the question 'Is "Is" Is?' It included the playwright Tom Stoppard, who handles metaphysics deftly in his stage comedies ('Jumpers', 'Travesties'), the pop writer Tony Palmer, and others. A sample, delivered at a furious pace:

'Though some might argue that the existence of the ideal "is" is not affected by whether or not there are any physical manifestations of "ises", it is only to the existing written or spoken "is" that the scholar can turn in his researches. Therefore, let us consider the two letters I and S. Together, they make "is"; they are the only physical components of the word. Here, it may seem, is a definite statement. And yet it is not definitive without further qualification. For instance, it must be specified that the letters should appear in that order. They can also make the word "si", which, though it is not used in English, is used as an affirmative in other languages. Are we therefore to conclude that the word "is" has affirmative connotations by contiguity with the word "si"? Or alternatively, does the word "si" partake of the ideal "isness", is it a part of the "is" form we seek to define?'

The listener did not have a chance to ponder the question. More came at a rush:

'It would seem that the answer to both these questions is "no", and they emphasize the danger of defining "is" merely in terms of structure of letters. Even with the strictures of order, one is no nearer to definition. The two letters I and S might mean "is", but they could also act as initials for a variety of subjects which bear no relation to the "is" syndrome at all. The concepts of

International Students, Indian Songs, Idle Sods and Interchangeable Spanners have nothing to do with "is" in its pure form.

'And "is" is susceptible to further diffusion if one considers it only as a sequence of letters. The I and S may occur in longer words. . . .'

The musicologist John Gould gave an analysis of a piano sonata which gradually descended into mind-numbing nonsense and reached a fitting climax.

'The first bar represents the exposition of the second series in retrograde by chords grouped mainly in fifths and consecutive thirds, characterising the underlying "bogen" or arch form of the first motif. This leads to a bridge consisting of the first and third rows, with 4-2-9-6 and 7-3-2-1-9 respectively missing, giving an inversion of the re-numbered row, which mirrors the previous backwards-facing underlying choral passage presented as 1-3-5-7-9 and 2-4-6-8-10 in slightly shorter note values. This itself becomes a pivot in inversion, now transposed after it has doubled back on itself and disappeared up its own arch.'

It was all done with a straight face: not a smile was heard.

*   *   *

Lastly, on the subject of media hoaxes, there is one that I myself thought up. This, unlike the others, is a hard news hoax in a hard news medium, and makes full use of the speed of modern communications. I feel I can tell it since it is one that will almost certainly never be perpetrated now, and it seems to me worth telling because it incorporates many of the characteristics of the *genre*.

A good number of years ago, I worked in the London bureau of the Associated Press. For a time, I worked on what was called then the control desk; this was normally manned by two people, and occasionally I was 'in the slot', meaning that I was in charge of the desk.

In those days, this desk controlled all A.P. teleprinter messages between Europe and America. It would transmit news and service messages from one to the other; this meant sending important news stories originating in Europe – which included the correspondents in the London bureau – in both directions, i.e. to America and all over Europe. The slot man would do this either by pressing a switch that allowed an incoming story from a foreign bureau to go through automatically, or, if it originated in London, by giving the story to the teleprinter operator sitting next to him to punch out on his keyboard and send down the wire. The desk man also exercised some editorial control. Thus, he had two functions: sometimes he was an editor, sometimes a traffic cop on a busy news intersection.

The emphasis was on speed. The teleprinter operator was under orders to stop what he was doing, in the middle of a sentence if necessary, in order to punch out a 'bulletin' story. This meant that at busy periods, there was intense pressure: the teleprinter operator, for instance, had no time to reflect on the import of the words he was punching out, or discuss them with anyone.

The control desk also passed on service messages between the European bureaus and America, like 'need more details rome's 11816 urgentest' or 'appreciate get confirmation your 20822 martians story since experts here believe it improbable.'

Now, in those days, I had not yet read Professor R. V. Jones' monograph *The Theory of Practical Joking: Its Relevance to Physics* (see Chapter One). But I and a few others, who regarded the job less reverentially than we might have, realised the potentialities for hoaxing of the slot man's position on the control desk. It exemplified Professor Jones' thesis that if a person can control the channels of communication, then he can also control what is being communicated. There was nothing to stop a slot man inventing a message and pretending that he was passing it on. He could write a story himself, sign it with any correspondent's name, and have it sent on the teleprinter wire to New York, and to Europe as well. Not only that; he could also intercept any service messages addressed to the correspondent, and reply in his name. The foreign desk in New York would believe that it was receiving a story from a correspondent out in the field somewhere in Europe, and was exchanging messages with him, whereas in fact it would be communicating only with the control desk in London.

One day, a few of us took refuge from the pressures of the moment in anarchistic fantasies, in which, from the key position on the control desk, we would foist outrageous news stories on the world.

bulletin. london–princess margaret has eloped with the soviet ambassador. (more follows)

bulletin. moscow–nikita khrushchev today announced his conversion to the russian orthodox faith, and said he intends to become a monk. (more follows)

bulletin. paris–the french government announced that it plans to launch a manned rocket to the moon, with president de gaulle inside it.

bulletin. paris–space second–the announcement came as a complete surprise. there have been rumours for some time that a french space program was under discussion, particularly in view of the progress of the french military rocket program, but no hint that any such role for the french president was being considered.

paris space third–one reporter asked the ministry of defense whether the announcement was some kind of a joke. a ministry spokesman replied: 'certainly not. general de gaulle has shown his bravery as a soldier in the past. he is determined to lead the way for his country in this historic step.'

And so on. As we worked it out, the slot man would have prepared service messages ready to send in answer to certain obvious queries that would follow the story, signed with the name of the correspondent, or perhaps the correspondent's bureau chief. Queries like '31755 jack your 1742 margaret elopement story sounds unbelievable. does eddy gilmore still have his marbles?' the reply: 'your 31755 gilmores story genuine have checked personally smith.' That sort of thing.

But this kind of hoax seemed to me to be too limited in its effects. It would be a half-hour wonder. It would doubtless be reported over many radio and TV stations, and might even get into some newspapers as a stop press item. It would cause a sensation. But after a short while–probably less than an hour–other news services would have checked, they would find the story was not true and shoot it down, and the hoax would be exposed. A few months later, it would be forgotten outside the offices of the news media. Here, and only here, it would be remembered, and the perpetrator's name also would be recalled, with chuckles and the degree of envy that people always feel for total irresponsibility. Within the journalistic profession, though nowhere else, the perpetrator would be famous, and also unemployable.

But I wanted something more. I wanted a hoax news story that would have some consequence beyond itself, that would make something happen in the real world, preferably something irreversible, and lasting, something that would make the history books, even as a footnote, as well as the trade press. Two or three of us pondered the matter one evening in the Hoop and Grapes, the friendly hostelry next door to the A.P. office. It was difficult at first to think of anything that would have this kind of impact. Since the story would be short-lived, any consequences would have to follow very quickly indeed. You could not start a war. No government would take military action solely on the basis of an A.P. news flash. A report of a mushroom cloud rising over Bonn as the city went off the air might create hysteria among some radio listeners but would have no other effect. None of us could think of anything that would change the world even slightly, so attention turned back to darts, sex and the state of British politics.

A few days later I came up with the answer: *We would devalue the pound.* This would have an immediate effect, and one that could never be entirely undone. In those days, the pound, like most currencies, had a fixed exchange rate in relation to the dollar.

At first, I contemplated a Government announcement devaluing the pound. But then I realized that an official denial carried by every other news agency would be too swift and too overpowering; the story would be killed within minutes. Instead, it would be a high-level, very short-range leak. Something like: 'A highly reliable source said today that the British Government intends to devalue the pound sterling by 15 per cent. The official announcement is expected later this afternoon, the source said.'

People would certainly take action on the strength of this, and would race one another to do so. The money markets and the stock exchanges in America and on the Continent would speed into action. Only someone more familiar than I am with the structure of international finance can spell out the precise consequences that would ensue, but some of these would surely be irreversible. Perhaps the British Government would have to really devalue the pound, in order to cope with the effects of people having believed that it was doing so.

As I saw it, the slot man would send this report that the pound was about to be devalued in mid-afternoon, when the stock markets are still open in Europe and, due to the time difference, the New York one has just started trading. The story would be a short one: just the brief statement, followed by a few paragraphs of background, telling when the pound was last devalued, and its new value in relation to the dollar. The story would, of course, be prepared beforehand, on several separate sheets, and slipped into the teleprinter operator's basket, among others in the flow of news. The first paragraph would be a bulletin, and the rest would have high priority.

The slot man would have to be prepared to keep the hoax going after that. The sequence of events would be something like this: U.P.I. and Reuter would hear about the story within minutes, and would send urgent messages to their London offices. These would contact the Treasury, which would deny the report strongly, and this would be reported on the U.P.I. and Reuter news wires. The A.P. foreign desk in New York would send an anxious query pointing to these denials. The slot man would have the reply ready: a message supposedly from the London bureau chief, saying that the denials were only to be expected and did not weaken the story. Subscribers to the A.P. would pour in their doubts in the light of the others' denials; the New York desk would be sweating, caught in the dilemma in which a newsman occasionally finds himself, torn between delight at finding himself alone with a story and anxiety that maybe the others who are not up there with him know what they are doing. But it would stand by the story. This might all be within 20 minutes.

The other wire services, and some newspapers, would now spur on their London staffs with messages like 'ap still stands by devaluation story despite denials. could you check urgentest with all possible unofficial sources?' This would produce another wave of even stronger official denials. Meanwhile, the international money markets and stock exchanges would have been galvanized into frenzied activity by the first story; now, perhaps, half an hour later, there might be some second thoughts, with some traders pausing and waiting anxiously for the latest word from the A.P.

In this tense atmosphere, the foreign desk would send back a message saying that everyone else seemed to be denying the story, was there no possibility of being more specific about the source? Again, the slot man would have the answer ready. After a suitable pause of a few minutes, he would send back another message in the bureau chief's name, something like: 'eye know source of devaluation leak and reasons for it, which concern high level dissatisfaction with british government economic policy. eye personally stand by authenticity of story.' The bureau chief, meanwhile, might be standing a few feet away from the control desk, unaware of the drama in which he was supposedly participating.

So the A.P. in New York would hold the line against the buffeting of denials. But it would probably ask its Washington bureau for guidance. A.P. men in Washington would contact the U.S. Treasury and the State Department, and would receive assurances that these knew nothing about any planned devaluation. This would be passed on to New York, while State Department officials telephoned the London embassy. Meanwhile, share prices would still be rising and falling on the strength of the impending devaluation, and the money exchanges would be busily translating huge amounts from one currency to another.

By now the A.P. day editor in New York would be sufficiently worried about the whole situation to take it to the most senior A.P. executive he could find, perhaps the General Manager. Then a message would come to the control desk over the teleprinter from the General Manager addressed to the London Bureau chief, saying he would be telephoning him immediately to talk about the devaluation story. It is also possible that by this time, British newspapers would have heard about the reports in America and on the Continent and, as A.P. subscribers, would be telephoning the news desk. Either way, the control desk would no longer monopolise the channels of communication.

At this point, the game is about over. The slot man would go home for the day, and, if prudent, would not return. He would leave secure in the knowledge that, unlike most mortals, he will not have lived out his days in this world unnoticed.

CHAPTER 5

Nom de Plume: Literary Hoaxing

> The reader has a traditional respect for print.
> The respect for print is first instilled in the
> child by schoolbooks; this is handed down by
> teachers, the continuation of parental
> authority. Nobody so far has been able to
> explain by conscious logic the ridiculous
> respect for printed matter in the average adult.
> EDMUND BERGLER,
> *The Writer and Psychoanalysis*

PART of the reward for literary hoaxing is the special status that accrues to anything between hard covers. It gains something in importance, and the likelihood of being accepted, something over and above the authority of appearing in more ephemeral media. It gets into libraries, and the information contained in a book is read over the generations, and absorbed, and perhaps transferred into other books.

In getting a lie into a book, the hoaxer has written it in the sands of time. He has inserted a frame of his own devising in the motion picture of mankind's history, that is re-run every now and again for reference and reflection. Dr. Bergler may not understand the respect for the printed word to which he has attested, but the ancient Egyptian rulers understood well what lies behind it when they gave writing a sacramental status, and restricted the knowledge of writing for several centuries to the priestly caste. They knew that it is the means by which a man can throw his thoughts and feelings beyond the range of his own voice, and beyond the life of his own body, and that, therefore, it partakes of the transcendental.

The motives for literary faking are the same as those for literature itself: the desire to see one's work in print and to know that it is being read; the desire for fame; a grasp at a little immortality; money. Buried somewhere in the literary fraud, however mercenary, there is nearly always a literary impulse. There is also an element of sadness in the achievement, even at

its most successful. A triumph of literary faking has an under-
tone of disappointment; for the faker, it is nearly always
second-best. If he sees his work in print under another name, he
would rather have seen it in print under his own name. If he
earns money by describing invented exploits and adventures, he
would rather have earned it by recounting real exploits.

E. B. White, that gentle, witty and perceptive soul who illu-
minated so many aspects of the modern world in the *New Yorker*
for three decades, knows well the wayward channels through
which the literary impulse can flow. Once, during the Second
World War, when there was a great scarcity of automobile tyres
in America because of the shortage of imported rubber, someone stole the tyres from a parked car in Norfolk, Virginia, but
left a diamond ring and a handbag untouched on the front seat.
On the windscreen the owner found a note saying:

> *Roses are red,*
> *Violets are blue,*
> *I like your jewels*
> *But your tyres are new.*

Many newspapers carried this story, and reported it as a case
of a thief with a talent for poetry. But White saw its deeper significance, and dismissed this interpretation.

'This is palpable nonsense,' he wrote. 'It was a case of a poet
who was willing to attempt any desperate thing, even larceny,
in order to place his poem. Clearly, here was a man who had
written something and then had gone up and down seeking the
precise situation which would activate his poem. It must have
meant long nights and days of wandering before he found a car
with jewels lying on the front seat and four good tyres on the
wheels.'*

Literary faking has a long history. Forgery must be almost as
old as writing, and plagiarism as old as literature. The Ptole-
mies' great library at Alexandria was full of forgeries which had
presumably been bought at a good price, including bogus
manuscripts by Themistocles, Aristotle, Euripedes and others.
When Petrarch became the model for poets in the Renaissance,

---

* From *The Second Tree From The Corner* by E. B. White.

NOM DE PLUME: LITERARY HOAXING

fakers wrote Petrarch sonnets, just as, in another century and medium, fakers would paint Corot landscapes and Modigliani portraits.

Money was by no means the only motive for literary forgery. The spread and influence of the printed word has given scope for others. The most influential forgery of the 17th Century was the *Eikon Basilike*, a book supposed to be a journal of King Charles the First. It was published shortly after he was executed by the Cromwellians, and showed him in a sympathetic light, as a devout Christian and conscientious monarch, concerned only for the well-being of his subjects in what he called 'Cromwell's bloody slaughterhouse'. It was read widely, and contributed to the anti-Cromwellian reaction and the restoration of the monarchy. It was a forgery, intended to have precisely this effect, the work of a Royalist clergyman, John Gauden. When the monarchy was restored, Gauden was rewarded for his cunning with the post of Bishop of Exeter.

The durability of deceptions in book form is shown in another fraud of the next century. This was supposedly a historical and topographical account of Roman Britain written in the 14th Century by Richard of Cirencester, and accompanied by a map. It was actually fabricated by Charles Julius Bertram, an Englishman who was a professor of English at the Royal Marine Academy in Copenhagen; he produced the manuscript as one that he had discovered, and it brought him some fame. It was accepted by scholars and published as a work of great interest. It contained more than 100 towns, roads and individuals that had not been named before in any account of Roman Britain, and added some important new facts, for instance, that Roman authority extended as far north as Inverness.

It became an important source book for historians, cited by Gibbon in his *Decline and Fall of the Roman Empire*. It was only in the late 19th Century, more than 100 years after it was published, that scholars decided that the work was a fake. By the time, Royal Ordnance Survey maps listed Bertram's Roman sites. These were purged, but the misinformation has been passed down to so many other books that it is probably impossible to eradicate entirely its effects.

This is unusual only in the seriousness with which scholars treated it. Historiography is replete with books that create legends. George Washington and the cherry tree, much of John Paul Jones' career, Betsy Ross and the story of Barbara Fritchie have this kind of dubious ancestry.

The social and intellectual history of 18th Century England contains many literary hoaxes, perhaps because the writer was now given an enhanced social status, and literary reputations became something worth stealing.

Horace Walpole, who was to become one of the most celebrated writers of his day, used fraud to make his debut as an author. He passed off his first novel, *The Castle of Otranto*, published in 1764, as a 200-year-old work which he had translated from the Italian. When it was well-received, he had a second edition brought out under his own name, with the following apologia by the author for his earlier deception: 'It is fit that he should ask pardon of his readers for having offered his work to them under the borrowed personage of a translator. As diffidence of his own abilities and the novelty of the attempt were the sole inducements to assume that disguise, he flatters himself that he shall appear excusable.'

However, he extended no such indulgence to Thomas Chatterton when Chatterton tried to emulate this, and helped to end his literary career before it had begun. Chatterton at 17 wrote a series of romantic poems, re-wrote them in old English, and issued them as the work of Thomas Rowley, a 15th Century monk. He was young and destitute, and when the authorship of the Rowley poems was revealed and he was denounced as a fraud, he felt rejected as well; he committed suicide in the attic where he lived and wrote. The poems were published in full after his death, and their merit was recognised.

The most famous of all the literary hoaxes of this century was perpetrated in order to bring fame and position to its author, James McPherson, a Scottish poet. These were the two epic poems *Fingal* and *Temora*, which were attributed to Ossian, a third century warrior and bard of the Scottish Highlands. McPherson said they had been transmitted orally over the centuries, and even published Gaelic texts which he said he had translated into English. In fact, he wrote the poems himself, drawing on old legends, but this was only established conclusively after his death.

The English world of fashion had just discovered Scotland

NOM DE PLUME: LITERARY HOAXING   103

and there was a great deal of romanticising of the qualities of primitive life in the old Highlands, and the simple, strong, proud Highland folk, a trend that was to continue, and 150 years later was to bring Queen Victoria under the spell of a strong, simple, proud Highlander who was a servant on her Balmoral estate, John Brown.

The Ossian poems were praised extravagantly for their vigour and poetic splendour, compared to the works of Homer, and translated into most European languages. There were skeptics, however; one of these was Samuel Johnson, who always had a very cool view of the Scottish character. One admirer of Ossian's poems, a certain Dr. Blair, asked him once whether any man living could have written the poems of Ossian. Dr. Johnson replied: 'Yes, sir, many men, many women, and many children.'

McPherson was a member of parliament for a Scottish constituency for 16 years and, at his own request, he was buried in Westminster Abbey.

The most audacious literary hoax of the century – some would say of any century – was the Shakespeare forgeries: the forgery of letters, poems, and eventually a whole play alleged to be by William Shakespeare, that was produced at a leading London theatre. The fact that they were the work of a 17-year-old boy makes the whole episode all the more extraordinary.

To write a five-act play and pass it off as a hitherto undiscovered work by Shakespeare is a feat of breath-taking daring. Yet it was not committed in a spirit of daring. The hoaxer was led on to each new forgery by the success of the last, and by a desperate desire to please, and to be recognised.

He was William Henry Ireland, the son of an elderly antiquarian bookseller and artist called Samuel Ireland, at this time a widower. He was one of Ireland's three children, but there are vague references in some letters to a mysterious circumstance of his birth. At any rate, young William Ireland seems to have been raised with a feeling of insecurity about his place in his father's esteem and affection.

This may have told on his life at school. He was a poor student, so much so that one school principal expelled him as incorrigibly stupid. His father made plain his low opinion of William's intelligence. But he did well when he went to school in France, presumably because this was away from the pressures of his home.

In 1793, when Ireland was 17, his father took him on an extended visit to Stratford-upon-Avon, which was then in the process of becoming a literary shrine as the birthplace of William Shakespeare. Samuel Ireland was quite captivated with the place, and succumbed to what is known today as 'bardolatry', the uncritical admiration of everything connected with 'the immortal bard'. He bought a few Shakespearian relics that were almost certainly fakes. He dreamed of finding one day, to add to his collection of antiquities, a manuscript in the hand of William Shakespeare himself.

This dream was not quite as fantastic as it might seem today. It was in this period that Shakespeare was first seen as a towering genius of literature; it seemed frustrating and, to some, mysterious that so little was known for certain about him, and that hardly anything remained that was written in his own hand. J. A. Boaden, writing about Shakespeare at this time, speculated that someone may have collected all his papers, and that one day, 'a rich assemblage of Shakespeare papers would start forth from some ancient repository, to solve all our doubts and add to our reverence and our enjoyment.'

Back in London, Samuel Ireland set to work writing a guidebook to the Stratford countryside and illustrating it himself with some views of the region, while his son Henry William was apprenticed to a lawyer, a post he found irksome and to which he gave little time or attention. Somehow, William conceived the idea of pleasing his father by manufacturing for him a genuine Shakespeare document, the thing he wanted most in the world.

He cut a piece of parchment from an old document, and got a workman in a bookbinders to make him up a bottle of ink that would look dark and aged when it was used. He carefully wrote out a title deed to some property near the Globe Theatre in London, and signed it with the name of William Shakespeare and one Michael Fraser. Then he told his father a strange story. He had met a wealthy country gentleman in a coffee house and, after he had expressed an interest in antiquities, this man had invited him to drop in at his house and look through an old chest which was full of old documents and papers; he said that if anything there interested him, he could take it away. He found there this title deed. The man gladly gave it to him, but only on condition that he promise solemnly to keep his name and address absolutely secret, as he shunned publicity. He referred to him only as Mr. H.

His father was delighted at the find, particularly after a distinguished scholar declared it genuine. He implored his son to go back and look for yet more Shakespeariana. Young Ireland, ever eager to please, produced more: a letter in connection with the property deal, and a receipt to Shakespeare from the actor John Hemynge, all written in Elizabethan English. When these produced admiration from many quarters, he found a copy in Shakespeare's own handwriting of a letter to the Earl of Southampton, thanking him in flowery language for his patronage. Then, when all these were displayed in Ireland's shop for the admiration of visitors (James Boswell knelt and kissed them in reverence), he wrote something more inventive still, a 'profession of faith', written by Shakespeare in the last months of his life. This pleased the Church of England because, they said, it gave the lie to suggestions that Shakespeare was under Papist influence, though it is hard to find anything in it that is specifically Protestant.

When the Profession of Faith was read to Dr. Samuel Parr, a distinguished scholar and clergyman of his day, he exclaimed: 'We have many very fine passages in our church service, and our litany abounds with beauties; but here, sir, is a man who has distanced us all!' This extravagant praise astonished young William Ireland, and it was to prove fatal to him. For it left him, as he wrote later, 'fired with the idea of possessing genius to which I had never aspired'.

Few people of 17, hearing their work spoken of in this way, would not succumb to an inflated opinion of their own talents. Ireland embarked on new inventions. He told his father that Mr. H. had now given him permission to ransack his country house for Shakespeariana. There, he found the rich repository which Boaden had imagined might exist. Buying new parchment, making the ink and working with great speed, he produced in one month letters, a love poem to Anne Hathaway, books from Shakespeare's own library with marginal notes by the man himself, and a letter of appreciation to Shakespeare from Queen Elizabeth. All these went into Samuel Ireland's shop off the Strand and swelled his reputation. The Prince of Wales joined the list of distinguished visitors. He had good reason to be pleased with his son.

Then William announced that he had found the most precious treasure so far: manuscripts of two of the plays in Shakespeare's own hand, *King Lear* and *Hamlet*. In forging them, Ireland took liberties which indicated confidence in his literary talent. He altered the texts and, as he saw it, improved them. He excised some lapses into ribaldry, and he also changed lines, flattening out the verse and substituting direct statements for metaphor and soaring imagery. One critic commented that this new, authentic text showed better Shakespeare's 'straight, manly style'. (The notion that Shakespeare had lapses which should be corrected was not such a startling one then; some years earlier the poet laureate, Nahum Tate, had re-written *King Lear* with a happy ending.)

Curiosity about the mysterious Mr. H. grew, and Ireland took steps to make his existence more plausible. He brought into his deception a young actor, Robert Talbot, and had him tell his father that he had introduced Ireland to Mr. H. He also forged some letters from Mr. H., including one to his father commending William Ireland as an admirable young man possessed of rare literary talents. Winning his father's good opinion still seemed uppermost in his mind.

There was now much argument about the authenticity of the manuscripts. Samuel Parr, who had so praised the profession of faith, led a group of well-known scholars in a joint statement attesting that they were genuine. But J. A. Boaden studied them and declared that they were forgeries, and others agreed with him.

Ireland was now at work on his most ambitious project so far. He told his father that he had found manuscripts of some hitherto undiscovered plays by Shakespeare. One was called *Vortigern and Rowena*, and was about Vortigern, the Anglo-Saxon king. He got the idea from a drawing of Vortigern and Rowena that hung in the family living-room. Writing much later about this, Ireland remarked on something that was noted in the Introduction: that once a false idea becomes fixed in a person's mind, he will twist facts or probability to accommodate it rather than question it. Ireland wrote: 'It is extraordinary to observe now willingly people will blind themselves on any point interesting to their feelings. When it was known that a play on the subject of Vortigern was coming forward, every person who inspected the manuscript admired the strange coincidence of Mr. Ireland's having so long possessed a drawing on the very subject of the drama. Yet I do not recollect, even in one instance, that the drawing in question excited the slightest suspicion.'

He worked hard on the play. In another passage in the same confession, he explained: 'I was really so unacquainted with the proper length of a drama as to be compelled to count the lines in Shakespeare's plays, and on that standard to frame *Vortigern*; as the play I had chosen happened to be uncommonly long, mine became so.'

Composing a five-act play in the manner of Shakespeare was one thing: forging it on old paper in old ink, with Elizabethan spelling, was just too much work. So Ireland said that Mr. H. would not allow him to remove the manuscript, but would let him copy out the play. Naturally, this was awaited eagerly.

He showed some scenes to Richard Sheridan, the playwright, and at that time owner of the Drury Lane Theatre. Sheridan wrote an opinion of the play that was percipient: 'There are certainly some bold ideas,' he wrote, 'but they are crude and un-digested. It is very odd; one would be led to believe that Shakespeare must have been very young when he wrote the play.'

He signed an agreement to produce it at the Drury Lane, his theatre, and to pay young Ireland £300, plus 50 per cent of the takings. As Ireland was still under 18, Samuel Ireland signed as his trustee.

He borrowed the story from Hollinghead's *Chronicles*, the source of many of Shakespeare's plots. It is about a nobleman consumed with ambition who murders his way to the throne, and has many echoes of *Macbeth*. It contains most of the standard elements of Shakespeare's plays: a capering fool who speaks whimsical prose, a girl singing a song, rhyming couplets at the end of each set. And it is faithful to the iambic pentameter of Shakespeare's lines, sometimes doggedly so.

It has a few flights of rich imagery which are worthy of com-parison with the earlier and more bombastic of Shakespeare's works:

> *... O sov'reign Death!*
> *Who hast for thy domain this world immense.*
> *Churchyards and charnel houses are thy haunts,*
> *And hospitals thy sumptuous palaces.*
> *And whenst thou would be merry, thou dost choose*
> *The gaudy chamber of a dying king.*

Or this, when Aurelius lands in Britain, and addresses the English earth on which he treads:

> *Fain would my feet play wanton on thy breast,*
> *And skip with joy to tread thee once again.*
> *Tis not to wound thee that I thus do come*
> *In glittering steel and dire array of war,*
> *But as my right to claim thee for mine own.*

But more often, the verse falls with the dull clunk of lead, and seems in Ireland's hands just an inconvenient way of getting across a lot of information and carrying forward the story:

> *Hengist hath pitch'd on t'other side of Badon;*
> *The noise of arms and distant hum of soldiers*
> *Bespeak their hasty preparation;*
> *'Twere best to attack them early in the morn.*

And like this:

> *Vortigern on the Scots hath laid the murder;*
> *But under this pretence much lies conceal'd.*
> *Til you arrive, he is to rule deputed:*
> *But as you prize your lives, return not yet.*

Sheridan entrusted the production of the play to the actor-manager John Kemble, who himself played the title role. This was a mistake. Kemble had joined the growing number of people who were convinced that *Vortigern* and all the other Shakespeariana were bogus. Committed by contract to do the play, he tried to sabotage its production by making it look ridiculous. He made his view of the play known widely, and decided to underline it by opening it on April 1st. But Sheridan would not have this, and he put off the opening until the next night. The play attracted enormous interest.

However, it did not stand a chance. Kemble had assigned a

heavy role to a poor actor with a piping voice whose very appearance in the part was so ridiculous that the audience laughed whenever he opened his mouth. Then, at a crucial death scene, the actor fell outside the curtain, so that as the curtain came down, the audience were treated to the risible spectacle of the corpse scrambling behind it. Then Kemble, according to Ireland's anguished account, laid special stress on the line 'And when this solemn mockery is ended' which once again produced a howl of glee from the audience. Some who had come to scoff kept it up, partisans of *Vortigern* tried to shout them down, and when the last-act curtain fell, fighting broke out. The play was not given a second performance.

Ireland was already at work on another newly-discovered Shakespeare play, *William IV*, though this was never to be seen on the stage.

After the fiasco of *Vortigern*, the tide of opinion turned against the authenticity of the Shakespeare finds. Old Samuel Ireland was accused of faking them. He himself clung stubbornly to his view that the finds were all genuine, and he beseeched his son to take him to see Mr. H. William found that he had unwittingly cast his father in the role of a fraud.

He made his first tentative confession to his brother and sister, and they passed it on to their father. Samuel Ireland's reply was consistent with his past attitude: he rejected the story as absurd, because his son quite obviously had neither the intelligence nor the wit to write *Vortigern* or the other manuscripts. Ireland, distraught and dejected now, wrote his father a lengthy letter in which he confessed to the whole Shakespeare hoax in contrite and filial terms, and even sent him some of the original manuscripts. Samuel Ireland's reaction was to reproach his son for this pack of lies. 'Do not suffer yourself from vanity or any other motive to adhere to such a confession,' he wrote. Finally, when he and his father were no longer on speaking terms, Ireland published a full confession, much to his father's disgust.

It often happens that the victim of a hoax comes to have a vested interest in arguing for its truth, because to admit that he had been hoaxed would be so wounding. In Samuel Ireland's case, this was doubly and triply so: he had won fame and distinction through possession of this unique collection, and he naturally did not want to accept that this fame was built upon a sham; he had himself revered these objects; and he had been hoaxed by the son whom he had always regarded as being unintelligent. He refused to the last to acknowledge the truth. He himself published *Vortigern*, along with *William IV*, in 1799, the only time it was ever published. He died four years later still insisting that *Vortigern* was genuine.

William Ireland married at about the same time that he published his confession. He had been cut off entirely from his father's money. But his successful forgeries and his break with his father seem to have given him confidence, and he was able to stand on his own feet. He started a circulating library, then actually produced some mock manuscripts in Elizabethan script which he sold as curios; he did some translation from the French, then lived in France for a while and became an educational administrator in Napoleon's regime. During his lifetime he wrote more than a dozen novels and plays. None were distinguished, and none had the fame of *Vortigern*.

*   *   *

Late in the last century, a stir was caused in literary circles by the fake Byron letters. These were the works of one Icodad George Gordon Byron, as he called himself, who claimed to be the natural son of the poet Byron by a Spanish lady. He resembled Byron in profile, and he was certainly of Spanish origin. He at one time owned a farm in Wilkes-Barre, Pennsylvania, before travelling to London. There, his wife and confederate sold packets of letters supposedly exchanged between Byron and Shelley, Keats and others, with a plausible story about inheriting them through her family. This was twenty-five years after the poet's death.

Though pure invention, the letters show some familiarity with the mind of Lord George Byron, and some of them are quotable. Like this, supposedly from a letter by Byron to one John Mackintosh: 'Rhyming is as easy as punning to one who will allow his thoughts to run more by the association of sound than of sense. ... Sometimes in the course of his life, under the influence of love, madness or some other calamity, almost everyone is silly enough to sin in rhyme.'

Some of the letters were published with an introduction by Robert Browning before they were found to be bogus. Icodad

Byron went to New York and announced that he was writing an authoritative biography of his father based on the unpublished letters. It's a pity about the letters; it might have been a good biography.

Patriotism has also played a part in literary forgeries. Some proud Veronese around this time faked a 14th Century manuscript telling of the lives and loves of the Veronese painters of that day, and also—and here is its historical significance—the formation of an artists' guild in Verona in 1303. This would make Verona rather than Florence the cradle of painting in Renaissance Italy. Honour for Verona is assumed to be the motive for the forgery, since none other can be discovered; the manuscript was not sold. The art historian Otto Kurz writes: 'The finger of suspicion points to Pietro Nanin, Director of the Academy of Verona until his death in 1889.'

Patriotism of a kind contributed to the faked letters perpetrated by one Vrain Lucas, a Frenchman. The best-known of these were letters exchanged between Isaac Newton and Blaise Pascal, which showed that Pascal, and not Newton, deserved credit for discovering the Laws of Gravity. These were taken seriously in academic circles until they were discovered to be forgeries. But it turned out that they were the plausible tip of an implausible iceberg, only a few of the thousands of forged letters which Lucas turned out over a period of nine years, all to cater to the demented chauvinism to which Michel Chasles, a French mathematician, had fallen prey in his dotage.

The letters supposedly dated back over thousands of years, and all, like the Pascal-Newton letters, added to the glory of France and her sons. There were letters from the Greek scientist Thales to a Gallic king, from Alexander the Great to Aristotle praising the qualities of the Gauls, from a Gallic physician to Jesus, and from Shakespeare acknowledging a debt to French authors. Chasles bought them all, eagerly, and paid out a total of £6,000. Lucas paid with two years in prison.

In our own century, most of the big literary hoaxes have been autobiographies, imposture in print. Rigorous scholarship makes it difficult to pass off new writing as old. But people have passed off fiction as fact, and have sold books by stealing or inventing another man's life, whether gangster, monk, war hero or relative of the great.

One of the most profitable of hoax books was *Carrying a Gun for Al Capone*. It was written by Jack Bilbo, a roistering young German writer, painter, adventurer and monumental egoist. First published in 1930, it purports to be an account of Bilbo's days as a member of the Capone gang in Chicago. Bilbo had indeed been to the United States, and he had travelled around the country, though as it happens, he had never been to Chicago. The book appeared first in Germany, and was translated into several languages and published in many countries, including the United States. It was a big-seller everywhere. Reviewers praised it. In London, the *Sunday Times* said: 'It contains dramatic glimpses into a sinister underworld, and . . . an excellent pen portrait of Al Capone.'

It was still being re-published in the 1940s. Bilbo himself made no sustained effort to keep up the fiction. Four years after he wrote it, he admitted to a newspaper that he had never carried a gun in his life, but this was somehow lost in the files, beneath other, more dramatic interviews. In 1939, when he exhibited some of his paintings in London, *Time* magazine reported the event as an exhibition by a former Chicago mobster, and a London newspaper recalled that he had killed at least a dozen people.

He was only 24 when he wrote *Carrying a Gun for Al Capone*. Born Hugo Baruch, the son of a wealthy German father and an English mother, he reacted against a rigidly conventional German upbringing by becoming a free-wheeling bohemian anarchist. When he wrote the book he was back in Berlin after some travels, broke and out of work. He gave an account of its success in his autobiography published in 1948, an engaging book but clearly the work of one of life's permanent adolescents: 'What I really wanted was to be a writer, but all my books, sent to publishers under pseudonyms, were returned. Now, with a juicy murder on every page, fifteen different publishers in fifteen countries were rushing to get their filthy hands on it.'

As he tells it, he met Stephen Lorant, then the editor of the *Muencher Illustrierte Presse* (one of the founders of modern photo journalism, he was later, in Britain, to be the first editor of *Picture Post*) and regaled him with stories of Chicago gangland. Lorant expressed interest in his story, and bought the manuscript for serialisation. From here it took off. Bilbo, a burly, bull-necked figure, helped by posing for publicity pictures wearing a hat with the brim turned down and a raincoat, and holding a pistol, the archetypal screen gangster. He looks as if he was enjoying it.

One can see today the reason for the book's success: it has pace and a lot of action, though its interest lies in the idea that it is really all true; the story is not strong enough for fiction. Also, it purveys something that was very acceptable then, a romantic fatalism that was seen elsewhere in those days in different forms: in the hunched shoulders and resigned face of Jean Gabin, in the doomed soldiers in *Journey's End*, and in the typical Hemingway hero. Bilbo, whose writing goes no deeper than the average goldfish pond, wears this attitude on his sleeve. Thus, from the preface:

'Writing this in Europe, I am far from Chicago. Conversation goes on around me, about film stars, horse races, fashions. Often in the crowd, in the midst of the noisy chatter, I grow suddenly silent. People look at me and think me strange. But I stare at the far distant horizon and think of Chicago, of friends of mine there who have probably died as I saw other gangsters die. I should like to die like that. I probably shall. I am 24 years old.' Many young men of that day leading hum-drum lives would identify with that passage when they read it, and young girls would shiver with excitement. One imagines that the young Bilbo was a knock-out with the girls.

In the book, Bilbo first works in an office for the gang, serves an apprenticeship as a gunman, and then rides about Chicago as one of Capone's bodyguards. There are accounts of fights, gun battles, a gangland execution, extortions, and the author's naïve idea of a gangland code of honour: 'A gangster cannot torture anyone; cannot give a friend away; cannot be true to one woman; cannot steal a fellow gangster's girl friend . . .' etc.

The centre-piece of the book and the biggest selling point, was the portrait of Capone himself. The boss is described in significant detail: 'Most of the pictures of Capone do not show him as he is. True, he did have a certain animal wildness in his face, but a wildness reminiscent of a wildcat rather than a gorilla. His eyes were small, with a very white background that offset the round pupils. His glance was piercing, strong, and a trifle sad. His nose was flat, sensual. His mouth was big and broad, and his underlip curled as if in scorn . . .'

He had Capone lecturing him and some others at length about Napoleon–' "We would have understood each other. He was an Italian like me," Capone told me.' He had him reeling off Napoleon's mistakes: lacking in ruthlessness, being too fond of his family, trusting Murat, and worst of all, marrying as he did.

'Capone brought his fist down on his desk with such force that the ashtrays rattled. "Why did that little man have to marry Marie Louise? As sure as my name is Al Capone, I'll never marry a Vanderbilt. You can call me a bedbug if I ever do that. . . . Napoleon wanted to become respectable! Write it in large letters, boys. HE WANTED TO BECOME RESPEC-TABLE! And he paid for it. Promise me that you'll never want that shabbiest of all things, respectability. Then you will never come to St. Helena. Meanwhile, I'll keep you out of all the other prisons".' This was Bilbo's Capone.

'That shabbiest of all things, respectability'. The phrase is obviously a part of a youthful bohemian credo. It seems surprising in retrospect that reviewers were hoaxed by this kind of thing, and took this as part of the strictures of a Chicago gang-leader.

Bilbo ends the book with yet another highly romanticised picture of the gangster as rebel, a successor to Robin Hood and Jesse James. Back in Berlin, he meets a cousin who works in the state prosecutor's office, and listens to him talking about the drive against crime. 'I thought afterwards of our gang, men who when they say "yes" mean "yes". No shifty-eyed standards, no hypocrisy. They are not interested only in prying you loose from your money. They are natural, not hypocrites. I am a gangster, and damned proud of it.'

Every age has its own sentimentality. Jack Bilbo evidently gave the 1930s the gangsters it wanted, and he was rewarded for it.

Another dramatic story of personal adventure, closer to the present day, was *The Man Who Wouldn't Talk*, written by Pierre Dupont* and Quentin Reynolds. Dupont was a French Canadian, at that time a civil servant living in the west of

---

* This is not his real name. He and his family have already suffered because of what he did, and it would be cruel to draw attention to him again.

Canada, and the book recounted his adventures as a spy and saboteur in Nazi-occupied France, and a prisoner of the Gestapo, during the Second World War. But it was all a product of Dupont's imagination, a series of fantasies that got out of hand.

Dupont lectured to young people and other audiences on Christian faith. Like many people, he had daydreams of adventures that he might have had, and trials of strength in which he might have triumphed. Gradually, he introduced these into his talks, as testimony to the power of faith in God. It seemed to him that his talks were more persuasive this way; they were certainly more interesting. The stories seemed to take on a life of their own.

One of the editors of the *Readers Digest* heard about his exploits, and asked Quentin Reynolds, as a veteran war correspondent and magazine writer, to help him write them down. The editor telephoned Dupont and asked him to come to New York to tell his story to Reynolds. Dupont agreed, but when he was told he would be paid a sizeable fee he seemed surprised, and said: 'I wouldn't want to make a financial profit. Please see if you can make a payment direct to the Canadian Boy Scouts.'

Dupont spent a week telling his story. It was an exciting one. He went to England with the Canadian Air Force and transferred to Intelligence. He parachuted into Normandy, posed as a garage mechanic in a village, and led a resistance group. They smuggled Allied airmen out of France, and also blew up troop trains and bridges. He was arrested by the Gestapo and they tortured him to try to make him tell who the others in his group were. They crushed his right hand in a vice, and poured boiling water down his throat, leaving permanent scars. Then he was released; he worked in a U-boat yard in Hamburg and carried out sabotage there, and eventually made his way back to England.

The power of a fantasy is strong when you have lived with it for a long time. In his autobiography, Reynolds wrote of his week with Dupont: 'He had a remarkable knack for describing people. I soon felt I knew them all—the priest, Père Gauraud; the doctor; Albert Baudoin, the blacksmith, and the brave young girls who had carried messages in the handlebars of their bicycles.' Yet Dupont had none of the slickness of the confidence trickster; he came across as a warm-hearted, decent, simple little man, which indeed he was.

Reynolds decided that his story was worth much more than a single article. He knocked it out quickly as a book, and went to see Dupont at home to check the manuscript with him. He met Dupont's employer and his neighbours, who were pleased that their friend was to get the recognition that his heroism deserved. But his wife was away at the time.

The book appeared, and went into a second printing almost immediately. The *Readers Digest* published a condensed version, as agreed. Then a man telephoned a Canadian newspaper to say that he had served with Dupont in the Canadian Air Force during the war, and that Dupont had been an intelligence officer at a bomber base in England, and never went to France. A newspaper reporter went to see Dupont.

Dupont was a day-dreamer who lost control of his day-dreams, but he was not by nature a liar. He had prepared no defences. Once challenged, he was a pushover. The reporter said he also had been connected with intelligence during the war, and asked: 'Which section were you with, A, B or C?'

'B Section,' said Dupont, promptly.

'Then you must have known dear old Colonel Kitchingham. He was in charge of that lot at that time,' the reporter said.

'Yes indeed. I knew him very well,' Dupont replied.

There was no section A, B or C, and no Colonel Kitchingham.

The truth came rushing out. Dupont had indeed never been to France. His hand and throat scars were from a boyhood accident. Dupont wrote Reynolds a pitifully apologetic letter explaining how he started making up some exploits and was carried away. 'Now I feel a huge burden has been lifted from me,' he said. His wife also wrote to Reynolds; she had lived constantly fearing his exposure, and was frantic with worry when his stories were turned into a book. She confessed that she had deliberately absented herself when Reynolds visited the Dupont household because she could not face him.

My Uncle Joe by Budu Svanidze was a book about Stalin, published in 1952 when Stalin was still the Czar of all the Russias, supposedly written by his nephew. It was published in several countries, treated seriously by reviewers, and serialised in

Britain in the *Sunday Dispatch*. It was a fraud, the work of a white Russian living in Paris.

For some reason, the white Russian communities scattered in the European capitals for 40 years or so after the revolution seem to have contained the champion forgers of books, documents and letters relevant to public issues. Throughout the 1920s and '30s, white Russians forged documents which purported to show the dark hand of Soviet subversion reaching into many corners of the world. Many documents were passed to American newspapers, mostly by people in Berlin and Paris, 'proving' that Soviet involvement was to blame when Mexico nationalised American oil companies; some falsely implicated liberal American senators, particularly Senator William Borah, an early campaigner for diplomatic relations with the Soviet Union. They also forged the famous 'Zinoviev letter', which linked the British Communist Party with the Comintern leader Andrei Zinoviev, tarred by association the Labour Party, and helped swing the 1924 election against it.

Curiously, *My Uncle Joe* is not in this vein politically. Though it was published when the Cold War was at its most intense, its picture of Stalin is a benign one. There is not a single slur on Stalin's character. It contains no political comment, but 'Svanidze' makes it clear that he defected to the West not because of any disillusionment with Communism or with his uncle's rule, but because he fell in love with a German girl who would not accompany him back to Russia.

It tells homely stories of Stalin from the time that he was a teenager in his native Tiflis through his years as an underground revolutionary to the time he was the big man in the Kremlin. Mostly, they are of no direct relevance to political events; there is little here for the serious historian to draw on—or to quarrel with. This is the Stalin the outside world never knew, nor, as it turned out, the inside world either, a dedicated, patriotic man of simple tastes and unassuming manner. Here is Stalin cooking his native Georgian dishes for other members of the politbureau; raising his strong, firm, kindly hand to stop the excesses of the 1930s purges; learning that the Germans had invaded Russia when he was out fishing with Svanidze, and reacting with calmness and wisdom; giving Marshal Rokossovsky a good luck charm to see him through the rest of the war.

Of course, the most famous fake biographer of our time is Clifford Irving, who sold his phoney biography of Howard Hughes, supposedly in Hughes' own words, for nearly a million dollars. The story is well-known, but there are three points that might be made about it, that bear on the general theme of deception.

One is the extraordinary case with which Irving practised forgery. The letters supposedly from Howard Hughes that Irving produced were shown to one of the leading firms of handwriting experts in America, who pronounced them genuine. Later, they revised their opinion and said they were forgeries and the real author was Irving. Yet he had never forged anything before.

A second point worth attention is that, as he tells the story, the fact that the hoax succeeded as well as it did for as long as it did was due to a remarkable coincidence – one might almost say an incredible coincidence. As recorded in his book *What Really Happened*, he decided to embark on the project when he was in Ibiza, after seeing some letters by Hughes in a news magazine. This version is apparently accepted also by the three authors who wrote *Hoax*,* the book about the affair, though there are signs of reservation on their part. Irving persuaded McGraw-Hill that he had Hughes' cooperation, and then he and Richard Susskind travelled around America doing research in newspaper libraries and talking to a few people who had known Hughes.

In Palm Springs, California, he called on his aunt, and she happened to take him over to see someone he had known years earlier, Stanley Meyer, a sometime TV producer and film agent. Meyer had a manuscript of a book about Hughes that was being written by Noah Dietrich, a longtime aide of Hughes, in collaboration with Jim Phelan, a magazine writer. He wanted to call in another writer to re-do it, and asked Irving whether he would be interested in the job. Irving demurred slightly, but Meyer asked him to take the manuscript to his motel and read it before making up his mind.

Irving and Susskind took the manuscript and made a photocopy before returning it. They drew on this for intimate stories

---

* *Hoax* by Lewis Chester, Stephen Fay and Magnus Linklater.

that were known only to Hughes and one or two other people, and for his way of talking and his mannerisms. It was these features that persuaded people that Irving's book was genuine even after Hughes denied that Irving had ever interviewed him. Only when Phelan was able to prove that the material had been taken from his and Dietrich's manuscript did Irving admit that he had lied about seeing Hughes, and tell of his meeting with Stanley Meyer.

Now, it is indeed a most extraordinary coincidence that Meyer, wanting someone to re-work a book about Howard Hughes, should have offered the job to the one writer in America who was already working on a book about Hughes, that was to be a fraud. Irving himself calls it 'an almost unbelievable and totally fantastic coincidence'. It is possible that it is a coincidence. It is possible that Irving was rash enough to tell his publishers that he was seeing Hughes, and promise them a book, without having any sources of information other than what was already printed and what came from his own imagination.

But it also seems possible that this was not a coincidence, that Irving knew he would have access to the Dietrich manuscript when he embarked on the project, and that this was part of his plan from the beginning. Particularly as an acquaintance of Irving reports him talking about a Howard Hughes book project two months before the time he says he first got the idea. Of course, to believe this would be to doubt Clifford Irving's word.

The third thing is that Irving perpetrated the worst kind of deception there is: he betrayed a trust.

It may be unfair to single him out on this score, since others have committed greater and crueller betrayals; his story is exemplary only because it is in the public eye. This betrayal overwhelms any feeling of grudging admiration that might otherwise accrue to his operation because of its style: his relaxed charm, the coolness of his lying, and the glamour of the small-part players in the drama.

Irving took advantage of the trust that McGraw-Hill editors had in him as one of their authors, and particularly of the executive editor, Beverly Loo, a personal friend who had been a house guest of his in Ibiza. He said in his own account of the affair that he had some scruples about this, but he appears to have overcome them. At one stage, after Hughes had declared that he had not given any interviews to Irving, Irving met with some McGraw-Hill executives, including Miss Loo, and outlined the possibilities. One of them, he said, was that he, Irving, was a fraud. Then he said: 'This possibility I intend to discard, and I hope you do too.' They agreed.

This is asking someone to drop his guard and then hitting him. It is the one kind of deception that is always to be condemned. It cuts deeper and lasts longer than others. It deceives, not senses, but emotions, which have been given freely. The person whose trust and friendship have been abused cannot easily give trust or friendship again; others involved are also affected. This kind of thing corrodes the bonds of affection and trust which bind human beings to one another, and pollutes the emotional environment in which we all live.

*　　　*　　　*

Not all the fake books in our time have been biography or autobiography. It would be nice to believe that readers today are more sophisticated than those of the eighteenth century who were readier to like Horace Walpole's first novel if it was translated from the Italian, and less susceptible to the whims of fashion; nevertheless, it does sometimes happen that the provenance of a novel decides its reception as much as its contents.

A novel that was presented to the public under false cover was a book as harsh as its title, *J'Irai Cracher Sur Vos Tombes* ('I Will Spit On Your Graves') published in France in 1947 as the work of one Vernon Sullivan, an American Negro, and as a book that was too hot for any American publisher. Bitter in tone, violent in action, it is the story of a Negro who passes for white, and sees his darker-skinned brother lynched. In revenge on the white world, he seduces two daughters of an upper-crust Southern family and then kills them. It was said to be translated from the English by Boris Vian, a well-known figure on the contemporary St. Germain-des-Pres 'existentialist' fringe, a cheerful jazz trumpeter and writer who favoured the bizarre and shocking. He was, as some people suspected from the beginning, the real author.

The book was treated seriously by a few reviewers. This was, after all, the America that French readers knew and understood, the true America, of race lynchings and gang war, of James

Cagney and Raymond Chandler. The book had a certain sensational success, boosted by charges that it was disgusting and obscene, and by the fortuity that a man strangled his mistress in a Paris hotel and left a copy by the bedside. The anti-pornography campaign succeeded in getting a prosecution against *J'Irai Cracher* and, facing a judge, Vian admitted that he was the author. By this time he had already churned out another Vernon Sullivan book that did not sound too different, *Les Morts Ont Tous La Même Peau* ('The Dead All Have The Same Skin'). The charges was dropped, the book went on selling, and Vian wrote more books under his own name.

The current practice, particularly in America, of promoting an author as much as a book with a publicity campaign encourages this kind of fraud. When twenty-four journalists sat down to write together the worst book ever written, a sex novel of the *genre* of Harold Robbins, Jacqueline Susann and Irving Wallace, they decided that they had to create an author as well. So they invented Penelope Ashe, put her photograph on the book's cover, and gave her the honour.

As nearly everyone knows now, the book was *Naked Came the Stranger*, and the authors were on the staff of *Newsday*, the Long Island newspaper. The thought had occurred to several of them, as it occurs at one time or another to most people who put words on paper for a living, that these days some novels that bear as much relation to literature as the average Tarzan film make grotesque amounts of money. So they were ripe when the hoax was proposed by Mike McGrady, then a columnist on *Newsday*, a chirpy Irish-American who was later to cover the Vietnam War for *Newsday* and to write a book called *A Dove In Vietnam*. McGrady thought up the scheme under the impact of interviewing Harold Robbins, and learning that Robbins had been paid advances totalling two million dollars on a novel solely on the strength of the title, *The Adventurers*. Payment of a million dollars a word must command serious thought, if not respect.

McGrady discussed it with some others, and then wrote a memo to all other members of the staff outlining the project, inviting participation, and laying down guidelines. Of these guidelines, the two key sentences were: 'There will be an unremitting emphasis on sex. Also, true excellence in writing will be blue-pencilled into oblivion.' Those who joined in worked out a rough plot, about a sexy suburban wife getting her own back on her unfaithful husband, and certain standard requirements such as two sexual encounters in each chapter, at least one of them bizarre – some of them were *very* bizarre.

Then they all wrote, and McGrady and a couple of others chopped, amalgamated and edited with gusto. They had their problems. They turned down the contribution by Marilyn Berger, now the White House correspondent of N.B.C., on the ground that it was too well-written and not dirty enough. The part written by Jack Schwartz, a young reporter, which involved a rabbi going wild with lust for the heroine, had force and Rabelaisian imagination, but the description of the rabbi and his background was, in the words of McGrady, 'intelligent and sophisticated, so much so as to be almost beyond salvage'. But they put it all into some kind of order, and imposed enough standardisation to make sure that the heroine was not flame-haired in one chapter and raven-locked in the next.

Then, laughing all the way, they sent the manuscript to Lyle Stuart, the publisher of the phenomenally successful *The Sensuous Woman* and other books about sensuous people, who agreed to publish and promote it. They devised a cover with an appealing nude on it.

This was all merely a literary (at least in the broadest sense) hoax. But the real imposture, the fraudulent performance on radio, on television and to newspaper reporters and magazine writers, was put in by the women who played the role of Penelope Ashe, in Lyle Stuart's big promotional campaign. This was Mrs. Billie Young, Mike McGrady's sister-in-law. She had the requirements for the part. She was 38, a Long Island housewife, good-looking and confident enough to wear a pink pant-suit and a daringly low-cut blouse for all her TV appearances. Best of all, she was, in the words of one of the book's authors, 'a natural'. She did not have the detached attitude of the others. She really believed. She believed in suburban living, in everyone trying to earn more money, and, most important, in best-sellers. A would-be writer herself with two unpublished novels in a drawer, she thought that Jacqueline Susann and Harold Robbins were first-rate writers.

Briefed by the others, but relying on her own resources for most of her answers, she put on a performance across the country as the writer/hustler and the liberated woman, answering questions with assurance and all the right cliches.

'It's a dirty book, isn't it?' an interviewer would say, on a TV or radio programme.

'It's a sexy book,' she would come back. 'Why do Americans feel that sex is dirty?'

Or the interviewer would say: 'I guess that just about every perversion that Dr. Albert Ellis has ever heard of is incorporated into your book. How did you become so experienced?'

And she would retort, 'Let me ask you, do *you* lead a sheltered sex life?'

The interviewer would ask her whether she approved of marital infidelity, and she would say: 'I think extramarital sex relations are beautiful for people that need them. I think it can save marriages. For myself, nix.'

The interviewer would ask her how many suburban families behave like the suburbanites in the book, in her experience. 'I would say 75 per cent, without hesitation', she replied. The real writers were as amazed as they were delighted by this whopper. As McGrady said, the book would have overstated the situation in Sodom. After Mrs. King's performance, any female sex writer who does the straight television interview either has a thick skin or no sense of humour.

A secret kept by twenty-four newspapermen does not remain a secret forever. When the hoax came out, it made a big story, because by now almost everyone had heard of the book. Yet it went on selling. People bought it and read it, even though they knew the joke was on them, even though they knew that the book's creators despised their creation. It sold 100,000 copies in hardback, and more in paperback. It was published in Britain. The pay-out for the authors was about $5,000 each.

Most of them felt uneasy about getting this money. The book was intended as a joke on a certain kind of writer who was very rich, not a con on the poor reading public. And when Bernard Geis, the publisher who specialises in big-money, sex-packed novels, asked them to write another book and talked of an advance of half a million dollars, McGrady, now a free-lance writer, turned him down. 'I think it was unanimous', he said later. 'We didn't take a vote on it, but it was a unanimously *felt* decision.'

When it came to it, Mike McGrady, like the others, was not a hoaxer in the classical mould. He did not really want to wield power over millions of readers. He did not want to deceive them, or hold them in contempt. A democrat and an American patriot to the deepest fibre of his being, he wanted to respect them as fellow-citizens of that republic where all people are equal, and no man looks down on his neighbour.

He wrote a funny book about the whole episode, called *Stranger Than Naked, or How To Write Dirty Books for Fun and Profit*. At the end of this, he expressed his gloomy, guilty conclusion on their deception: 'It was all too easy; it all went too smoothly, America, You sit there, you plump beauty, still buying neckties from sidewalk sharpies, still guessing which walnut shell contains the pea, still praying along with Elmer Gantry. America, sometimes I worry about you.'

*   *   *

If he is in that sort of mood, the Lobsang Rampa phenomenon might set him worrying about Britain.

Lobsang Rampa is the author of *The Third Eye*, a book which sold 40,000 copies in Britain and was translated into ten languages. It told a remarkable story of the author's life as a Tibetan lama, a story of physical and occult adventures. It described, in readable prose, his upbringing in Lhasa, the Tibetan capital, and, as the culmination of his spiritual education, an operation on his brain that opened his 'third eye', a physical organ that enabled him to practise clairvoyance, astral projection and other wonders. He travelled abroad, learned to speak English, suffered torture in a Japanese prisoner-of-war camp, then returned home in time to see the Chinese Communists arrive, with their evil auras visible to his third eye, and repress Tibetan religion.

The book was published in London in 1956 by Secker and Warburg. The author sent in his manuscript as Dr. C. Kuan, explaining that 'Lobsang Rampa' was a pseudonym to protect himself. The Chairman of the firm, Frederic Warburg, found it exciting; he lunched with Dr. Kuan and decided that he was telling the truth. He showed the manuscript to two scholars who knew Tibet, and asked for their opinion. One, while hesitating to go all the way in vouching for the extraordinary stories, said the author had clearly been brought up in Lhasa, as he said. Another said it was all culled from Western writings, and declared flatly: 'The fellow is a complete imposter and has never been to Tibet.'

When *The Third Eye* was published, it was reviewed seriously in a number of papers (it was also praised in the *Times of India*). The *Reader's Digest* considered reprinting some of it but, perhaps remembering the unfortunate episode of *The Man Who Wouldn't Talk*, its editors said they first had to have proof of Lobsang Rampa's story. An American publisher who received the manuscript said he had shown it to some scholars who knew Tibet well, and they had cast doubt on its authenticity. Warburg wrote to say that he had met Dr. Kuan and believed in him. Eventually, the book was published in America, but without any acclaim.

This seems to be one of those cases where the victims were ready to be hoaxed. Publisher and agent were persuaded that Dr. Kuan was a Tibetan holy man. But one of the few people from the media to be allowed to meet him, John Irwin, a television producer, reported that he encountered a tall, obviously occidental man who talked with a West country accent, wearing a saffron robe.

A group of Oriental scholars became so annoyed at the sensational picture of Tibet and its religion that people were accepting from the book that they hired a private detective, Clifford Burgess, to track down Lobsang Rampa. He turned out to be Cyril Hoskins, a Plymouth man who had not been far east of the Thames. The story was given to the newspapers.

And that, one might have thought, would be that. The end of Lobsang Rampa. But it was not, any more than blowing the whistle on Penelope Ashe was the end of *Naked Came The Stranger*.

A paperback publisher reissued *The Third Eye,* still under the signature of Lobsang Rampa. Then Hoskins wrote another book under the same name, explaining that his first was not a fake, but that the mind of a Tibetan lama had taken over his body, gradually blanking out his own mind and memories, and this was the mind that remembered, and wrote *The Third Eye*. Lobsang Rampa went on writing more books, fourteen altogether, which the paperback publisher issued. They were rambling books about the occult, life after death, flying saucers, and a secret world inside the earth reached through tunnels at the North and South Poles.

People went on buying his books. They were willing to be taken in, evidently, willing to forgive him for taking them in, willing to forget that they had been taken in, so that it could happen again. Some of them even wrote to him recounting their spiritual adventures, and asking for guidance. It seems that for many people, in need of some dimension of life beyond that of the material world about us, a fake lama is better than no lama at all.

CHAPTER 6

Strictly for Money

'Why do you lie to me? You tell me you're
travelling to Minsk because you want me to
believe that you're not telling the truth and
you're going to Pinsk. But I happen to know
that you're really going to Minsk.'
                                    OLD RUSSIAN JOKE

VICTOR LUSTIG, a confidence trickster of almost legendary
powers of persuasion, once found himself in the county jail in
Eagle Pass, Texas, awaiting trial for fraud. He passed the time
chatting with the sheriff, Quentin Richards, and discovered
that Richards was fascinated by his tales of big money. Lustig
soon wormed out of him the reason. Richards, as county tax
collector, had been slipping tax money into his own pockets,
amounting to $30,000 over the years; now the auditors were
coming, and he was frantic.

Lustig scoffed at him for filching such a piddling amount, but
offered to help him out. He would sell him a machine for
duplicating 100-dollar bills, which he would first demonstrate
to him, and with this the sheriff could manufacture the money
to pay back the county. The price would be a mere $25,000, 250
turns of the handle of the machine, plus his freedom. After
listening to Lustig for two days, Richards was not only willing,
but grateful for the offer. He stole $25,000 more from the county
and gave it to Lustig, and turned his back while Lustig escaped.
Then he put a 100-dollar bill in the machine, turned the handle,
and watched nothing at all happen.

Propelled by a rage that was almost incandescent, the Texan
tracked Lustig down to a swank hotel suite in Chicago, by a
stroke of luck, and confronted him with a pistol. Lustig pointed
out coolly that killing him in revenge would not placate the
auditors. However, now that Richards was in Chicago, he
would give him a chance to get off the hook. The machine was

a fake, of course, but he was working on a counterfeiting scheme now that was foolproof. Once it got going, he could give Richards the money and hardly miss it. The only trouble was, they were stalled for lack of capital. . . . There was some more talking, and Richards examined the evidence of Lustig's counterfeiting scheme. Then he went back to Eagle Pass, reached into the county safe for another $65,000, and gave it to Lustig, who of course disappeared.

This is a supreme example of the swindler's art, and also his ruthlessness. It also points up a key facet of his skill. The swindler plays on the expectation of gain, or perhaps the need for it. He plays on this with skill and sensitivity. Because he understands it; he too, is an entrepreneur, driven by the profit motive. In his campaign against his victim, greed is his ally in the enemy camp.

Another episode illustrates the same point. No swindler has ever been more successful over a long period in turning his victims into his allies than Oscar Hartzell, with the Francis Drake legacy swindle. He dreamed up a deception that induced 70,000 people to part with their money, in a scheme that was supposed to make them rich, and he had most of them resisting allegations that it was a fraud just as vigorously and for just as long as he did himself.

He was an Iowan who, in 1921, wrote from London to some friends back in Iowa to say that he had found the heir to the estate of Sir Francis Drake, thought to have died childless, and that the value of the estate had grown over the centuries to $22 billion. Hartzell was helping him to raise money to fight the legal battle to claim his inheritance. He was soliciting loans from other descendants of Drake, that is, people named Drake, and the loans would be repaid at the rate of $500 for one dollar. Mysterious forces were at work to prevent the heir recovering the legacy, so his name had to be kept secret. Amazingly, people in Iowa believed this and sent money. By popular request, Hartzell dropped his insistence that investors be limited to people named Drake. He appointed eleven people as agents to collect money, all in the Midwest, and they talked up the scheme. Thousands of dollars were sent to him every week for more than ten years. Some people mortgaged their homes or farms to contribute.

Because of the sinister forces at work, all investors were pledged to secrecy. Any violation of this pledge brought instant dismissal from the scheme. In exchange for their money investment, they were admitted to an exciting world of conspiracy and intrigue, of the kind they could not imagine in their own home towns but might well take place in far-off England. From his luxurious pad in London, Hartzell sent a stream of messages to all investors relating the latest moves and counter-moves. New documents were discovered, there were secret negotiations with the Crown, the President of the United States was involved, there were new attempts by perfidious Albion to stifle the truth, sometimes with covert U.S. Government support. The upheavals in the British economy through the 1920s were interpreted solely in terms of the likelihood of the Government having to shell out what now turned out to be the sum of $400 billion.

This fantasy world was self-sustaining. Every attack could be used to strengthen it. When Federal authorities eventually arrested Hartzell's agents for fraud, this showed that Washington was in collusion with the British Crown. When Hartzell himself was deported from Britain and arrested on his arrival in America, this was further proof of the unholy alliance, and proof also of the lengths to which it would go. At Hartzell's urgings, the true believers sent in money for his bail. Investors were loath to break their promise of secrecy. The witnesses who were called to give evidence in court about the thousands of dollars they had lost went on to insist that Hartzell was an honest man. When he was sent to prison for ten years, no one protested more loudly than his victims. Many continued to believe for the rest of their lives that they, Hartzell and Drake's still secret heir were all the victims of a plot.

If, as was said in the Introduction, the hoaxer is someone who creates a fantasy world and persuades other people to live in it, the swindler also collects rent. The person who enters his world pays money for an illusion.

Stories of swindles have come into previous chapters, but these have been by-products of a particular talent or inclination. The literary fraud can usually be trusted not to cheat in any other way. But the swindler is a professional criminal, and the criminal impulse lies behind his deception. There are many instances of a person turning from some other kind of crime to fraud, but none of a practical joker who has suddenly started to apply his talents to crime.

Some swindles have been elaborate as well as ingenious, and have involved many people in creating the deception. Typically, this may be a supposed plan to cheat a bookmaker of a large sum of money in which the bookmaker and the other clients are all play-acting; when the victim puts a lot of money into the scheme then it somehow goes wrong and he loses his money. The film *The Sting* was a fictionalised and probably exaggerated account of this.

I encountered a humbler and more common version some years ago when I was a youthful tourist in Italy. I was bumming around, but because I was in Milan on this day I was wearing a summer suit, and might have looked like someone affluent enough to be worth cheating, as well as simple enough to be cheated. I was gazing up at Milan Cathedral when two men struck up a conversation with me, and suggested that I should see something that most tourists don't get to see. I set off with them through some narrow streets. We came to a stretch of waste ground where a simple game was going on. My companions led me straight over to it, and I realised that this, and not some neglected gem of Quattrocento architecture, was what we had come to see.

The game was a version of the shell game involving slats of wood with rubber bands around them. A card was on the underside of one. The banker would shuffle them around and then ask the others to guess which was the one. But one of the three other men playing the game had slipped the rubber band at an angle, so that it was easy to tell which one it was. The banker, I was to presume, was either as blind as a bat or else remarkably careless, because the others would guess which one it was each time, and he would hand over thousand-lire notes with equanimity. My companions started betting and winning money, and urged me to do the same. The talk was fast and in Italian, they were digging me in the ribs, and I wasn't quite sure for the moment what was going on. But I could not believe that it was a heaven-sent opportunity for me to pay for my holiday, so I left the scene, and, as I suddenly realised that there was no one else within earshot, I did so rapidly.

Getting someone to participate in a trick that goes wrong is such a common kind of con game that there is a saying among some con men that 'you can't cheat an honest man'. Actually, this is not so. Those who say it are taking a maxim for one kind of swindle to cover every kind, and justifying themselves by pretending that the victim is always at the same moral level as the con man, and therefore deserves to be cheated. All that is necessary is that the victim has the ordinary amount of desire for more money, just enough hunger to make him snap at a bait.

*   *   *

Alves Reis, a Portuguese with a considerable and well-deserved reputation for business acumen and flair, could, if he wanted to, reasonably claim to have perpetrated the most ingenious financial deception of the twentieth century. It was also probably the most far-reaching in its effects and, while it lasted, one of the most profitable. When some of its consequences were being debated in the British House of Lords, Lord Macmillan of Aberfeldy, a man not customarily given to hyperbole, called it, in convoluted prose, 'a crime for which, in the ingenuity and audacity of its conception, it would be difficult to find a parallel'.

Alves Reis's crime, complicated in its execution, rested on a single idea that was beautiful in its simplicity. He hoaxed the British printing firm that printed Portuguese money into printing some for him. The bills were not forgeries, but genuine paper money. The only thing was, they were not made for the Portuguese Government, but for Reis.

Reis perceived that money is simply printed pieces of paper, that must be manufactured like any other objects. Indeed, in Europe at this time, in the early 1920s, it was being manufactured very freely in some places. In Germany, million-mark notes had poured off the printing presses until paper money was worthless. In Austria, paper money was reduced to one per cent of the value it had ten years earlier, in 1914, with catastrophic results for millions of people. In his own country, Portugal, more and more paper money was being printed, and the rocketing inflation touched 100 per cent in one year.

The great art forgers raise the challenging question of the real value of a painting; Reis raised the question of the real value of money. A piece of paper money is a promissory note: in theory, it is a promise by the National Treasury to pay the bearer a certain sum in gold, or silver. But after the First World War, most countries in Europe went off the gold standard, including Portugal. It was coming to be realised that governments themselves, as well as the general public, did not altogether understand the real nature of money. The question is a philosophical one in a period of stability. but in the Europe of the early 1920s, it was thrust before many people by the events around them.

One of Reis's defenders, the Portuguese writer Eugenio Battaglia, threw back the charge that Reis's money was not genuine. 'What about the Government's?' he demanded. 'Could anyone in 1925 exchange 20 escudos in paper money for 20 escudos in gold?'

Reis himself argued at one point, after he was caught, that his money was real money, and nobody had lost anything because of what he did. It was difficult to refute this. Indeed, years later, in the light of Lord Keynes' economic theories, which have been the guiding principles of national economic management since the Second World War, it could be said that he was a benefactor. The five million dollars in escudos that he put into the Portuguese economy went some way towards fulfilling Keynes' recipe for climbing out of economic depression: increase the money supply and the amount of credit available in a 'pump-priming' operation.

Though the fraud raises some interesting questions, Reis's purpose was not an experiment in macro-economics: he wanted to be rich. In fact, like most ambitious businessmen, he wanted to be *very* rich, and to be powerful, and esteemed in his country. His career indicates that he had the drive and the chemistry of talents needed to achieve all this honestly; he only lacked patience.

He achieved success very young, and the fact that a faked document started him off was almost incidental. He would have gone far without the faked document.

The son of an undertaker in Lisbon, he studied engineering for a while, then quit to get married. Intensely ambitious, yet without money or social position, he did what young Europeans in his situation had done for two centuries, and turned his eyes to the colonies. In 1916, with his bride of a few months, Alves

Reis set out at the age of 21 to seek his fortune in Angola, Portugal's West African colony.

He took with him a forged diploma in engineering and applied sciences from the non-existent Polytechnic School of Engineering of Oxford University. It was stamped with the similarly non-existent 'golden seal of Oxford'. He probably felt the need of something a little more substantial than his wits to start him off.

His career was meteoric. With his phoney diploma, he got a job as an engineer in the civil service in Angola, rose rapidly in its ranks, showing dynamism and organising ability, then quit to become an importer and exporter, and prospered immediately. He moved his business back to Lisbon and soon, when he was still in his middle twenties, he was one of the most successful businessmen in Portugal.

Reis was small in stature, only about five foot six, but, according to all accounts, he possessed an air of command rare in one so young. He was quick, coolly decisive, and not without charm; at any rate, he was a good listener. His only nervous habit was chain-smoking day and night.

He wanted everything too quickly. He over-reached himself, and tried to buy control of two big Angola companies with money that he did not have. He was arrested for embezzlement and spent two months in prison. He got the charges against him dropped only by selling all his assets, including his wife's jewelry, and raising enough money to satisfy his creditors.

It was while he was in prison that he conceived his plan. He was sure that his take-over bid for the Angolan companies was a sound idea, and would have worked if he had had enough cash in hand. He would not be in this position again. He would, literally, make money. As the only body entitled to do this was the Bank of Portugal, he studied all the published material on the structure and workings of the national bank, which was only partly owned by the state, and was entrusted under its constitution with the task of supplying the national currency.

Once again, he turned to forgery. The fact that he had never acquired any skill as a forger did not inhibit him, any more than his limited knowledge of engineering slowed his career in Angola. If a forged document was needed, then he would forge one. The document he drew up was a contract between the

Bank of Portugal and a group of international financiers. The financiers were to lend some five million dollars to Angola, to boost the colony's sagging economy; in return, they would be authorised to print five million dollars' worth of Portuguese money, which they would also invest in Angola.

Reis typed it on official paper, had it notarised by a dozey notary whom he knew would not bother to read it, and then simply traced the signatures of the Angolan High Commissioner and Minister of Finance from a public document. He bound it with tape and sealing wax, stamped the wax with the Portuguese coat of arms, and clipped on a 500-escudo bill and a 1,000-escudo bill, which presumably were the bills that were to be printed.

He had already chosen his three confederates in this crime, but they were also dupes. For he was not going to tell them the whole story. Two of them were foreigners, both men with extensive experience of international trading who were none too scrupulous about legalities. They were Karel Marang, a Dutchman who had built up a prosperous business on the basis of wartime black market deals; and Adolf Hennies, a German who had been in business in several countries and found it expedient to travel on a Swiss passport. The third was Jose Bandeira, a young man with a shady background which included a prison sentence; he had some useful contacts as the brother of a Portuguese Embassy official in the Hague, and it was he who had first introduced Marang to Reis.

Reis persuaded these three that the document was genuine, though dishonest. That is to say, he had been given the contract because he had bribed some well-placed friends in the Bank of Portugal. He suggested that once they got the five million dollars, they need not worry about actually lending money to Angola. He said the Government was keeping the matter secret because it did not want people to know how bad the economic situation in the colony was.

He wanted the others to arrange secretly for the printing of the money in another country. He warned them not to contact the firm that did print Portuguese money. He did not give them the reason for this caution; he imagined that this firm would be in constant contact with the bank, and would soon find that no arrangement to print money for Angola existed.

The ensuing events are involved, but Marang saw a Dutch firm that printed money for several governments, and they gave him a letter of introduction to Waterlow & Sons, the British firm that printed most of Portugal's money. Armed with this, Marang passed himself off as a member of a legitimate financial syndicate that had made the agreement with the Bank. The Chairman, Sir William Waterlow, believed his story. He was eager to believe it; Waterlow & Sons were competing with other firms to keep the lucrative Bank of Portugal printing contracts. Sir William readily agreed to keep the arrangement secret, and gave him a price for the printing job–£1,500. He needed specific authorisation from the Bank of Portugal, and the serial numbers that were to go on the bills.

Bandeira and Marang went back to Lisbon and reported to Reis. Reis was furious; they had gone to Waterlow & Sons, just what he had told them not to do. The next day, he told them that he had seen his friends, the High Commissioner for Angola and the Governor of the Bank. They were ready to call off the whole deal, but he had placated them, and they had agreed to provide the authorisation. However, they would not exchange any letters with Waterlow's because this would endanger secrecy. All exchanges must be by personal contact.

Then Reis manufactured a second forged document, the authorisation that Waterlow & Sons required, which was intended to fool Marang and Hennies as well as Waterlow. On this one, he traced the name of the Governor and Vice-Governor of the Bank of Portugal from a 10-escudo bill. Marang and Hennies accepted it as genuine, and took it back to Waterlow & Sons in London.

In the involved series of events that followed, luck was with Reis. Things could have gone wrong in a lot of ways. Waterlow & Sons could have contacted the Bank of Portugal directly at any time (in fact, at one point they *did* write a letter to the Bank about the matter and, incredibly, it seems to have been lost or pigeon-holed). Waterlow had an agent in Lisbon who expressed to them disquiet about the whole affair; he was told to stay out of it and say nothing to anyone since it was secret. Marang, Hennies and Bandeira continued to believe that they were taking part in a dishonest deal–they were not going to have to send five million dollars to Angola; but they had no idea that they were purveying a false contract, and that the arrangement with the Bank of Portugal was pure invention by Reis.

They agreed at one stage to share out the money and drew up a contract to this effect. Reis was to receive, in addition to his share, $800,000 for 'expenses he had incurred', which, so far as the others were concerned, meant bribes to the heads of the Bank of Portugal.

Marang collected the money in three huge suitcases, and the four of them shared it out, and set about filtering it into the economy. First, they exchanged a lot of it for foreign currency in small exchanges in Oporto. Rumours arose that counterfeit 500-escudo bills were in circulation. The Bank of Portugal examined various of the new bills that were arousing suspicion, subjecting the paper, the ink and the engraving to expert scrutiny, and pronounced them genuine. It issued a statement denying that counterfeit bills had been found.

Given the value of money at the time, and Portugal's parlous economic state, this wealth made all four among the richest men in the country. Marang and Hennies spent their money as shrewd businessmen, buying properties and investing some abroad; Bandeira became a playboy, driving around Lisbon in a Rolls Royce with his actress mistress, Reis also spent conspicuously, but he used his money to become a man of importance, and to pursue his vaulting ambitions. But again, he lacked patience, and his sudden and conspicuous wealth inevitably raised searching questions about how he had acquired it.

He turned his attention to Angola again, and bought a majority of the shares in the Ambaca company, which owned mineral resources there. This avenged an earlier defeat; it was his attempt to gain control of Ambaca that led to his arrest for embezzlement. Then he got a charter to open a new bank, the Bank of Angola and Metropole ('Metropole' is the term in Portugal, as in France, for the homeland as opposed to overseas territories). The bank had its own building in the financial district of Lisbon and another as a branch office in Oporto. Almost immediately, it invested in several Angolan businesses.

Reis had more far-reaching ambitions still. He knew that a majority of shares in the Bank of Portugal were privately owned.

He started buying shares, some of them through nominees, apparently aiming to become nothing less than the majority shareholder in the national bank, a position no one had ever held. This would make him one of the most powerful men in the country. It would also give him virtual immunity from prosecution – and this doubtless figured in his plans – since charges on currency offences could only be initiated with the consent of the Bank of Portugal.

Throughout 1925, banks closed down in Portugal, but the Bank of Angola and Metropole flourished, and opened branches in Angola. Reis called a Press conference to announce his next move; he said he was leading a group of development experts on a mission to Angola to look at ways to resuscitate the colony. The announcement was widely applauded. If things were tending to go to Reis's head, it was not altogether surprising. It was less than two years since he had had to sell his wife's jewels to stay out of jail.

Some Portuguese recalling the affair today exaggerate Reis's importance, making him out to be the harbinger of a short-lived economic boom, during which unemployment dropped and business prospered. More sober historians deny that he had this impact, but they agree that his investments in Angola turned the colony's economy around and started it on an upswing. Small wonder that Reis has been called a Keynesian before his time.

On his trip to Angola he was given a reception suited to Royalty. He was entertained by the Government of the colony, and hailed in the Press as a native son returning, and 'Portugal's Cecil Rhodes'.

Naturally, some people persisted in questioning the source of all this wealth, and the Bank of Angola and Metropole's vast supply of capital. There were hints again that forged money was behind it. Again the national bank's experts checked the bills over, and pronounced them genuine. But there was now so much mystery surrounding this money that officials checked further. At last, one found the flaw. It was not in the printing but in the serial numbers; some of the numbers of the bills in Reis's bank duplicated numbers on bills already issued. They quickly checked with the printers, Waterlow & Sons in London, and the game was up.

Reis was on the high seas on his way back from Angola, and he was arrested on his arrival in Lisbon. This caused a sensation. The Bank of Portugal did not know how much of the money printed on his instructions was in circulation, but it tried to identify the bills by serial numbers. It asked anyone possessing these bills to hand them in, and get others in exchange.

Accusations were flung about wildly. Everyone had his own theory of who in high places was responsible. Public confidence in the republic, already weakened dangerously, dropped still further.

For a while, Reis himself behaved like a demented nihilist, determined to wreak as much havoc on the state as he could. He named names wildly, implicated directors of the Bank of Portugal, and even forged receipts for bribes from the Governor of the Bank in his prison cell. The directors of the Bank offered to resign. He also wrote, in his prison cell, a small book which was a disjointed attack on the Bank of Portugal and the League of Nations.

When he had calmed down, he fought for time. He delayed his trial for more than four years, helped by clever lawyers, the difficulties of pursuing all the tortuous pathways of the affair, and the upheavals in the country. For this period took in the overthrow of Portuguese democracy by a military junta, and the assumption of power by Antonio Salazar, the ascetic, reactionary economics professor who was to rule Portugal with a tight hand for forty-two years. Reis's blows at the integrity of Portuguese democracy contributed to this, just as Stavisky's swindle was to weaken the Third Republic in France.

Reis argued that he had cheated no one, that he had been motivated by a desire to help Angola. In the end, he confessed in court, in a detailed recounting of the planning and execution of his crime that sounded more boastful than repentant. He also fought to get various Portuguese assistants acquitted, including his wife; she was released. He was sentenced to twenty years' imprisonment. Bandeira and several smaller fry were given lesser sentences. Hennies and Marang were abroad and were sentenced *in absentia*, and they remained *in absentia*.

In prison, Reis underwent a religious conversion. From being an occasionally practising Roman Catholic, like most Portuguese, he became a convert to the Evangelical Protestant faith.

He threw his bountiful energies into the pursuit of spiritual goals, and proselytising as well; he wrote Evangelical tracts.

He was released from prison in 1945. His funds had all been seized, and his wife and three sons were living in very modest circumstances. He became an unpaid lay preacher for a while. His sons ran a small import-export firm, and Reis joined them. Briefly, he was carried away by his old habits. Two years after his release, he negotiated on behalf of the firm a big deal to import rice from Brazil. He flew to Rio de Janeiro, difficulties cropped up, he started to bend Brazillian law, and he was deported. This was his last deal. When he died of a heart attack in 1955, at the age of 59, he was nearly penniless.

In Britain, the Portuguese money affair became the Waterlow affair. Waterlow & Sons were a distinguished firm; its Chairman, Sir William Waterlow, was Lord Mayor of London. He resigned his chairmanship when it was found how he had been hoaxed, and was replaced by his cousin. The Bank of Portugal claimed that Waterlow & Sons were at fault in printing the money, and sued them for the cost of replacing it. Some Portuguese newspapers said the Portuguese national bank would not stand a chance in a British court against such a prestigious British firm. They were wrong; a court ruled against Waterlow & Sons, there were appeals all the way up to the House of Lords, and the ruling was upheld.

In the course of the trials and appeals, some interesting questions were raised. Waterlow's chief defence counsel, Gavin Simonds, argued that the Bank of Portugal had lost no real wealth through the fraud, because Portugal was not on the gold standard and the money did not represent gold, and Reis's notes were only replaced by other paper money. 'If the liability of the bank is to pay gold,' he said, 'their liability would be measured by so much gold, but if the notes are only to be honoured in paper, the value of the paper is their only liability; and it has been found by the courts that there was no probability of a return to gold.'

Despite this intriguing line of argument, the House of Lords agreed that the Bank of Portugal, because it had replaced the false notes with genuine ones, had lost the face value of the genuine notes, and not just the value of the paper on which they were printed. Less the amount recovered from Reis and his associates, this amounted to £70,000, and Waterlow & Sons had to pay this, plus costs.

*   *   *

Most financial swindles come into that rather uninteresting class of deceptions that are primarily falsification of *things*; the deceiver stands back at a distance, and carries out his deception through pieces of paper. Alves Reis put his whole personality into his deception; he was right there in the ring throwing the punches himself. So did the Musica brothers, who perpetrated one of the longest-lived and most extraordinary financial swindles that the American financial world has ever seen.

In December 1938, Wall Street received a shock. One of its most respected figures was arrested, and charged with filing a false statement with the Securities and Exchange Commission. He was F. Donald Coster, a financier and President of McKesson & Robbins Inc., the pharmaceutical firm.

Both Coster and his corporation were, in Wall Street's favourite term of approbation, thoroughly 'sound'. McKesson & Robbins was 105 years old, and in recent years it had expanded to become the third largest drugs firm in the world. It had assets of $80 million and an annual turnover of $160 million. It had come under Coster's control twelve years earlier, and under his guiding hand it had expanded its national and international operations. Coster himself hardly seemed like a natural candidate for the state penitentiary. He was a director of three trust companies, a member of the Bankers' Club, the New York Yacht Club and the Lotos Club, a married man and a Methodist, with a gracious, spacious, Colonial-style mansion in Fairfield, Connecticut. He had a background that was particularly useful in the pharmaceutical field, since it included a PhD from Heidelberg University and two years as a practising physician in New York City.

Coster's arrest followed the discovery that $18 million worth of assets supposedly belonging to the crude drugs department of McKesson & Robbins were missing, and quite likely, had never existed. The discovery was made by the corporation's treasurer, Julian S. Thomson. But he was almost as shocked as the rest of the financial world at the significance of his discovery. He was still more surprised when two other men connected with McKesson & Robbins were arrested along with him: George Dietrich, the Deputy Treasurer, and also a good friend and neighbour of Coster's in Fairfield; and George Venard, a trading agent who dealt with the company. All three men were released on $5,000 bail.

Wall Street buzzed with surprised talk. Coster's slightly old-fashioned style of dressing, with spats that matched his suit, his pudgy face, his round glasses and his owlish expression all seemed to guarantee respectability, not to say dullness. People were saying that old Coster might be a bit of a stick-in-the-mud, but he was as honest as the day is long, and a victim of bureaucratic New Deal interference.

The following day ,there was an announcement that was more startling still.

When the F.B.I. arrested the three men, they fingerprinted them as a matter of routine. Also as a matter of routine, they checked these fingerprints against their files.

They found that the man they had arrested in his Fairfield mansion was not Frank Donald Coster, born of American parents in Washington D.C. He was Philip Musica, born in Naples, who had come to America when he was six years old. Coster's American birth, his w a s p background, his educational and professional qualifications, his name, even, all recounted in *Who's Who in America*, were pure invention.

And more. The two men arrested with him were also not the people they said they were. They were his brothers. George Dietrich, the deputy treasurer of the company, was George Musica. George Venard, the trading agent was Arthur Musica. A few days later, yet another Musica brother was discovered. He was another senior official of the company, supposedly George Dietrich's brother Robert Dietrich, actually Robert Musica.

The news was greeted with incredulity. Coster had a wife and a wide circle of business associates, and a life-style of restrained affluence suitable to his position. He was not much of a party-giver, or party-goer, nor did he frequent night clubs. But he entertained small groups of friends aboard his 123-foot yacht, the Carolita, which had a crew of ten. He suffered from heart disease, and had founded a heart clinic in Bridgeport, Connecticut, where sufferers who could not afford big medical fees could be treated. Friends and acquaintances looked again and again at the picture, and could find no flaw in it.

It does seem incredible that his claims about his background did not trip him up. Did he *never* let slip his Italian origin? He was supposed to have been a practising physician. Was there never a circumstance in which he was called upon to show some knowledge of medicine? He was supposed to have been at Heidelberg University (for a time he had a forged degree from Heidelberg framed on his office wall). Did no one ever, even jocularly, address him in German? He must have been a very skilful performer.

Julian Thomson, the man who had brought about his down-fall, said he could not believe it. Coster's doctor, Dr. Petrovic, who was involved with him in his heart clinic, reacted with stunned bewilderment. Days later, he told reporters: 'I think I'm still dreaming. I can't believe it.'

His wife, Carol, could not believe it. She had been married to him for twelve years. They had met when she, newly divorced, opened a pet shop in Jamaica, Long Island, and he walked in to buy a dog. She evidently knew nothing about his real background until the bombshell burst. The gardener who worked for the Costers reported that on the day after his arrest, he came upon the two of them engaged in an anguished emotional exchange. She was kneeling before him and saying, 'My Donald, why didn't you tell me this, why didn't you let me know?'

Now the newspapers turned up the career of Philip Musica, from police files and their own. He seems to have been one of those people who was dishonest as soon as he was anything. His father, Antonio Musica, was a barber. Over the years, he saved money and started a small business importing foodstuffs from Italy, and young Philip joined him in this. He persuaded him that he could reduce his costs by bribing customs inspectors instead of paying import duties. It worked, and the business prospered. Then they were caught. Philip Musica insisted in court that he alone was to blame, and he was sentenced to a year in prison, in 1909. Even in those days, he was remarkably plausible; his appearance in court persuaded several of the jurors to ask for leniency, and he was pardoned by President Taft before he completed his sentence on the ground that he had been led astray by a dishonest customs official, something which in the light of his later career seems unlikely.

Then his father branched out from barbering into the human hair business, and once again the Musicas started to prosper. Young Philip used the business as the basis for borrowing large sums from banks on stocks of hair and other properties that did not exist. His life-style now was that of the playboy, patent leather Italian-American 1900s version. He lived at the Knickerbocker Hotel, was an operagoer, and dined regularly at Delmonico's, often accompanied by an opera singer or an actress. He also became a figure in New York's Italian-American community, making donations to charities and sitting on committees.

Then the banks started asking for the repayment of loans, and the bubble burst; some $300,000 was missing. Philip, his father Antonio, and a sister disappeared. They were arrested some weeks later on a ship in New Orleans harbour that was about to sail for Costa Rica, with $80,000 and a lot of jewelry on them. The father, who had once again been talked into a crooked venture by his son, tried to commit suicide while he was in custody.

In court Philip explained his abrupt departure from the New York scene in the bland, business tones that he was later to make his own: 'We left the city because we were not in a position to meet our obligations at once.' Later, he admitted that he had been 'money-mad, and obsessed with the notion of becoming a financial power'. He repented and promised to try to repay the money.

By a process that is not altogether clear from the surviving records, he received a suspended sentence in exchange for promising to act as a police informer. He did this for a while, and assisted in counter-espionage operations during the war, operating under an alias now for the first time. He impressed officials with his earnestness and dedication. When, in 1919, a Senate committee questioned the practice of using criminals as informers, and Musica's name was raised, New York State's Deputy Attorney General, Alfred R. Becker, said he was totally convinced that Musica had repented and wanted to be a good citizen. He said he had become a personal friend, and declared: 'His life convinces me that there is such a thing as reform. There is no person in the world I trust more than Philip Musica. I stand alongside him.'

He, too, was to be disillusioned, as others were later. A year after this, Musica was charged with procuring perjured evidence for a mobster accused of a gangland murder, but was not convicted. After this, there was no trace of Philip Musica on the public records, or, it seems, anywhere else.

F. Donald Coster was born around this time, middle-aged and already in business as the head of Girard & Co., a firm manufacturing hair tonics and lotions under several brand names, located in Alexandria, Virginia. This company too, it turned out, was known to the police. It was during the Prohibition era, and Federal prohibition agents had suspicions that some of the large quantities of alcohol that Girard & Co. was buying for the manufacture of its lotions was ending up in the kind of medicine that is usually drunk with soda water or ginger ale. Police visited the firm several times, but could find no proof. One police officer, recalling these visits, said that Coster had several times referred him to his partner, Mr. Girard, but he had never met him, and he eventually concluded, correctly, that Mr. Girard did not exist.

In 1926 Coster decided to expand. He met Julian Thomson, then the head of an investment bank, and asked him to help him raise the money. Thomson looked over his books. These were all cooked to make the company seem bigger and more profitable than it was, but they also contained an audit by a reputable firm of auditors. Not unnaturally, Thomson accepted Coster as the head of a thriving business. He helped him negotiate a loan and then another million dollars, and with this Coster obtained control of McKesson & Robbins, persuading the stockholders to merge it with the apparently prosperous Girard & Co. Thomson left banking to join the new firm as a director and treasurer.

Under Coster's stewardship, McKesson & Robbins weathered the 1929 crash, and set up a nation-wide chain of wholesale drug distribution houses. It marketed 238 different pharmaceutical products. When Prohibition was repealed, it went into the wholesale liquor business as well.

Thomson's help was invaluable in all this, but there was never any doubt about whose was the guiding brain behind it.

Thomson was to tell a court in evidence: 'Mr. Coster was always the dominant person. He had put the merger through, and he was the largest stockholder. Everyone deferred to him in the fundamental decisions.' (This did not always apply to matters that were less than fundamental. He often sent his chemists suggestions for new products, and they were almost all rejected. McKesson & Robbins chemists came to have a fairly low opinion of their boss's abilities in the medico-chemical field, which is not surprising.)

Yet Thomson, too, was a victim of Musica's plausibility. Even after all the arguments over the missing millions, even after he had forced an investigation, he told a *Wall Street Journal* reporter when Coster was arrested: 'If you knew the man as I do, you could not believe that he had anything to do with the missing money.'

The day after the F.B.I. discovered that Coster was Philip Musica, they decided to re-arrest him on additional charges. They also wanted to increase the bail to $100,000. Coster, after the scene with his wife, was brooding, and drank quite a lot.

Evidently, having lived for eighteen years as F. Donald Coster, he did not want to live as Philip Musica again. In his bedroom, he heard the two F.B.I. agents driving up to the house, and probably saw them from the window. He took a revolver from a chest of drawers, went into the bathroom, locked the door, faced the mirror, and, as the F.B.I. men's footsteps sounded on the wooden porch, he shot himself through the head.

It took the law enforcement agencies eighteen months to unravel the case. McKesson & Robbins' crude drugs department was a blind, through which money was being siphoned off. The deception was transferred from Girard & Co., where the false statements of dealings had been used to inflate the firm's paper profits. At McKesson & Robbins, the operation was carried out on a suitably larger scale. Millions of dollars worth of crude drugs, which actually did not exist, were sold through another company, W. W. Smith, which was in reality only an office in Brooklyn staffed by George Venard, alias Arthur Musica. False bills of sale were made out to many firms, and W. W. Smith collected the commission. The profits were supposedly poured back into more crude drugs. The drugs, the sales and the profits all existed only on paper. The only thing that was real was the commissions that McKesson & Robbins paid to W. W. Smith, which amounted to some three million dollars over the years.

Thomson had become worried about the figures that were being given for the crude drugs division, which on paper was the most profitable part of the corporation. The division was kept under the personal control of Coster and George Dietrich (alias George Musica). Thomson felt it was his duty to stockholders to investigate; if anything was wrong, they would be the losers. Coster always turned aside his questions about the crude drugs division, but Thomson continued to press him for details. Eventually, despite their long friendship and business association, he refused to sign the company's annual report unless he was allowed to examine this division and its assets personally. Thomson, scrupulous, courageous and doggedly conscientious, was clearly the stuff of which Wall Street's heroes are made.

The whole deception seemed so incredible that the police and the F.B.I. were convinced for a while that still more must lie behind it. They told reporters that dummy trading in drugs concealed large illegal trafficking in arms with European governments in violation of the U.S. Neutrality Act, but dropped this idea after a while. New York Attorney-General Thomas E. Dewey described the Musicas as 'the smartest bunch of thieves I ever heard of'. The three surviving Musica brothers were all sent to prison.

Coster had assumed another identity for eighteen years. He lived his business and social life in this *persona*. His wife knew him in no other, and could not accept any other. After his death she had built for him an ornate mausoleum, with a marble slab that read: 'F. Donald Coster, 1884–1938'.

But while he was alive he did not, unlike some other imposters, bury completely his former identity. Philip Musica still lived.

For one thing, he was being blackmailed by a person or several people who knew his former identity, and until his death he paid them to keep quiet. But this reminder was not needed. Philip Musica lived on as part of the Musica family. It was not only that he brought his three brothers into the scheme with him. All four were devoted sons. They supported their mother in comfortable style not far from Fairfield, and saw her often.

When she was ill they sometimes visited her daily. In fact, Coster stretched his concern to the point of allowing the two lives to touch; when the doctor prescribed medicines for his mother, they were delivered in a McKesson & Robbins van.

The brothers also kept in touch with their two sisters, and sent them money from time to time; one was married to a gardener in upstate New York, the other lived with their mother, under the name of Girard. (The Musica brothers seem to have had difficulty inventing names; they only thought of a few, so that the same ones keep cropping up. Girard was supposedly the maiden name of Coster's mother, in the *Who's Who* entry. Three of the four brothers took out birth certificates appropriate to their new identities, and they all gave as the person who attended the birth the same name for the midwife, which would have been a remarkable coincidence considering that two of them were supposed not to be related.) Coster was a loyal brother to the last; he left behind him when he died an eight-page confession which he wrote in longhand the night before he killed himself, attempting to vindicate his brothers and saying that he alone knew of the dishonest dealings at McKesson & Robbins.

There was one other tie that Coster kept with the identity of Philip Musica. F. Donald Coster was a Methodist. But in the wallet that police found on his body, there was a leather pouch. It contained a small silver crucifix in a setting of five silver medallions. On the back of one of these was inscribed the words 'I am a Catholic. In case of accident, notify a priest.'

CHAPTER 7

Faces and Masks: The Hoaxer as Imposter

> If one realises that social interaction is role-playing and appearance, one can play the game without getting lost in it . . . The crucial matter is, does the social mask come off or does it stick?
>
> 'The Psychopath: Hero of Our Age',
> article by MICHAEL L. GLENN
>
> I'm not singing, I'm impersonating Caruso.
> Remark attributed to JOHN BARRYMORE

THE Musica brothers were not just swindlers; they were also imposters. Imposture, the assumption of another person's identity, is a creative act requiring enormous resources of imagination and ability. Unlike many other kinds of deception, it requires histrionic talents. It appeals to a theatrical impulse, to the contradictory tendencies to exhibitionism and concealment that makes up the motivation of the actor, exhibiting himself to an audience, but at the same time concealing himself behind the guise of another identity.

Furthermore, to play a role for most of the hours of the day over a long period of time, to *live* the role, and to subsume one's own identity, is so difficult, and so complex psychologically, that it usually involves an element of self-deception. Sincerity and insincerity are terms too crude to encompass the ambiguities involved. If a person is in the habit of defining himself primarily by his past, then in pretending to have another past, he is a hoaxer; but if he defines himself primarily by his present activities, then, once he has played a role for a while, and is engaged in it most of his waking hours, the lies about his past become less important than the sense of identity with his daily life.

Literature contains many examples of people who play a role and find themselves becoming the person whose identity they have taken, and history has quite a few; for instance, the Russian Yegov Azov, who was infiltrated by the Czarist secret police into the Social Revolutionary Party as a double-agent, and was so carried away with his role as a revolutionary that he organised the assassination of the Minister of the Interior.* There is also negative imposture, which is much less difficult. When John Stonehouse, the runaway British Member of Parliament, arrived in Melbourne and set out to start a new life under the name of Clive Mildoon, he was not so much pretending to be Mildoon as pretending not to be John Stonehouse.

An early practitioner of imposture both for profit and also, evidently, to meet some deep-seated need, was George Psalmanazar, the Formosan. He was not a Formosan and Psalmanazar was not his real name, but no one has ever discovered any other. He was one of the last of a long line of hoaxers that began with the great age of exploration, who would feed public curiosity with their accounts of travels to far-off lands and marvels they had seen, without troubling to make the journey. Psalmanazar went further in that he not only pretended to the England of the 1700s that he had been to Formosa, but that he was a Formosan, though his accounts of that exotic land outdid most writers of exploration fiction.

Psalmanazar arrived in England from the Continent in 1702 under the sponsorship of an army chaplain, the Reverend William Innes. He passed himself off as a native of Formosa who had spent six years travelling in Europe, and had been converted to Christianity. He spoke what he said was the Formosan language, as well as several others, and knew Latin. He said the inhabitants of Formosa looked more like Westerners than Orientals, which explained his own Occidental features.

Psalmanazar was adept at flattering English vanity with grateful accounts of his conversion from his heathen religion and customs to the superior culture of England. He pleased the right people, was entertained widely and well, and received a grant to study at Christ Church College, Oxford, and train missionaries. His imposture earned him a good living, but he

---

* This switching of roles is a recurring theme in the history of underground revolutionary and counter-revolutionary activities in pre-1917 Russia. The Revolution of 1905 was actually started by a police spy, the priest Father Gapon, who became the workers' leader that he was pretending to be.

was intelligent, well-educated and sophisticated, and could probably have succeeded in any profession he chose. He chose this one, partly, perhaps, because of the same kind of desire for notoriety which sometimes prompts schoolboys to invent exploits, but also in his case, it seems, a need to conceal from the world his real background, perhaps for deep-rooted psychological reasons which he did not himself perceive.

At Oxford, he produced what he said was a translation of the Church of England catechism into Formosan. Then he wrote a book about Formosa that gratified the public appetite for sensation. He said that most Formosans lived to be a hundred, that gold and silver were plentiful there, and that elephants, giraffes and rhinoceri inhabited the island. He devoted a lot of space to the Formosan religion, which outdid the Aztec in its cruelty. This required that for one annual ceremony, 18,000 boys under the age of nine should be slaughtered, and their hearts burned as a sacrifice to the gods. Not surprisingly, in view of this practice, there were many more adult women than men on the island, and polygamy was practised. His account was challenged by a Dutch Jesuit who had been on Formosa, and gave a far more prosaic account of life there; Psalmanazar denounced him as a fraud, and for good measure threw in some stories about the depradations of Jesuit missionaries on Formosa; his exciting inventions were accepted more widely than the other's dull facts.

Psalmanazar remained a Formosan for twenty-five years. Then, in his early fifties, he fell ill, and underwent some kind of religious experience. When he recovered, he confessed as a penitent that everything he had said about Formosa was lies, and that he had profited from these lies to lead a life of 'shameless idleness, vanity and extravagance', to quote from his memoirs. Yet these memoirs were only of the years of his imposture. He had buried his original identity too deep to resurrect it, and he said almost nothing about his early life. After his confession he retained many of his friends, including Samuel Johnson, who enjoyed discussing literary and other questions with him until the end of his days. But they knew him only as George Psalmanazar.

An aristocracy of birth provides both temptations and opportunities for imposture. The notion that people are born to different stations in life is frustrating to the person of high ambition and talent who is not well-born. Small wonder that some have been tempted to jump the gulf to another station, by falsifying their parentage and simulating what in any case lies hidden in the genes. Romantic literature is full of the stories of the peasant who throws off his rough cloak to reveal himself as the rightful earl.

An early and very ambitious imposter was the sixteenth-century Italian con man who pretended to be King Sebastian of Portugal. Sebastian, a bold and dashing warrior-king, was killed fighting the Morrocans in the battle of Alcacer-El-Kebir in 1578, when he was only 25. Because his body was never found, there were rumours that he was alive, and prophecies that he would return one day to rule Portugal again, particularly after the Portuguese kingdom was merged with the Spanish.

Twenty years after the battle of Alcacer-El-Kebir, a man stepped forward in Venice and claimed that he was the missing King Sebastian. He was, as it turned out later, Marco Tullio Catizzone, an Italian who had already spent time in prison for impersonating a Spanish duke. Catizzone, as King Sebastian, told a story of adventures beginning with his escape from the battlefield, and of journeying across Africa and the Middle East. He proved to be a clever and inventive liar; he said that he had sent a messenger from Constantinople to Portugal with news that he was alive, one Marco Tullio Catizzone, an Italian from Calabria, but he had never returned. The authorities checked and found that there was indeed a Marco Tullio Catizzone from Calabria, who had vanished.

Catizzone probably never intended to go to Lisbon to claim his throne but only to grab what he could abroad before disappearing. He spoke only poor Portuguese, and could hardly have hoped to carry off his imposture there. But the Venetians put him in prison while his claim was tested. Several Portuguese supported it at first, some of them prominent figures, no doubt having their own political reasons. But then others who had known Sebastian refuted the claim, Catizzone's wife and children, whom he had deserted, were brought as witnesses, and he was sent to Spain, where he was tried and executed.

The story was repeated in later centuries. A monarch or heir to the throne dies, but in circumstances which leave the possibility of doubting that he really did die, at least to those who want to doubt it. And claimants come forward.

The last Dauphin of France, the son of the executed King Louis the Sixteenth, died at the age of ten in a French prison, where he had been cruelly treated. Of course rumours abounded that the boy did not really die but was smuggled out by Royalist sympathisers. In later years, various people claimed to be the Dauphin. One turns up as a comic character in Mark Twain's *The Adventures of Huckleberry Finn.*

Oddly enough, the only claimant to receive any kind of official recognition in France *was* an American. He was a Protestant missionary named Eleazar, who, so far as he knew, was the son of a frontiersman and an Iroquois woman. His background was a strange one. When people first knew him, as a child, he was mentally retarded. Then, at the age of 13, he was hit on the head by a stone, and found an intelligence and memories that had apparently been lost.

In 1841, the Prince de Joinville was travelling in America when he met Eleazar, and was struck by his Bourbon features. He questioned him. According to his account, Eleazar said he seemed to remember from his childhood a lady with a rich dress and a train. He also remembered a terrible person, and reacted with fright when he was shown a picture of Simon, the Dauphin's jailer. By this time another monarch was on the French throne, Louis Philippe. He had Eleazar paid a pension from Government funds, apparently because he did not want anyone questioning his right to the throne.

In our own century, claimants have come forward to fill the role of the Princess Anastasia, the 16-year-old daughter of the last Czar and Czarina, who were killed along with their immediate family at Ekaterinburg in 1919. In Russia, an almost religious aura attached to Royalty, and some of the stories about the Princess's escape from the massacre contained touches of the miraculous. There was a lot at stake in the claim to Anastasia's identity: money and jewelry which belonged rightfully to the Romanoff family.

Back in American colonial days, Sarah Wilson fooled the colonists into accepting her as a Royal princess instead of an indentured servant, a remarkable feat.

Sarah began life in London as a housemaid, and even here,

she showed that she was bold, ambitious and had no strong regard for the law. Deep in her heart, she did not really believe that the lords and ladies on whom she waited, and even Royalty, were of a different breed to her. The lady she worked for travelled in Royal circles, and sometimes stayed in the Royal palaces, with her personal maids, of course. On one of these visits, Sarah stole some clothes and jewelry from the apartment of Queen Charlotte, the wife of King George the Third, and she was caught. Only hanging seemed an appropriate penalty for such an enormous offence, but her employer asked for mercy, so Sarah was transported to America as a bondswoman. This was in 1771.

She was sold to a William Devall at Bush Creek, Maryland, obligated by law to work as his servant for a period of years. But she ran away. Somehow, she acquired some fine clothes; some have said that she even managed to keep one of the Queen's dresses that she had stolen. Certainly she still had a locket. Anyway, she next appears in the accounts of the time in Virginia, causing a stir as Princess Susanna Caroline Matilda, Queen Charlotte's sister. She must have been very quick-witted and intelligent, but even so, without formal education or suitable background, she could not have carried off the imposture for five minutes in England. But Virginia was a different matter; the Royal court was a long way away, and the personages, their manners and histories were known only distantly.

Sarah travelled as a house guest from one mansion to another through Virginia, the Carolinas and Georgia. Sarah delighted all her hosts with her tales of London court life. Sometimes, she would show them the locket containing the picture of her dear sister, the Queen. In Williamsburg, the Rev. James Horrocks packed his church by letting it be known that she would attend the service. In North Carolina, she was entertained by the Governor. The stirrings of rebellion did not affect the social attitudes of the leading families of the South.

She needed some travelling money, and she acquired this by the promise of Royal patronage. Many people asked favours of her, for themselves or relatives: promotion in the civil service, or in the army. She would promise to take up the matter, but hint that the way things worked, money would be useful in getting things speeded up. The hint was usually taken.

One of the people who had paid her in the expectation of Royal favours became suspicious, and then saw the offer of a reward for the recovery of an escaped bondswoman. She was exposed in a dramatic denouement to her adventure, at a plantation party in Charleston. She was returned to Bush Creek to work as a bondswoman again.

She did not end her days there, however; she was not the stuff of bondswomen. She ran away again, taking advantage of the confused beginnings of the War of Independence. She made her way to New York, and there she met and married a British officer, Lieutenant William Talbot, of the 16th Light Dragoons. Here, she disappears from historic records, but she had travelled a long way: marriage to an officer was almost as far beyond the reach of most housemaids in London as the life of a princess.

In the present day, it is not unknown for a girl to advance herself by inventing a suitable background, though the social currents on which she rides upwards may be different ones.

Marlon Brando discovered this when he married a beautiful, dark-complexioned Indian actress, Anna Kafshi. The newspapers described her as the daughter of an engineer in Madras. But a British reporter discovered that she was Joan O'Callaghan from Cardiff, who had gone to Hollywood to try her luck a little earlier. The marriage ended almost immediately. (Brando seems to be prone to this kind of mistake. In 1973, he was awarded an Oscar for his performance in *The Godfather*. He did not go to the award ceremony, but sent in his place an Apache princess, Sasheen Little Feather, in Indian dress, to stage a demonstration on his behalf against the treatment of Indians. Sasheen Little Feather turned out to be a Marie Cruz, a small-part actress from Salinas, California, who can claim only a little Indian blood. Brando was again a victim of ethnic chic.)

*   *   *

The champion of all the imposters of aristocracy, in achievement, tenacity and sheer, unblinking gall, is undoubtedly the Tichborne claimant. He persuaded a remarkable number of people in Victorian England, who were otherwise reasonably well anchored to reality, against a weight of evidence, that he was the man they had once known as Sir Roger Charles

Doughty Tichborne. He persuaded a large section of the British public that he was the rightful possessor of the Tichborne title and estates, for the case was so sensational and so widely publicised that almost everyone had an opinion, and it was argued across glittering dinner tables and in village markets. He persuaded one of the lawyers who fought his case in court so thoroughly that the man spent the rest of his life trying to prove it.

His fraud was pure, and unmixed with any element of sincerity or self-deception. Yet so stubbornly did he cling to his aristocratic name, so completely did he bury any other, that no one knew what to call him other than 'the Tichborne claimant'. Contemporary photographs of him have this as the caption, or sometimes, just 'the claimant'; no one ever had to ask which claimant.

In the almost two years of arguments in court, the opposition set out to show that he was really Arthur Orton, a butcher's son from Wapping, London, who was wanted in Australia on a charge of horse-stealing, but this was never universally accepted. Gerald Sparrow, the author and former judge who has written on the subject, does not accept it.

To tell the story, one must go back to the life and disappearance of the real Roger Tichborne. The Tichborne family, Roman Catholics, had owned large estates in Hampshire for a thousand years. As nephew of the baronet, Roger did not seem a likely heir to the title. But the baronet died unexpectedly, leaving no children, and his successor, Sir Edward Doughty, grew old without producing children. Roger was born in Paris, and lived there for his first sixteen years. His father, James Tichborne, had married an aristocratic and wealthy Frenchwoman, Henriette Felicité. She was by all accounts beautiful, highly emotional, and strong-willed; she usually had her way with her husband, and everyone else too. There were two sons and two daughters, but the two daughters died; Roger was the eldest and much-loved child.

Roger moved to England when he was 16, and went to Stonyhurst, then as now a prominent Catholic boarding school. At the age of 20, his father obtained for him a commission in the 6th Dragoon Guards.

When he was 23, Roger fell passionately in love with Katherine

Doughty, his first cousin, a girl of 18. They wanted to marry, but her parents opposed the match: one objection was that the Catholic Church forbids marriage between first cousins, and special dispensation would have to be sought. Sir Edward told Roger that they must part, but promised that if after three years they still wanted to marry, he would give his blessing.

Young people obeyed their parents in those days, and Roger agreed reluctantly. He wrote a letter which he showed to Katherine on their last day together, and which she copied in her own hand. Then he gave it to a friend to keep. This letter was to play a part in subsequent events, and it shows the depth of his devotion. In it, he wrote: 'I make on this day a promise that if I marry my cousin Katherine Doughty this year, or before three years are over at the latest, to build a church or chapel at Tichborne to the Holy Virgin, in thanksgiving for the protection which she has thrown over us, and in praying God that our wishes may be fulfilled.'

If he had to go away from Katherine, he would go far away. In 1852, he resigned his commission to travel the world. He went to South America, and after some months there, sailed from Rio de Janeiro for New York aboard a small British ship, the *Bella*. The *Bella* disappeared in a storm, and was never seen again. Her logbook was found floating 400 miles from land. Three years after Roger left England, a court pronounced him dead. When his uncle, the baronet, died, Roger's younger brother Alfred, inherited the estates that would have gone to him Alfred died at the age of 27, and his baby son Henry became the baronet.

Roger's mother, the Dowager Lady Tichborne, was a tragic figure. She had lost her three other children, and she refused to believe that her beloved Roger was dead. Strong-willed as ever, she would no more accept the dictate of fate than that of her husband or anyone else. Some years after the *Bella* sank, she began advertising in newspapers for news of her son. A missing persons bureau in Australia repeated the advertisement.

In the small Australian town of Wagga Wagga, a butcher named Thomas Castro chanced to see the bureau's notice in a lawyer's office. He studied the description, and then told the lawyer, William Gibbes, that he was Roger Tichborne. Gibbes contacted the bureau.

Probably, Castro (almost the only thing that is certain about him is that this was not his real name) hoped at this point only to get some money out of Lady Tichborne, not to press the claim to its conclusion. But each success must have encouraged him to press on further. He was uneducated; his wife, an Australian servant girl, was illiterate. But he was quick-witted, and acquired early on the knack of playing back information that had been given to him. This is shown in the succession of letters that he wrote to Lady Tichborne. In each, he asked for money so that he could return to England, and in each he commented on what she had said in her last letter.

His first letter, dated 17 January, 1866, addressed to 'My Dear Mother', contained almost no reference to the family. Her response to this was to write immediately to the missing persons bureau asking for more information about 'the person you believe to be my son'. At the same time, however, she grasped at this opportunity to believe that her favourite son was still alive. She wrote a letter to Castro beginning: 'My dearest and beloved Roger, I have never lost the hope of seeing you again in this world. . . .'

In this letter, she wrote that his brother Alfred and his father had both died within the past year. Castro had not asked about either of these, and presumably did not know of Alfred's existence, but now he wrote back: 'I was very sorry to hear of poor father and Alfred's death. I hardly know, my Dear Mother, how you have borne the suspence of not knowing my fate so long. You must not blame me mother for I believe fate had a great deal to do with it.' (The grammar and spelling are characteristic, and would hardly be a credit to his schooling if he were Roger Tichbone.)

Lady Tichborne had one sound idea. She wrote that an old Negro servant of the family called Bogle now lived in Sydney, and would know Roger. Castro collected what facts about the family he now had, and went to the address he had been given. He greeted the elderly Bogle warmly by name, and talking about his dear father and poor Alfred and other members of the family, he soon persuaded him that he was Roger Tichborne. Lady Tichborne needed no further confirmation.

She sent him some money, and Castro sailed for England with his wife and two children, and Bogle. Roger Tichborne had left

England a slender young man; the Roger Tichborne who
returned twelve years later was middle-aged and fat, weighing
280 pounds.

Lady Tichborne was living in Paris, and after a few days in
London, Castro went there. She accepted him immediately,
and gave him an allowance of £1,000 a year, a considerable
amount in those days. She also brought his old tutor, Henri
Chatillon, to see him. Chatillon addressed him in French, the
language they had spoken together, and found that he did not
understand him. After a short conversation in English, he told
him he did not believe he was Roger Tichborne. This gave
Castro a foretaste of what he was up against.

Castro went back to England to begin his campaign. He read
up on the Tichborne family, and memorised a lot. He had
dinner with the family solicitor, Robert Hopkins, and, talking
about the family's affairs, he persuaded him that he was really
Roger; this was his first success. Using what he had learned from
conversation with Hopkins, he called on a few of the family's
neighbours in Hampshire, and, chatting about old times, persuaded some of *them* that he was Roger. As well as information,
he was learning a way to talk, and to behave.

Then he began on the Sixth Dragoon Guards. Moving slowly,
he found two old soldiers of the regiment who had known young
Roger from afar, and invited them to come and stay at his
house, as servants. After they had been there for a while, and
doubtless after many evenings exchanging regimental reminiscences, he invited a few more old soldiers to visit them, and then
felt sufficiently well briefed to call on some of his fellow-officers
and talk about old times. Some of these were persuaded that he
was Roger Tichborne.

Roger's closest friend had been Vincent Gosport. Roger had
given Gosport the letter he had shown to Katherine, containing
the promise to build a chapel if they were married. Gosport was
impressed when Castro talked of the old days, and at first
seemed ready to believe him. But then he asked him what was
in the sealed letter he gave him before he left England; Castro
said he could not remember. This convinced Gosport that he
was an imposter.

Now Castro swore an affidavit in the Chancery Division of the
Court, which governs the disposal of estates and wills, asserting

his identity as Sir Roger Tichborne and claiming back the estates from the infant Henry Tichborne, the son of his dead brother Alfred. He was questioned by a lawyer retained by Alfred's family.

Castro's affidavit contained a long account of his rescue from the wreck of the *Bella* by a ship bound for Australia, along with eight other seamen, none of whom was ever traced. He was cross-examined, and came out of it so badly that it seems astonishing that the case got any further. The knowledge he had acquired was shown now to have some gaps, despite Lady Tichborne's support in court. He had spent his boyhood in Paris, but now spoke no French. He could not remember the name of any of his boyhood friends, though he remembered one servant. Questioned about Stonyhurst, the school he attended in England for two years, he could recall none of his teachers, nor one book he had read there.

Then Gosport was cross-examined. He told about the sealed envelope, and said only that it contained a letter concerning Katherine Doughty. He said he had destroyed it after he learned of Roger's death. Castro could not know what the letter said, so he had to invent something. His invention was cunning and cruel and gave the case a new and sensational twist.

He said the letter told Gosport that Katherine had given him to understand that she was pregnant, and had pressed him to marry her. He did not believe she was pregnant, and said he thought she had made it up only to get him to marry her. If, however, it turned out to be true, then Gosport was to arrange for her to leave England.

To say a girl pretended to be pregnant in order to get someone to marry her is to accuse her of being a scheming bitch. But in Victorian England, the accusation that she was unchaste was just as damaging. Passions were aroused, among family, friends and the public. From now on, to come out for the claimant was to come out against Katherine Doughty (now married to one Joseph Radcliffe). J. B. Atley, writing at the time, expressed many people's feeling about this short statement by Castro: 'A blacker lie was never committed to paper, and a more diabolical plot was never framed by the heart of man.'

Before the main case came to court, both sides wanted more time to assemble their evidence. While they did so, two of the

claimant's principal witnesses died, the Dowager Lady Tichborne, and Robert Hopkins, the family solicitor, the only close
friend of the family to accept his claim.

The Tichborne claim was now becoming a cause. Castro
raised money from supporters to help pay the expenses of the
case. Both sides spent a good deal. He said at one point that during his travels in South America, he had stayed at a Chilean
village called Melipilla. He went with a lawyer and a lawyer's
clerk to Chile, a journey not undertaken lightly in the 1860s.

But the evidence gathered there was very damaging to his
claim, and was made available to the court. A lot of people
remembered an English youth there, a teenage boy called
Arthur Orton, who told them he was a butcher's son and had
deserted his ship. This was the first identification of Castro with
Orton. His stay there was three years before Sir Roger Tichborne left for South America.

The court hearing did not start until early in 1871. The first
part was a lesson in human credulity. Soldiers in the Sixth
Dragoons, then officers, then a former governess employed by
the Tichborne family, all went into the witness box to testify
that the claimant was the Sir Roger Tichborne they had
known. They gave different reasons for being sure of this
identification: 'a peculiar expression of the eyes', said one;
'dimples on his hands', said the governess; some said they
recognised his voice. Castro had done his persuasive work well.
Eventually, the witnesses who said they recognised him totalled
ninety.

Then the claimant himself went into the witness box. He
showed himself again to have little recollection of his boyhood
in Paris, and an embarrassing ignorance of all the subjects he
had studied at school, and of the Dragoons' drill procedure.

The Tichborne Family's lawyers had traced his movements
immediately after he came from Australia, and found that he
visited Wapping looking for the Orton family the night he
arrived in England; he later gave some money to members of
the family. He said he had done so on behalf of Arthur Orton,
who was a friend of his in Australia. The lawyers had also
ascertained that one Arthur Orton was wanted by police in
Australia on a charge of stealing a horse, and had disappeared
when the theft was discovered. The counsel asked him why he

had not written to his family during his eleven years in Australia, and he said he had been working hard, and it was due to 'carelessness and neglect'.

Katherine, now Mrs. Radcliffe, went into the witness box. She was asked about the sealed letter, and she told in hushed tone of Roger's promise to build a chapel if they should marry.

Other witnesses went into the box, to swear that this man was not Roger, including two aunts of his. The claimant did not have much of a case left by this time, but what remained was destroyed when several witnesses produced a new point: Roger was tatooed with his initials on his forearm.

The jury gave their verdict that the claimant was not Roger Tichborne. The case had lasted 102 days. The Lord Chief Justice immediately ordered him arrested on a charge of perjury. Three policemen arrested him at his hotel in Jermyn Street. He was taken to Newgate prison and, as he arrived at the gate, a crowd gathered outside cheered him.

This was a foretaste of what was to come. The many witnesses for the claimant, and his own composure throughout, had persuaded a lot of people that his claim was just. He was released on bail provided by friends, and because some witnesses had to be found in Australia and brought over, it was a year before he was brought to trial. During the year, a campaign of public support for him swept the country, and he played his part to bigger audiences than the courtroom. He spoke at public meetings, and he was cheered when he appeared at music halls and open air fetes. A subscription fund was started to pay for his defense. Society abounded in Tichborne buffs.

The trial was a re-play of the civil case, with most of the same witnesses giving the same testimony, but with a few important differences. One was the introduction of perjured testimony for the claimant: a sailor said he was in the lifeboat with young Roger Tichborne after the *Bella* sank, and was also rescued by the *Osprey* and taken to Melbourne. But it was proved that the sailor was actually in prison when the *Bella* sank. This testimony was almost certainly arranged by the claimant himself, without the knowledge of his lawyer.

A piece of damning evidence for the prosecution was the production of a notebook that had been brought from Australia containing some entries in the claimant's handwriting. It contained the name of Thomas Castro, and the added note: 'Rodger (sic) Charles Tichborne, Bart, some day, I hope.' It also contained two sentences which, however clumsily worded, constitute an aphorism: 'Some men has plenty money and no brains, and some men has plenty brains and no money. Surely men with plenty money and no brains were made for men with plenty brains and no money.' The claimant said the notebook was a forgery, which was all he could do.

Another distinctive feature of the trial, as against the civil case, was the presence as the claimant's counsel of Dr. Edward Kenealy, an Irish lawyer of some eminence but little judgment, who pleaded the defence case in court with a zeal bordering on fanaticism. His summing-up speech took twenty-three days.

The jury, to no one's surprise, found the claimant guilty. They further said explicitly that they believed he was Charles Arthur Orton, and that there was no evidence that Roger Tichborne was ever 'guilty of undue familiarity' with Katherine. The judge, taking into account, he said, the henious nature of the claimant's perjuries, passed two sentences of seven years' each to run consecutively. The trial had taken 188 days, and was the longest criminal trial in British history until that date.

The claimant continued to find supporters. Dr. Kenealy became a rabid champion of his cause. He addressed public meetings and published a weekly paper called *The Englishman*, to protest against the persecution of 'Sir Roger Tichborne'. A society formed to support the cause held meetings attended by thousands. Kenealy stood as an independent candidate for Parliament in 1875 and won. Once in the House of Commons, he asked for a Royal Commission to inquire into the trial, but this was rejected unanimously. Eventually, his obsession bored people, and at the next election he lost his seat. He died soon afterwards.

The claimant himself, Arthur Orton or whoever he was, was a model prisoner, and was released in 1884. He went back on the boards to argue his case, but he was no longer the draw he once had been and he drifted from job to job. He continued to use the name 'Sir Roger Tichborne', and when he died in 1898 in a cheap boarding house, someone inscribed this name on his coffin.

*   *   *

The mixed motives that can lie behind the fabricating of another's identity are nowhere more apparent than in the career of Stanley Weinberg, the famous American con man who once visited President Harding in the White House in one of his bogus roles. He was after money, certainly, but he also suffered from thwarted social ambition; he liked the grand style of living for itself, and he liked the trappings of status, particularly uniforms. He was small in stature, a fact which probably shaped his destiny. Put simply, little Stanley Weinberg wanted to be a big shot.

The son of poor immigrants in Brooklyn, he clearly felt strongly that he was born for better things, as strongly as any would-be nobleman of another time. But Weinberg was a child of the age of democracy, and the land of the free and equal. Every American is taught that he can be proud of the name he is born with, and that there is nothing to envy in noble lineage. Weinberg altered his name very slightly, to Weyman, but he disdained to go further than this. Indeed, he flaunted this name; he used it in all his exploits. But if he would not disguise his name, he was prepared to adorn it: he was, on different occasions, Dr. Weyman, Professor Weyman, and Lieutenant-Commander Weyman.

He had the natural equipment for an impostor: a quick wit, persuasive powers, and an air of authority that enabled him to start on his career very early, and compensated for his youthful appearance. When he was only 21, and working in an office in Brooklyn, he spent a few evening running up bills in smart Manhattan restaurants while proclaiming himself the U.S. consul-delegate to Morocco; but he also stole a camera in this guise, and was sent to reform school. Out on parole, he impersonated a naval officer and was sent back again.

In 1915, when he was 24, he emulated the hoax perpetrated five years earlier in England by Horace de Vere Cole and his friends on the battleship *Dreadnought*. He telephoned the U.S. Navy Department's office in New York, represented himself as Stanley Weyman, the Romanian consul-general, and said that the Queen of Romania had asked him to pay his respects to the Navy. A visit was arranged to the battleship *Wyoming*, which was then anchored in New York harbour. He decked himself out in a light blue uniform with gold braid—he could not bear to be the only person not in uniform – and was taken out in a launch. The *Wyoming* flew the Romanian flag alongside the Stars and Stripes. He inspected a guard of honour, appreciatively but, on occasion, critically, and was entertained in the officers' wardroom. There, he told the officers that he would like to reciprocate their hospitality by entertaining them to dinner at the Hotel Astor. He booked a private dining-room in the name of the Romanian consulate, and chose the menu. The hotel sent out an advance press notice of the occasion, and a New York detective chanced to see it, with the name of Stanley Weyman. Weyman was arrested at the dinner table, and the *Wyoming*'s officers were stunned. The captain told reporters: 'All I can say is that little guy put on a hell of a show!'

He would have appreciated the compliment. He tried to put on the same sort of show two years later in the custom-tailored uniform of an Army Air Corps officer, but was arrested while inspecting a regimental armory in his native Brooklyn.

All these were juvenile frivolities, but as Weyman grew older, he had to take seriously the problem of earning a living. He did very well for a while as Dr. Weyman; when a development company advertised for a medical consultant on a construction project in Peru, he got the job over other applicants, and spent a year there living in a company villa with a girl friend and giving lavish parties.

He pulled off his biggest coup in 1921, when Princess Fatima of Afghanistan visited the United States with her three sons. She was an exotic figure, with her Afghan robes, a jewel in her nose and, on her person, a fabled 42-carat diamond. She received a lot of Press coverage, but as this was not a state visit, little official notice. Then Lieutenant-Commander Weyman called on her at the Waldorf Astoria Hotel. He explained that, as well as being a naval officer, he was the State Department's chief protocol officer, and he had been asked to bring her to Washington, where the President was anxious to receive her. He also explained that it was the American custom to give cash presents to junior officials who organised such visits, and he collected $10,000 from her which he said was to pass on to various such people.

He arranged the visit to the White House by telephoning the State Department on her behalf, and the party travelled to

Washington. He took them to the White House, and introduced them personally to the President, then chatted with Mr. Harding for a while. They posed for photographers on the White House lawn. They made an odd group: the tall, mannish-looking Princess dressed in billowing white robes, her three sons beside her, standing rigidly at attention in their morning suits, President Harding, looking slightly uncomfortable, standing next to the Princess, and on the President's other side, and nearly a head shorter, Lt.-Commander Weyman, with his Navy whites positively gleaming in the August sunshine, looking proudly at the camera.

Weyman collected money from the Princess to pay the Washington hotel bills, which he neglected to do, and more for payments to the news media, which he told her was customary in America. Then he vanished.

He paid the penalty for this three or four frauds later. He was arrested for milking the patients of a visiting Viennese surgeon while posing as a hospital official, and given an additional two-year sentence for impersonating a naval officer.

He was drawn back to medicine. When Rudolf Valentino died, he turned up as an old friend and doctor of the star, helped to make the funeral arrangements, and became Pola Negri's personal physician for a while. He turned to the legal profession and was sent to prison twice for pretending to be a lawyer. He made himself at various times a visiting lecturer at universities in both medicine and law. During the Second World War he set himself up in New York as a 'selective service consultant'; in fact he instructed people in draft-dodging, and he was jailed along with nine of his pupils.

He emerged in 1948 and took up a new profession: journalism. With phoney credentials, he became the United Nations correspondent of the Erwin News Service, and the stringer for some radio stations. His writing was not outstanding but he had news sense, and he got interviews with the right people. He became a familiar figure at the U.N. building.

Then Thailand's ambassador to the United Nations offered him a job as press officer to the Thai delegation, with full diplomatic accreditation. For once, authentic V.I.P. status seemed to be within his grasp. Surprisingly, he hesitated, and did something extremely unwise for him: he wrote to the State

Department asking whether accepting such a job would affect his American citizenship. Someone in the State Department found that they had a file on Stanley Weyman. The Thai ambassador to the United Nations was contacted, and the Erwin News Service also. Weyman did not get the post, and he lost his job as a U.N. correspondent.

He died nine years later, in 1960, ironically the victim of a crime. He was working as night manager of a small motel in Yonkers, New York. One night, a gunman held him up and tried to rob the motel safe. Little Stanley Weyman resisted, and the gunman shot him dead.

For pure imposture for its own sake, evidently to gratify some psychological need, but unmixed with any profit motive, there is nothing to equal the career of Ferdinand Waldo Demara. The story is widely known, and there is no need to do more than recall it here as an illustration of the extraordinary feats of imposture that are possible. Demara's feats justify the almost extravagant terms used by the psychologist Phyllis Greenacre, in a paper called 'The Relation of the Imposter to the Artist': 'The ability of the imposter to put on convincing acts of impersonation, including facsimile reproductions of special skills, may seem to be almost miraculous and inspired.'

Demara, who never finished high school, occupied a number of academic posts, each time taking another person's identity and credentials, and filling each post with distinction. After deserting from the army and navy in quick succession, he joined a Roman Catholic order as a trainee priest, and, with a phony PhD in psychology, he studied scholastic philosophy at De Paul University and earned high marks. He taught psychology at Gannon College, California, and St. Martin's College, Washington. After a spell in a navy prison when his service desertions caught up with him, he joined a Catholic teaching order in Maine posing as a graduate biologist and physician.

He joined the Canadian Navy as a surgeon-lieutenant, served on a destroyer in Korean waters during the Korean War, and in addition to normal medical services, he removed a bullet from the heart of a wounded Korean soldier under difficult circumstances, and carried out the rare operation of resection, or the removal of a lung, at an aid station. When he was exposed as a fraud, whose only knowledge of surgery was gained from the solitary reading of textbooks, the incredulous officers on his ship poured out testimonials to his medical skill, his humane care for his patients, and his untiring efforts on their behalf.

In interviews, he has expressed contempt for convention, and the straight way of achieving a professional status. His career does seem to raise the question of whether some of the conventional qualifications that are required for carrying out professional functions are not too rigid.

At this writing, Demara's whereabouts are unknown. Is he instructing scholars in some advanced science? Piloting a jet airliner? The possibilities are almost limitless.

*   *   *

One of the most ambigous of impostures was that perpetrated by the man called Grey Owl, who came out of the Canadian North Woods in the 1930s with several fascinating and moving books about life in the wilds. He became a celebrity for a while. As a lecturer, he entranced audiences in Britain and America with his stories of Indian life and lore, including the British Royal Family and the present Queen. He died at the height of his fame, and with his death came his exposure.

His hoax was imposture more than literary fake, since the literature was genuine – it is still being re-published and read today. Only his own identity was fake. Even here, the lie was only a small part of the whole.

Grey Owl had a message to put across to the world, a message about the need to respect and understand the wilderness instead of conquering it, about the need for a balance between the world of man-made things and the world of nature. Today many voices tell us about the implications of the destruction of much of the natural world; but when Grey Owl spoke his message, it was rare and prophetic.

He represented himself to his audiences as a man wise in the ways of the woods and their animal inhabitants, wise with love as well as knowledge, a man who was at home in this world of wilderness, and who cared passionately about its preservation. He was all of those things. He also said he was Wa-Sha-Quon-Asin, an Indian name meaning Grey Owl, the son of an Apache mother and a Scottish-born Indian scout, born in Mexico. He was not. He was Archibald Belaney, an Englishman.

He had always wanted to be an Indian. His assumed Indian background gave him an identity with which he could stand up in public, strengthened his purpose, and gave more weight to his message. It is dangerous ever to justify lying to the world, becasue of the slippery slope that leads down from even the most well-intentioned falsehood. (There is a Spanish proverb 'The perjurer's mother told white lies.') But in the case of Grey Owl, one can, at least, withhold condemnation.

Archibald Belaney became a likely candidate for alienation from his environment when he was four years old. His father, the wastrel son of a comfortably middle-class family, went to Central America to become a remittance man, and little Archie was taken away from his mother and his baby brother to be raised by two maiden aunts in the genteel seaside town of Hastings. In later years, he was to represent himself as unschooled, but he attended the local grammar school and seems to have been an intelligent pupil. His aunts' home was starch and prim and he found their discipline cramping, but they made sure he had plenty of books.

Lovat Dickson, the Canadian author who was his publisher in Britain for a while, has traced his story painstakingly for his biography of Grey Owl, *Wilderness Man*, published in 1973. It seems that Belaney was something of a loner as a schoolboy, and, even then, was fascinated by the small animals that were found in the woods and fields around Hastings, and kept snakes, rabbits and small rodents.

Dickson quotes a pen portrait of Belaney at the age of 11, in a publication of the Hastings Grammar School, which is uncanny in its unintended foresight: 'Archie Belaney did not conceal firearms in his pockets, but just as likely might produce from them a snake or a fieldmouse. . . . What with his camping out, his tracking of all and sundry, and wild hooting, he was more like a Red Indian than a respectable grammar school boy.'

Like many boys at the time, young Archie was fascinated by Indians. Unlike most others, he never settled down to an interest in more prosaic things closer at hand. In one way, his whole life is a glorious story of pursuing a childhood dream, and accomplishing it.

He told his aunts that he wanted to go to Canada and learn more about the Indians, and perhaps write a book about them; neither their doubts nor his progress to the relative maturity of his late teens swayed him from his purpose, and he sailed for Canada at the age of 18, in 1906.

He landed in Toronto, but a city held no interest for him. He went into the woods in Ontario some 200 miles north of there, took up with a local guide well-known in the area, Bill Guppy, and helped him in exchange for an apprenticeship in woodcraft. He became an adroit and hardy woodsman himself, then went to live with a tribe of Ojibway Indians, learned their language and their ways, worked variously as a guide and mail carrier, and married an Ojibway girl, Angele. But he did not settle down for long. He drifted, as he was to do for many years, always in the North woods and its little towns, leaving Angele and the Ojibways and promising to return. He had some brushes with the law caused by a touchy temper, and earned a living for a while as a trapper.

He joined the Canadian Army in 1915, served as an infantry-man in Flanders, where he let others think he was part-Indian, then was shot in the foot, had a toe amputated, and was invalided out. He spent some time in a military hospital near Hastings, and met again and married a girl he had known in his child-hood, Florence Holmes. Many years later, Florence would recall in a newspaper interview one of the games they had played together when they were children: 'I was his squaw, Dancing Moonbeam, and he was Big Chief Thunderbinder.'

The marriage was bigamous; he did not tell Florence, of course, that he was already married to an Indian girl. In any case, it lasted only a few months, and Archie returned to Canada alone at the end of 1917. All his life, he was to take up women and leave them again irresponsibly. After his death, a woman came forward with persuasive evidence that he had married her in Ontario in 1910.

He went back to the Ojibways and his Ojibway wife, and was shocked at the changes in that part of the country since he had last seen it. These changes occupied much of his thoughts, and later were to be the subject of much of his writing. They were wrought by the inroads of civilisation in the form of mines, rail-roads and timber mills; whole stretches of forest had been felled, the old ways of life were going, particularly Indian ways, and the frontier was being pushed back. He pushed on with it, still a drifter, right through his twenties and thirties, following the receding frontier as a guide and trapper.

His face was permanently tanned by sun and wind, and now, he wore his dark hair in two long plaits, Indian-style, dressed in buckskin and moccasins. He usually told people that he was half-Indian and had always lived in the North woods since he was brought from Mexico as a child. Working as a tourist guide near Bear Island, he fell in love with a dark, slender Iroquois girl of 19, with high cheekbones and narrow, almost Oriental eyes. She was Gertrude Bernard or, in Iroquois, Anahareo, and unlike his first Indian wife, Angele, she was town-bred and educated. They went to live for the winter in a log cabin in the woods, and he trapped animals all day, an increasingly uncertain way of earning a living as more hunters and trappers came through the woods, sometimes slaughtering wildlife wantonly.

If the wanton slaughter by strangers who had no respect for the ways of the wild angered him, his attitude to his own more discriminating killing was altering. As he told it later in his book *Pilgrims of the Wild*, the presence of Anahareo, and her unspoken compassion for animals, was making him more sensitive to some of his own feelings about animals which he had been pushing to the back of his mind.

The decisive change was brought about by two beaver kittens, the infants of a beaver that had died in one of his traps. Anahareo insisted that they rescue them, and take them home to their cabin. They found them affectionate, intelligent and intimate companions, and came to love them; reading his fascinating account of his life with them, it is clear that this word is not too strong. He came to see his trapping in a new light, and to see the approaching disappearance of the beaver population not only as a threat to his livelihood, but as a desecration in itself, a theft of something from the natural world. He wrote later about the way that the presence of these little animals changed his life. 'With their almost child-like intimacies and murmurings of affection, their rollicking good fellowship not only with each other but with ourselves, their keen awareness, their air of knowing what it was all about, they seemed like little folk from some other planet, whose language we could not yet quite understand. To kill such creatures seemed monstrous. I would do no more of it. Instead of persecuting them further, I would study them, see just what there really was to them. I perhaps could start a beaver colony of my own; these animals could not be permitted to pass completely from the face of the wilderness.'*

With gentleness and almost infinite patience, over many months, he made friends with other animals of the forest that came by his log cabin: moose, lynxes, and mongeese.

He was in his late thirties now, a time when most people have become fixed in their character and way of life, but he was changing in many ways at once. He found that he wanted to put on paper some of the things that were happening to the landscape that was his home. In his cabin, writing in longhand on lined paper, he produced a 3,000-word essay, an evocative picture of the landscape of the North woods, which he called *The Fall of Silence*. He sent it to a woman in England with whom he had recently started corresponding: his mother, now re-married as Mrs. Hazel Scott-Brown. She sent it to the British magazine *Country Life*, which published it. The editor wrote to Belaney inviting him to send in more contributions, and they started a correspondence. Belaney started gradually to alter the picture in the editor's mind of an English emigrant in the Canadian woods, by telling him first that he had been adopted by the Ojibway Indians as a young man, and then that he was known as Grey Owl. The editor suggested that he write the story of his life, and said that *Country Life* would be interested in publishing it as a book.

He knew now that he had something to say, and at about this time, in 1929, he created another part of the act he was to put on before the world, though without realising it. The two beavers had gone back into the woods, and now he and Ana-hareo had another as a pet, whom they called Jelly Roll. Turning their backs on trapping, they left the woods for the little town of Metis Beach, Ontario, on the upper reaches of the St. Lawrence River. They attracted a lot of attention when they camped beside the river with Jelly Roll. He started to talk to people in the town about his idea for a beaver sanctuary, intro-ducing himself always by his Indian name, Grey Owl. Someone

* From *Pilgrims of the Wild.*

asked him whether he would care to give a talk about the subject to a public meeting, and he agreed. He worked hard preparing it, and wrote out the whole speech in longhand.

As a younger man, he had always been popular in the frontier towns as a campfire entertainer. Now he found that he could hold an audience at a formal gathering, and hold them with the gentleness and cunning with which he tamed woodland animals. Later he told the story of his first talk in Metis Beach with some pride, but judging by his performances it can be believed. As he recounted it, the talk was a great success. One man in the audience, a retired British colonel, rose to congratulate the speaker, and said that what they had heard was not just a lecture but a poem; others applauded this. He was invited to talk to the local boy scout group about wild life, and then to other audiences in near-by communities. At each talk, the hat was passed around, and to his surprise, he found that he was earning more money by talking than he had by trapping animals.

It was always Grey Owl that he presented to the public, in buckskin clothes and moccasins, sometimes with a feather in his headband. The pose was becoming more pronounced, more a part of everything he had to say. The Canadian writer and naturalist Lloyd Roberts visited Grey Owl in his forest home in 1930, and wrote that he found him 'the first Indian who really looked like an Indian – an Indian from those thrilling, Wild West days of covered wagons, buffaloes and Sitting Bull. The stamp of his fierce Apache ancestors showed in his tall, gaunt physique, his angular features, his keen eyes, even in his two braids dangling down from his fringed buckskin shirt.'*

In the meantime, Grey Owl had written to the editor of *Country Life* saying that he intended to write, not an autobiography, but a series of sketches of the Canadian North; the editor wrote back a letter of encouragement. He wrote it in a year and a half, and called it *The Vanishing Frontier*.

Now, all trace of Archie Belaney had gone, so far as his relationship with *Country Life* was concerned. When he sent in the manuscript, he sent with it a long, rambling letter such as an uneducated, backwoods Indian might write to a literary gent, apologizing for any mistakes in grammar or punctuation,

* Quoted in *Wilderness Man: the Story of Grey Owl* by Lovat Dickson.

and saying that none the less it all came straight from his heart. But the editor found out just how shrewd he was and how sensitive to the meaning of words when he changed the title without telling him, and published it, not as *The Vanishing Frontier*, but *The Men of the Last Frontier*.

Grey Owl wrote angrily: 'The original title has the lure of the vast, though disappearing frontier, which in the nature of such a work as I tried to produce, dwarfs and belittles that of mere, diminutive, short-lived man. That you changed the title shows that you, at least, missed the point of the book. You still believe that man as such is pre-eminent, governs the powers of Nature. So he does, to a large extent, in civilisation, but not on the frontier, until that frontier has been removed . . . I speak of Nature, not men; they are incidental, used to illustrate a point only.'

By now, he was acquiring a reputation. He wrote articles for a Canadian wildlife magazine, *Forest and Outdoors*, and lectured; the Parks Department film unit made a film about his beavers. A correspondent wrote about him in the London *Times* as 'An Indian Thoreau'. *The Men of the Last Frontier* received enthusiastic reviews when it was published in Britain and America. Grey Owl went on writing, and in the next three years produced a children's book and *Tales of an Empty Cabin*. In this, he described vividly the hard life of the woods, and the comradeship of the men who lived it. Yet sometimes he wrote with a new self-consciousness. He was aware now of his new-found audience, city men who lived softer, more circumscribed lives, and he seemed at times to be trying to impress them, like some latter-day Robert Service.

His publisher, Lovat Dickson, invited him over to England to lecture and so promote his books. Grey Owl, once he accepted, threw himself into the project with enthusiasm.

This was the full flowering of Grey Owl. He was a great success in England. He looked all Indian, as he had to Lloyd Roberts in Canada, more than the Hollywood Indians, all feathers and warpaint, that his audiences saw on their screens. He usually wore a sombrero-type hat, a neckerchief and moccasins, with his black hair hanging down in plaits—a more unusual sight then than it is today. A photograph of him by Karsh shows him as a tall, proud figure with a strong, almost beak-like nose, alert eyes and a stern, lined, face that could have been sculpted from stone. He had the appeal of the noble savage, and he held his audiences enthralled with his picture of the life of the wilds, and his anxieties about what was happening to it. It was recalled only much later than when he lectured in Hastings, he said that if there was anyone named Belaney in the audience, he would like them to come around and see him afterwards.

He was concerned with the impact he was making more than the money it earned him. He was astonished and then worried when he found how much authorship and lecturing was bringing in to his bank account. The B.B.C. cancelled a talk he was due to give on 'Children's Hour' because he refused to delete a passage in which he asked children never to take part in blood sports. The B.B.C. said this was 'too contentious' for a children's programme.

He was appointed Chief Conservation Officer of the Prince Albert National Park in Manitoba. He went back to his log cabin there, and wrote *Pilgrims of the Wild*, about his life with Anahareo and their beavers. Ironically, at about this time, he left Anahareo for a French-Canadian girl, Yvonne Perrier, though he did not let his audiences know this.

He agreed to do a second lecture tour of Britain, followed by one of the United States. A high spot of his second tour of Britain was a command performance at Buckingham Palace. This was arranged mainly to please the two young princesses, Elizabeth and Margaret, who had been enchanted by his children's books and by what they had read of Grey Owl. He made sure they were not disappointed, and he brought a whiff of the North woods to the Palace plush. He made a dramatic entrance, in his fringed buckskin suit and beaded belt with a knife at his waist, and greeted King George the Sixth with outstretched arm and a salutation in Ojibway, which he then translated: 'I come in peace, brother.' His Royal audience was as charmed as others had been, and when the lecture was over, he stayed to answer questions by the princesses.

Grey Owl was tired by the end of his British tour, and the American tour proved a strain. He broke it off to go back to his cabin in Manitoba, and there he suddenly fell ill with pneumonia and died, in April, 1938. He was 51.

The day after he died, the Toronto *Star* carried an article by a noted wildlife writer to say that he had known for some time that Grey Owl was not a half-breed Indian but an Englishman named Belaney; apparently, a Government department had once traced his origins through official documents. Friends and publishers rejected this as absurd. The argument went on in Britain and Canada. Anahareo said she had only known him as the half-Indian Grey Owl. Two soldiers who had served with him in Flanders said he crawled up hills and through No Man's Land as only an Indian could. But the two Belaney sisters were still alive in Hastings, and in England, the *News Chronicle* published an interview with them along with his birth certificate and childhood photographs. After this, it all came out.

It turned out that he had one confidante in Canada, a Mrs. Harry Ross, the mother of a childhood friend. He told her that he wanted to meet his father, and that after this, he planned to write the true story of his life. He had buried his origins, but not out of his own sight.

Grey Owl never pretended to care about things he did not care about. He never lied about his motives, or what he was doing. He lied about who he had been in the past. But surely, for the most part, in his final years, he *was* Grey Owl. The public person was hardly different from the private person, probably less so than most public figures. His was the achievement of the hero of *The Great Gatsby*, of whom F. Scott Fitzgerald wrote: 'The truth is that Jay Gatsby of West Egg, Long Island sprang from his Platonic conception of himself . . . he invented just the sort of Jay Gatsby that a 17-year-old boy would be likely to invent, and to this he was faithful to the end.'

Belaney too, was faithful. When he had completed his transformation, the world was not much poorer for the loss of Archibald Belaney, and it was richer for the presence of Grey Owl.

CHAPTER 8

Since the Trojan Horse

Force and fraud are in war the two cardinal
virtues.
THOMAS HOBBES, *The Leviathan*

ONE day in March 1938, Claude Cockburn, a left-wing British
journalist who was fighting in Spain with the Republican forces,
went to Paris on leave and looked up an old friend, Otto Katz.
Katz, an international Communist operator, was at that time
working in the Paris office of the Spanish Republican news
agency, *Agence Espagne.* He immediately recruited Cockburn for
a project he had in mind.

The French Government was engaged in one of its periodic
debates about whether to allow the passage of arms across the
Spanish frontier to the Republican Government. It had permitted it during some periods since the civil war had begun in
Spain, and barred it at other times. Right now there were field
guns and other weapons waiting for shipment. Things were
going badly for the Republic, and these were needed urgently.
Katz had decided that a sudden setback for General Franco at
this moment would strengthen the hands of the pro-Republican
men in the French cabinet, and might sway the issue. He wanted
Cockburn to help him invent one.

Cockburn threw himself into the task with enthusiasm. Katz
had already decided what the event would be: an uprising
against Franco in Spanish Morocco, an area firmly in Franco's
hands, and the base from which he had launched his rebellion.
This would point to trouble in the very heart of the Nationalist
camp. Neither Cockburn nor Katz had ever been to Spanish
Morocco, but they worked with imagination, some guidebooks
and a street map of Tetuan, the capital. They described bloody
fighting in Tetuan street by street, in vivid detail. They decided
that some doubt on a few details would land the story veris-

similitude. So they said that, for instance, it was not certain whether the Captain Murillo who died bravely in the fighting outside the barracks was the same Captain Murillo who, months ago in Madrid. . . .

The report was believed for a little while, and is credited with helping to persuade the French Government to re-open the Spanish frontier and allow arms to cross.

Cockburn recounted the episode with characteristic gusto some years afterwards, in a series of articles about the 1930s, as part of a portrait of Otto Katz. Richard Crossman, the Labour Party intellectual and future cabinet minister, himself a propagandist during the Second World War, wrote shortly after this deploring the tone in which Cockburn talked about concocting the Battle of Tetuan. Crossman accepted that sometimes one had to lie in wartime, but this was not something to be recounted with cheerful pride. 'It may be necessary in war, but most of us who practised it regretted what we were doing,' Crossman said.

Cockburn, writing later in his autobiography, derided this. 'To me, at least,' he wrote, 'there seems something risible in the spectacle of a man firing off his propaganda-lies as, one presumes, effectively as he knows how, but keeping his conscience clear by detesting his own activities. After all, if he does not think the cause for which he is fighting is worth lying for, he does not have to lie at all, any more than the man who sincerely feels that killing is murder is forced to shoot at those enemy soldiers. He can become a conscientious objector, or run away. . . . At any rate, Katz had none of those inhibitions, and did his work *con amore*.'

The issues involved in lying in wartime are rarely brought out so sharply. Telling a lie caused an agonising dilemma for Crossman, a humanist intellectual dedicated to the truth, but dedicated also to the struggle against fascism. For him, it is morally repugnant, and it is important that it should be seen to be so. Yet to another kind of man, no less committed to combatting fascism and, in the case of Cockburn, who fought at the front, committed body as well as soul, this was just another weapon, like a gun, and telling a lie raised no more moral or philosophical questions than firing a gun. If you are in a war and you really want your side to win, then you do it, and if you do not want to do it, then it is wise to avoid getting involved in a war.*

Deception of some kind plays a part in most wartime operations, just as it plays a part in most crimes. Any attacking force wants its attack to be unexpected. But in modern times it has developed into a separate branch of warfare, with its own specialists. Sometimes, these specialists have been upright and honourable men who, under pressures of war, show a hitherto hidden talent for deceiving people, just as some otherwise kindly men show an unexpected talent for killing. Sometimes, they have found an outlet in wartime deceptions for talents which they would otherwise direct into different channels, like practical jokes, as Professor R. V. Jones did, or writing complicated mystery novels, like Sir John Masterman, the Oxford University historian who ran a network of double-spies. (Cold War can also provide an outlet for such talents. The practical joker Hugh Troy was in the CIA until his death in 1967.)

Some deception campaigns in contemporary warfare are subtle and psychological; some are aimed at civilian populations rather than military forces.

The most important single deception campaign in the Second World War, however, was a purely military one, simple in its conception, complex and elaborate in its execution. This was the D-Day deception, the campaign to mislead the Germans into thinking that the Allied invasion of France would take place in the Pas de Calais area. The deception continued even after the landings in Normandy had started; then it was an effort to persuade the Germans that the main attack was still to come, and it would be in the Pas de Calais. It succeeded far better than its perpetrators imagined it could. After the landing, German forces that could have been thrown against the beach-head were held back to meet a second landing further to the North. Three weeks after D-Day, the German High Command still believed that this was not the main thrust.

By early 1944, the British and Americans had a number of means of deception at their disposal, principally double-agents

---

* It is also relevant that for men like Katz and Cockburn, in the desperate political atmosphere of Europe in the 1930s, all political life was warfare, and it did not require an outbreak of shooting in a particular sector to justify lying. Some people have this view at all times. Thus Gordon Liddy, one of the men involved in the Watergate break-in, said of the burglary and the subsequent cover-up, in a television interview: 'It was just basic politics.'

who were known now to be trusted by the Germans, a good deal of experience of dealing with German Military Intelligence, the Abwehr, and an administrative structure that could direct and co-ordinate these. (There actually was in the British Army at one stage a post called 'Controlling Officer, Deception'. He was Lieutenant-Colonel John Bevan.) This made possible the promulgation of a false picture over many separate channels.

The Allied officers controlling the project did not at any point leak a set of false invasion plans to the Germans. They made the Germans work. They let them gather pieces of information that could, with skilful interpretation, add up to the picture they wanted to convey. As one of those involved used to say: 'An item of misinformation that someone has worked out for himself is worth ten that he has been told.'

The deception was built into the planning of D-Day from the start. Among the specific moves were these:

The operational headquarters of Allied forces preparing for the invasion was near Portsmouth. But the radio signals all went along radio lines to a communications centre in Kent, further to the East, and were transmitted from there. Other radio signallers kept up a steady hub-bub of signals traffic in South-eastern England, as if large forces were stationed there, in the part of England nearest the Pas de Calais.

Dummy forces were scattered around Kent. There were balsawood gliders visible from the air, inflatable models of tanks, wooden landing crafts, and vehicle tracks leading into forests. (One of those designing and building these models was Major, as he then was, Basil Spence, better known today as the architect of Coventry Cathedral.)

A Belgian businessman who served as a double-agent reported to the Germans that Allied officials were drawing on his extensive knowledge of the commercial and economic circumstances of the area around Calais to make some kind of survey.

Another double-agent reported over a period of time that he had made friends with a railway clerk who told him about the D-Day plans to move American divisions by train to Dover and other ports in South-eastern England.

In the months immediately before D-Day, there was built up an exaggerated idea of the number of American divisions that were gathering in Britain for the invasion. Different agents sent in reports so that a picture was created of a non-existent American force, the First U.S. Army Group, FUSAG. This, supposedly, was under the command of General George S. Patton. Patton was not due to go to Normandy for three weeks after D-Day, so the impression could be conveyed that he was in command of another army group that was being held in reserve.

Allied bombers raided the Pas de Calais area repeatedly in the weeks before D-Day, ostensibly to soften it up.

On June, 6th when the invasion was still in its first day, a double-agent in Britain who claimed to have a good friend in the Ministry of Information reported that he had visited his friend's office and had seen a directive to be sent to all departments. This said there must be no reference to the possibility of any further assaults, and the decisive importance of the present landings must be emphasised. The agent said there was consternation at the Ministry because General Eisenhower himself had violated this directive in his D-Day message to the French people, and cited the words: 'Frenchmen! A premature uprising may prevent you from being of maximum help to your country at the critical hour. Be patient. Prepare!'

This agent, whose code name was Garbo, also reported two days later that he had received reports that Allied landing craft were still seen moored in the river in South-eastern England.

The Germans swallowed it all. The German Army's Intelligence assessment of the situation immediately after D-Day stated: 'The forces employed comprise only a relatively small portion of the troops available. Of the sixty large formations in Southern Britain, only ten to twelve divisions, including airborne troops, appear to be participating so far. . . . The indications are that further large-scale operations are planned.' It went on to suggest that the Pas de Calais was the likely area of the next attack. This was precisely what the Allied deception officers wanted them to think. Actually, of these 60 large formations, 25 of them did not exist.

In the ensuing days, two Panzer divisions that were 100 miles away were held back on the other side of the River Seine, ready to counter-attack an invasion of the Pas de Calais. Even three weeks after D-Day, when General Rommel had now decided that he needed to throw everything he had into the battle for

Normandy, he was overruled by his superiors, and forces were held in reserve for the second invasion that never came.

The network of double-agents in Britain, the principal channel of misinformation to the Germans, was a phenomenon of the Second World War. Some of them were agents, either Britons or foreigners, who were captured and 'turned', in Intelligence parlance, in other words induced to work for the other side. Two were Britons who had gone to work for Germany with this in mind. Two were citizens of German-occupied countries who had agreed to spy for Germany only as a means of getting to England. British Intelligence believed that there must surely be other German spies in Britain they did not know about, but after the war, studying captured German Intelligence files, they decided that they had actually controlled every German spy in Britain.

In order to co-ordinate the misinformation, a committee was set up with representatives from all the services and government departments. It had twenty members and so was called the 'Twenty Committee'. Then someone saw it written in Roman numerals as the XX Committee, and decided that double-cross committee was an appropriate name, and this is what it became. Its official history was written immediately after the war by the man principally concerned with the double-agents, Sir John Masterman, for internal circulation among government departments. In 1972 it was published, under the title *The Double Cross System*.

It contains some excellent lessons on the art of deception. One of them has been seen in many other episodes: the victim, once he is convinced, is likely to become the principal ally of the deceiver, defending the falsehood. An Abwehr officer gained success in his career by creating and manipulating reliable spies. Hence, once he had a spy, he was likely to defend his reliability against doubts.

A lesson Sir John says they learned in controlling double-agents was an extension of this same one. It was never to assume that a deception had been discovered, and do anything irrevocable. Often they would have an agent feed information that some military operation was about to take place; they would assume that when it did not take place, the Germans would know they had been fooled and would not trust the agent any longer. But they found the Abwehr was more likely to make excuses for the agent, or say the information was correct but not his conclusions, or to assume that *he* had been fooled.

Of course, not all the deceiving in the Second World War was done by the Allies. The other side had some successes. One of the longest-lived, and most tragic for the victims, was the one called Operation North Pole, in German-occupied Holland. This was almost a counterpart of the double-cross operation, though the Germans did not turn agents around.

'Operation North Pole' was the code name given by Major H. J. Giskes, who ran it, and it arose out of a subordinate's joke before it really got going. Giskes was in charge of German counter-intelligence in Holland in 1941. His radio detection unit reported that no secret radio transmitters were operating in Holland. So when one of his n.c.o.s, Sergeant Willy Kupp, came to him with a report from an informant saying that one was being operated, Giskes threw the report back at him with the pencilled note 'Go to the North Pole with your stories!' Kupp quietly gathered more information, and then sent him a second report saying that the transmitter was being manned by two agents of the British SOE–Special Operations Executive, which ran underground activities in occupied Europe. He headed the report: 'Concerning Operation North Pole'. Giskes grinned, and allowed the joke against himself to stand.

The radio detection unit was wrong and Kupp was right. Two Dutchmen had been parachuted in from Britain to set up a resistance network, and the radio operator, Hubert Lauwers, was communicating with London from an apartment in the Hague. Giskes tracked them down, surrounded the apartment house, burst in and arrested the two at gun-point. The owner of the apartment threw the radio out of the window. By a fluke, it landed on two clothes lines and bobbed up and down there, for Giskes to see, undamaged. This fluke made Operation North Pole possible.

Giskes had the two SOE agents sent to Haaren Prison and held there. After eight days he went to see Lauwers in his prison cell, offered him a cigarette, inquired solicitously about his treatment, and then made his pitch. He said he would like Lauwers to send back to London over his radio the message he had on him when he was arrested. This gave the location of a German warship, and could hardly be of help to the Germans. He said he respected Lauwers and his companion as brave soldiers, and would like to be able to save them from execution as spies by saying that they had co-operated with their captors. Lauwers agreed, and sent the message. Then SOE in London sent a message saying that they proposed to parachute in another agent, and asking him to arrange a drop point. Giskes asked him to do so. This time, Lauwers refused. Giskes tried to persuade him that he should not fall in with British plans to involve the whole Dutch civilian population in a struggle, which would bring down reprisals. He also promised him that if he co-operated, no Dutch agents who were captured through this operation would be executed.

Eventually, Lauwers agreed. But he was only pretending to co-operate. In sending the message, he left out the agreed security checks. This was a mistake on every sixteenth letter. It had been arranged before he left London that if a message did *not* contain these mistakes, it was to be considered that it was sent under duress, or by someone else. Lauwers thought SOE would recognise the position. But they did not. Lauwers was horrified when another agent was parachuted to the waiting Germans, and joined him in prison.

Lauwers tried to insert a warning in the next message he sent; the Germans caught it in time, and sent him back to prison. Giskes sent a message in Lauwers' name saying he was handing over his radio set to another member of the resistance so that he could carry on more active work.

The SOE dropped in another agent, Hendrik Jordaan, with his own radio set, and Giskes tricked him into telling him his security checks.

Giskes was now operating two radio sets, one containing all the right security checks. Sending messages over these, he gave SOE a picture of an active resistance organisation, and arranged for more Dutch SOE men to be dropped in. The pattern was the same. The parachutist would be greeted by Dutchmen working for the Germans but posing as members of the resistance. They would chat with him, to pick what crumbs of information they could, then German soldiers hiding nearby would pounce and arrest him. Then messages would be sent back to SOE reporting his safe arrival.

This was a pure communications hoax. Professor Jones knew all about this before he wrote his paper on the theory of practical joking. There was only one channel of communication, or rather several channels that were all the same, because some of the SOE agents parachuted in brought their own radio sets which Giskes put to use. At the height of the operation, Giskes was running fourteen sets, which SOE believed were fourteen separate links with an underground resistance spanning Holland.

R.A.F. planes parachuted arms, weapons and explosives to the phantom resistance force. They made 150 airdrops altogether. In July 1942, SOE asked the resistance to destroy a radar station at Kootwijk, on the Dutch coast. Giskes, a regular army officer, sat down and worked out this attack as a tactical exercise, placing himself in the role of the leader of the attacking force. Then he sent back an account of the attack as he would have carried it out. He said it was led by Thijs Taconis, one of the Dutchmen he had captured on landing. He said the attackers had stumbled into a minefield, and had been driven off after an exchange of gunfire with German guards; three men were killed, but Taconis got away. London sent a message regretting the loss of life, and saying that Taconis would receive a medal.

On another occasion, Giskes decided to provide some supporting evidence for the picture that was being fed along the radio links. He loaded an old Rhine barge with some useless parts of airplanes, covered the lot with tarpaulin, so that it looked like a bargeload of German planes, then had it blown up as it travelled through Rotterdam, apparently by a bomb planted by saboteurs. A large crowd saw the barge sink. He was sure that SOE would receive some report of this.

He also made other uses of his North Pole deception. He would arrange a time and place for an air drop, and then pass on the information to the Luftwaffe, so that German fighters would be waiting when the British transport plane arrived. Twelve R.A.F. planes were shot down in this way.

The deception was blown through Dutch bravery and perseverance. Two of the men who had been parachuted into SOE to follow the usual route to Haaren Prison, Pieter Dourlein, a burly ex-sailor, and Jan Ubbink, escaped from prison, and made an adventurous journey across German-occupied Europe to Switzerland. There, they told their story to the military attache at the Free Dutch Embassy, who expressed his thanks and passed it on to London immediately. The s o e asked them to return to London, so they went underground again and crossed occupied France to Spain, from where they were flown to England. Then, to their astonishment, they were placed under arrest for several weeks. s o e did not know who to believe at this point, and they were taking no chances.

Giskes requested more airdrops, but received no answer. Eventually, he guessed that the deception was over. He also suspected that s o e was sending in men to form a separate network. So he decided to bow out in style. On April 1st, he sent a message over all ten radios that were then operating. It was couched in the phrases of a formal business letter, and addressed to the two heads of the Dutch section of s o e, whose names were supposed to be secret. It also contained a reference to the anticipated Allied invasion of Europe. It read: 'To Messrs Blunt, Bingham & Co., London: We understand that you have been endeavouring for some time to do business in Holland without our assistance. We regret this the more since we have acted for so long as your sole representative in this country, to our mutual satisfaction. Nevertheless, we can assure you that should you be thinking of paying us a visit on the Continent on an extensive scale, we shall give your emissaries the same attention as we have hitherto, and a similarly warm welcome. Hoping to see you.'

Operation North Pole had several sequels. Giskes kept his promise not to execute any of the North Pole agents, so far as he was able. But then Himmler's s s took over control of all the prisoners in Holland. The captured agents were sent to Mathausen concentration camp, where they were all killed in a single afternoon. After the war, a Dutch Parliamentary commission investigated the catastrophe, and concluded that s o e had shown a 'failure to apply even the most elementary security checks'. The British Government would admit only to 'errors of judgment'. s o e had taken into account the fact that the original radio operators were on their first missions, and had been working under stress, and simply assumed that the security checks had been forgotten.

Giskes was brought to Holland after the war to face war crimes charges, but the judge ruled that there was no case to answer.

*   *   *

All these deceptions were between military forces. The 'black radio' operation, that beamed broadcasts from Britain to Germany and German-occupied territory during four years of the Second World War, was total war, aimed at the civilian population as much as the military forces. It is difficult to find anything anywhere that equals it for cunning, subtle, ingenious and savagely effective lying.

It raises all the questions of morality that are raised by total war, and it was this that caused Richard Crossman, when he was engaged in propaganda himself as the director of the Political Warfare Executive, to agonise.

Some hoaxes make you wonder how people were ever induced to believe them. This one makes you wonder how you can ever believe anything.

The term 'black' when applied to propaganda, means that it conceals its source, as opposed to 'white' propaganda, which consisted of Allied messages to the German people.

The black radio pretended at all times to be a German radio station broadcasting to Germans, sometimes a home front station, sometimes a forces station speaking for the ordinary soldier, sailor and airman. The propaganda message was slipped in subtly

An Allied broadcast telling the Germans that the American and British armies were stronger would be received as just another 'Yah, boo, we're better than you!' message. But it is a different matter when a German radio announcer says with approval: 'Gauleiter Jordan created a new slogan at the conference of the Gau Labour Chamber in Magdenberg. "Our enemies may boast," he said, "that they have the largest number of aircraft and tanks, the most numerous labour force and the most money. For us National Socialists, however, it is decisive that we possess the best philosophy!"' The second thoughts that may follow once this message is absorbed are not encouraging.

Or, as a chilling booster to home front morale, an announcer would follow a report on the situation on the Russian front with: 'Some people have their priorities wrong. It doesn't matter that five hundred of our soldiers were killed in the battle, or five thousand. What is important is that we have a victory to present to the Fuehrer on his birthday!'

It specialised in patriotic propaganda that gives rise to treasonous thoughts.

When the battle of the Atlantic was at its height, German submariners based in the French ports heard over the servicemen's radio complaints that inexperienced, glory-hunting U-boat commanders were taking their submarines on foolhardy missions and risking the lives of their crews, just to try to win an Iron Cross for themselves. That must have been something to think about when going into action.

Sometimes, the message was so indirect that even the British authorities began to wonder what side the black radio was on. Sir Stafford Cripps, then a cabinet minister, was horrified when he saw the script of a broadcast which referred to the British war leader as 'that flat-footed bastard of a drunken old Jew Churchill'. He said he wanted the whole operation closed down. 'If that's the only way we can win the war, then I'd rather we didn't win it!' he exclaimed, a gut reaction that he might have modified on reflection.

The guiding hand behind the black radio was Sefton Delmer, a man uniquely qualified for the job by background and temperament. He was a well-known figure on Fleet Street with a good popular journalist's sense of how to grab people's attention. Delmer was born in Germany of British parents, raised partly in Germany, and was totally bilingual, speaking and even writing German as well as English. He had been the Berlin correspondent of the *Daily Express* during the 1930s, and knew personally many of the Nazi leaders. Though as British as John Bull, whom he resembles somewhat in physiognomy and build, he has an unusual ability to empathise with Germans. Indeed, some people who worked in his black radio unit, smarting under his overbearing manner, used to call their boss 'the gauleiter'.

He decided from the beginning that the black radio would be, if anything, more patriotic than the official German radio stations, and more vigorous in its appeals on behalf of the

German war effort. As Delmer explained the philosophy behind it some years afterwards: 'In the propaganda struggle, it was like judo. Instead of struggling against your opponent's force, you use his energy to throw him over your shoulder. We were using the impetus of the Germans' own propaganda.'

He broadcast himself from the beginning, under the name of 'Der Chef', but his other broadcasters and script-writers were all Germans. To ensure authenticity they were, in so far as possible, anti-Nazis recruited from prisoner of war camps, or fairly late emigrants from Nazi Germany. He found that Germans who had been living in England or America for several years were already alienated from the German public and out of touch.

He and his staff monitored conversations among prisoners of war, not just for information, but to pick up the latest slang and the current topics of conversation, and get an idea of the flavour of life in the Third Reich. They read German newspapers assiduously. One of his first instructions to his staff was that it was always to be 'We Germans', never 'You Germans'.

One theme which the radio hammered home constantly was that Nazi officials were corrupt and venal, abusing their position to escape war service and line their pockets. Their targets were not the internationally-known Nazi leaders like Himmler, Goering and Goebbels, but local party officials, the equivalent of a precinct chief or an urban district council leader, who would be identified by name and position.

An idea of the ruthlessness and cynicism with which Delmer set about his task can be gauged from his own explanation of this campaign. 'I made the Nazi Party functionaries the number one target of our attack because in my opinion, the fanatical and dedicated officials of Hitler's organisation were doing an amazingly effective job as the driving force behind the war effort of the German people. I was immensely impressed by the way Goebbels and his underlings, high and low, were succeeding in cheering and goading the Germans to ever greater efforts and ever greater sacrifices. If we could blacken these men in the eyes of the German public as a venal and slothful privilegensia, which demanded everything from the common man but made no sacrifices itself, then we would have struck a mortal blow at a vital nerve of Germans' war morale. Not only that, we would be giving the ordinary German a splendid excuse for any falling short in his devotion to duty.'*

As well as other kinds of corruption, he denounced Nazi officials for sexual malpractices, because he knew that stories of sex scandal always have a ready audience. He spiced these up with accounts of orgies and depravity, and took a certain satisfaction in getting the details of perversions from a book on the subject by Dr. Magnus Hirschfield, a book which, since the author was a German Jew, was burned by the Nazis.

Much of the output of the black radios was straight news in the approved Nazi jargon, i.e. American and British bombers were 'terror raiders'; the radios also broadcast Hitler's speeches live, relayed through some technical wizardy from the official German radio stations. The music programmes were later to cause Marlene Dietrich some embarrassment and annoyance. They broadcast some songs that she had recorded in German, for the Allied 'white' broadcasts beamed at Germany. After the war, she was accused of having sung over German radio stations. She denied the charge angrily, but some people in Germany went on saying that they had heard her. They did not know, of course, that they had heard her songs over Delmer's pseudo-Nazi stations. Nor did she.

The indirect routes along with the black radio broadcasts backed into their lies were many. For instance, when children in cities under heavy bombing were being sent to evacuation centres in the East, the black radio decided to spread the belief that there was an epidemic of diphtheria in these centres. They praised the work of a medical unit that had brought the deaths from diptheria down to sixty a week.

Sometimes, they would create a rumour by denying it. When German troops were being airlifted to North Africa in 1943 to meet the Anglo-American breakthrough, a servicemen's radio denied rumours that the transport planes were unsafe. 'It is perfectly true,' it admitted, 'that there were some tragic incidents a

---

* From *Black Boomerang* by Sefton Delmer, an engrossing though subjective account of black radio.

To set against Delmer's ruthlessness, it should be recalled that the officially assigned tasks which these Nazi functionaries were carrying out with dedication included hounding down surviving members of racial minorities, and ensuring that treatment of imported slave labourers was suitably 'harsh and pitiless', to quote an official directive.

while ago when planes crashed on taking off, but this was due to a defect that has now been corrected. There is nothing wrong with our planes now. Do not believe anyone who says there is.' Any volunteers for the airlift?

Another technique was to use true information which they had received from either overt or covert sources to build up a false situation.

Thus, one of Delmer's team read in a German Navy newspaper an account of an unfortunate submariner based in Calais. He went to a doctor with a rash on his private parts and the doctor diagnosed syphilis. The sailor became depressed, and hanged himself. Then it was discovered that he did not have syphilis at all. One of the black radio stations, Soldatensender Calais, which purported to be broadcasting from Calais, used this story as the basis of a campaign, supposedly on behalf of sailors, to have a doctor aboard every U-boat, a quite impractical demand.

One of Delmer's own favourites was the one about Dino Alfieri, the Italian ambassador to Berlin. From an Intelligence contact, Delmer got a tip-off that Alfieri was shortly to be transferred, in a routine diplomatic reshuffle. This seemed like an unexciting item of information, but Delmer went to work on it.

His home front station went on the air with a story of the shameful betrayal of a decent ss officer. Returning home unexpectedly from the Russian front, this officer found his wife in bed with the Italian ambassador. He was about to shoot him dead, but 'this craven Macaroni', the radio said, begged for his life, and even had the nerve to plead diplomatic immunity! The officer beat him up, bundled him into a taxi, and sent him off to the Italian Embassy. The radio repeated the story over several days, with some sarcastic comments on the character of 'our gallant Italian allies', until it could at last report that Alfieri was being recalled to Rome. It said this was because of his disgraceful behaviour, although to preserve the façade of good relations with Italy, this was not being said officially.

Mussolini seems to have believed this particular story. His Foreign Minister, Count Ciano, referred in his diary on July 3rd, 1941, to an incident involving Alfieri which was not specified, and said: 'The affair has amused the Duce, even though he considers the incident quite serious.'

Another use of this technique was in a multi-media black

propaganda campaign, for by this time Delmer had expanded his operation to take in other media as well. This was the Colonel Mölders operation. A German who has written a study of Second World War propaganda, Ortwin Buchbander, says this was the most effective black propaganda campaign of the war. It was certainly one of the nastiest.

Colonel Werner Mölders was a Luftwaffe fighter ace and war hero. He was also a devout Catholic. British Intelligence learned from prisoners of war that he was becoming critical of the anti-religious tendencies of the Nazi regime, and was being investigated on suspicion of having made treasonable statements. Then he was shot down by German anti-aircraft fire over Breslau, and killed. This was undoubtedly a normal wartime accident, but of course the black radio suggested that this brave airman had been murdered on the orders of certain Nazi Party crypto-Bolsheviks.

They then forged a letter supposedly from Colonel Mölders to the Roman Catholic provost of Stettin. This said that more and more of his Luftwaffe comrades were turning away from the 'godless ones' and seeking religion. It contained the words: 'There is nothing more beautiful for a man than to have struggled successfully through all the slime of lies, injustice and perversion in order to find his way to knowledge, to light and to the true faith.' They forged a short introduction to the letter by a Luftwaffe friend of Mölders, made thousands of copies on Luftwaffe stationery, and had these dropped over Germany by the R.A.F. Any German finding one might assume that they had been dropped by Luftwaffe planes. The letter was accepted widely, and some brave priests read it from their pulpits.

Delmer and his team even used astrology for black propaganda purposes. They produced fake copies of a German astrological journal, *Der Zenit*, which were backdated. Thus, one printed in July, 1943, was dated April, and contained forecasts of unfavourable circumstances for U-boats on certain days when, as was known by then, U-boats had actually been sunk. These were circulated in German submarine ports, and were intended to unnerve the U-boat sailors, who would believe that these grim forecasts had been dead on target.

They also included predictions supporting other black propaganda lines, fomenting a split between the ss and the Nazi

Party, for instance. These were produced with the expert help of Louis de Wohl, a Hungarian astrologer, who cast the zodiacs to make these forecasts.

De Wohl worked for the Special Operations Executive in an earlier black operation in 1941, which was directed against the man the British secret service, or a section of it, believed was Hitler's astrologer, Karl Ernst Krafft. A copy of a letter forged in Krafft's hand-writing was leaked to some journalists in America in the expectation that it would reach the German Embassy in Washington (this was before Pearl Harbour). The letter contained speculation, based on astrological data, that Germany might lose the war, and that Hitler might suddenly disappear. Both suggestions were obviously treasonable in Nazi Germany, and it was hoped that this would lose Krafft his influence and possibly his life.

The operation was pointless: the secret service was misinformed about Krafft on several points. Hitler did not follow astrological advice, and did not know Krafft. Krafft, a Swiss with Nazi sympathies living in Germany, did have a certain following in some Nazi Party circles. He had also been used by Goebbels' propaganda department to disseminate anti-British propaganda in the form of astrological predictions. However, when this fake letter was written, he had already been arrested in the panicky purge that followed Rudolf Hess's flight to Britain, and he died en route to a concentration camp.

Most sides employed a certain amount of black propaganda during the war, though none on the British scale. The Germans had a black radio beamed at American audiences from Bremen. It featured two homespun Midwesterners called Ed and Joe, who gave their fellow-countrymen the lowdown on 'that goof Roosevelt and his Jewish war'. They explained the poor quality of its transmission by saying that their transmitter was mounted on a trailer somewhere in the Midwest and was moving around to keep one jump ahead of the FBI. Its broadcasts carried very little conviction.

The Germans also had one broadcasting in Russian, supposedly manned by old Bolsheviks. This managed to call Hitler a fascist swine, but also called Stalin a bloated bureaucrat who had murdered all the decent Communists.

The OSS carried out black propaganda operations in the

Pacific, but these never twisted the knife in quite the same way as Delmer's, either because the men operating it had different temperaments or because the requirements were different. Indeed, one of its black operations was designed to disseminate the truth. This was in Japanese-occupied Thailand. The newspapers there received their news from the official Japanese news agency, Domei, by radio from Tokyo. They were obliged to print all the war communiques. In 1945, the oss set up a radio station in Burma that transmitted on almost exactly the same wavelength as the Domei transmitter. It would send fake Domei reports of the Allied advances in the Pacific that were actually taking place, and these were printed in Bangkok newspapers. At this time, the oss was arming and helping to organise a Thai anti-Japanese guerrilla force, and they wanted to swing around the Thai population to the idea that Japan was the losing side.

oss had a deception section in the Far East, which had its headquarters outside Calcutta. It included a number of Japanese-Americans, and was under the command of Major James R. Withrow, now a lawyer in New York City with the law firm founded by the oss chief, William J. Donovan. One of its activities was a black radio, modelled loosely on the Delmer operation in Britain, which transmitted to Japan from Saipan. It started broadcasting in July, 1945; it only had a month of operation before the war ended, and most of this time it was jammed. It represented itself as the radio voice of a group of dissident farmers, accusing the Japanese military of sacrificing the people in a war effort that was now futile, and misleading Emperor Hirohito. One of the directives for all black operations against Japanese was never to attack the Emperor.

One of the most ingenious and dramatically successful of the oss deception operations was carried out at the front, in Burma. The oss had acquired some official Japanese documents and rubber stamps left behind by retreating Japanese forces. With these, they forged a high command directive ordering a crack Japanese regiment fighting near the Chinese border to pull out of the line immediately. Then, in a carefully co-ordinated action, they gave these documents to a Burmese agent working with the oss behind the lines. They had air force planes strafe a Japanese staff car, killing the occupants. The Burmese planted the fake orders in the car, then told the nearest Japanese soldiers he found about the wrecked car. The orders were retrieved, of course, and the regiment pulled out.

There is an important operational principle to be seen in most black propaganda. This is to avoid, wherever possible, a direct statement of a lie. A direct assertion is a permanent invitation to question the truth or untruth of what is being said. A simple statement like 'German transport planes are unsafe', or 'Family evacuation centres are rife with diphtheria', is easily denied, and a denial will at least weaken the hold of the story on people. But to refute one of the black radio's untruths, one would have to go through a tortuous explanation to even *get* to the part that is untrue.

(It is interesting to note that advertisers tend to follow this principle these days. The advertisements of a generation or two ago contained a statement about the product. Often, it was a simple and a memorable one: 'Ponds makes you lovelier'. 'Guinness is good for you.' 'Lucky Strike means fine tobacco.' If they told a story, the message was similarly straightforward: taking this tonic regularly will give you more energy and transform your life. Nowadays, most advertisements, whether in the form of a poster or a television commercial, do not contain any single statement that can be called true or false, or that you can even put your finger on, but identify the product with a way of life or a set of qualities that seems enviable. Look, just for instance, at the advertisements for Coca Cola, Canadian Club or Marlborough cigarettes.)

Another important principle is to conceal the intention of the propaganda as well as its source. A leaflet dropped over Japan during the Second World War by the U.S. Air Force carried at the top the words in Japanese: 'Warning. This is an enemy publication. The finder is commanded to take this to the nearest police station immediately.' Most of them were taken to police stations, which was what was intended. The propaganda was aimed at the police.

Black propaganda did not begin with the Second World War, though it was raised at this time to a high peak of sophistication. The most notorious example of it dates back to the first years of this century: the *Protocols of the Elders of Zion*, a justification for anti-Jewish violence in Russia and elsewhere, that has been published in Middle Eastern capitals in recent times. It was supposedly the proceedings of the first Zionist Congress in Basle in 1897, with plans to blow up the main cities of Europe and overthrow Christian civilisation, and was forged by a Russian employed by the Czarist political police.

Black propaganda certainly did not end with the Second World War either. It is practised today by the Intelligence services of most major powers, in the Cold War they wage constantly. Here are a few known instances from the 1960s and 70s.

In the Middle East, the CIA translated into Arabic some Russian anti-Moslem tracts dating back to the 1900s, reprinted them under the rubric of the local Soviet Embassy, and had them distributed. In Lima, Peru, the CIA organised a raid on the Cuban Embassy by a supposedly independent group of anti-Castro Cuban exiles, who then produced CIA-forged documents they said they had found there indicating that Cuba was financing subversion in Peru. In Uruguay, when a leftwing 'People's Congress' was held with strong Communist participation, the CIA forged leaflets signed by the Congress organisers calling for an insurrectionary strike, resulting in an anti-Congress backlash. Also in Uruguay, the CIA forged Soviet documents indicating that the Soviet Embassy was trying to subvert student, cultural and labour organisations; this resulted in the expulsion by the Uruguayan Government of four Soviet diplomats, and a celebratory party at the CIA's Uruguayan desk.

In 1968, the KGB forged a letter to the Bombay newspaper *Free Press Journal* which had the Delmer touch; purporting to come from a senior U.S. Navy officer, it assured Indians that no harm could result from the United States stockpiling bacteriological warfare weapons in Thailand and Vietnam. This was carried by newspapers all over the world. In Turkey, the KGB forged letters supposedly exchanged between U.S. Embassy officials and an American spy in the Turkish Justice Department which indicated that the United States was plotting to purge the Turkish Army and undermine the Liberal Party; they were brandished in the Turkish senate. The KGB appear to have a 'disinformation' department.

In Northern Ireland, the British Army forged IRA posters urging a softer line, and other documents designed to cause dissension within the IRA ranks.

Whatever Claude Cockburn says, there are men who are willing to shoot at the enemy, but not to participate in certain kinds of black propaganda. Black propaganda involves a different dimension to a direct act of violence.

For one thing, it is a lie told about an enemy rather than to him. The initial victim is a third party: Arabs, Turks, Indians or us, who are deceived about the world we live in, and induced to act upon false information.

It attacks a person's standing in the eyes of other people, and does not merely frustrate his efforts but alters their direction, so that his impact on the world is changed. The participants in the People's Congress in Uruguay were trying to do something, but it was made to seem as if they were trying to do something else. Colonel Mölders was a man of strong religious feelings. After he died, these were falsified, so that the Werner Mölders who lived on in people's memories was the author of that letter, not the real Werner Mölders, but one manufactured by people in Britain for their own purposes.

A really effective black propaganda lie is different from a straightforward, short-term, tactical lie in the same way that a nuclear explosion which sheds radioactive fallout is different from a high explosive shell: its effects are widespread, undiscriminating, and continue long after the deed itself is done.

Truthfulness as well as truth is damaged. It is surprising how often this point is missed. Recently, a former CIA official wrote a book extolling the CIA's ability to dissemble, to forge black propaganda, and to conceal its traces even from the American Government. In the book, he also made a number of questionable statements about CIA activities and international affairs which he presumably expected the reader to take from him on trust.

Sefton Delmer was furious when he found after the war that some people in Germany were using his black propaganda lies to whitewash sections of the German Army, and even the Nazi Party; it was said that traitors were responsible for many of the war crimes, and even for the defeat. Yet he should have known that once you have started this kind of a lie, you cannot call a halt. Its very effectiveness makes it almost impossible to get the genie back into the bottle.

*   *   *

All these deceptions were carried out by Governmental organisations with large resources at their disposal. Yet one of the most remarkable deceivers of the Second World War, and certainly one of the most engaging, was an individual who worked alone for a lot of the time and had the laugh on the Intelligence services of both sides.

He was a citizen of a neutral country, Spain, and though he is dead now, having died of malaria in West Africa some years after the war, his anonymity is preserved resolutely by his friends and former colleagues. So in telling his story, just to give him a name, we will call him Juan.

Juan's involvement with the Second World War began one afternoon in January 1941. Like many Spaniards in the aftermath of the Civil War, he was at a loose end. He had studied engineering for a while, but at 29, he had no profession. During the Civil War, he had been revolted by the violence of the Left, and, serving in the Republican Army, he deserted to the Franco forces; then he found himself disliking the Nationalist side equally, perhaps because he came from a Basque family.

On this particular afternoon, he walked into the British Embassy in Madrid and offered his services to the British Government as a double-spy; he proposed that he get himself recruited as a spy by the Germans and then feed them false information. He said, truthfully, as it turned out, that he was strongly anti-Nazi. He must have seemed very naïve and quite possibly an *agent provocateur*, and he was given short shrift. He went to the U.S. Embassy and was also sent off.

So he offered his services to the German Embassy saying that he was an admirer of Hitler and wanted to work for his New Order. He proposed that he go to Britain as the representative of a Spanish firm of fruit exporters and spy for Germany. Someone there recognised talent when he saw it, and Juan was taken on.

A German Intelligence officer gave Juan his briefing, and invisible ink and code instructions, and agreed with him on a monthly salary. He said communications would be by way of Lisbon, and he must find a courier to take his messages to Lisbon. The courier would leave them in a bank safe deposit box, where they would be collected by a member of the Abwehr based in Madrid. The courier would also have to collect instructions for Juan from the safe deposit and take them to London. Juan said he would travel by way of Lisbon, since going directly from Spain was very difficult at this time.

He went to Lisbon, and sent a telegram from there to say that he had his visa for Britain and was on his way. Two months later, the Abwehr received Juan's first message in the safe deposit box, saying that he had established himself in London and had found a courier. This was a steward on the BOAC flying boat that travelled regularly between Southampton and Lisbon, who carried his messages past the censor for small payments in the belief that they were simply business letters that he did not want held up, in return for payments. Then he started sending regular reports on the effects of the German bombing and the state of British morale, the two topics on which they had particularly asked for information.

But Juan was not in London. He did not go there. Instead, he went to Cascais, the seaside resort some 15 miles out of Lisbon, a sunnier place in 1941, both literally and metaphorically, than wartime London. There, armed with a tourist guide to Britain, a map, a British railway guide and the daily newspapers, he produced his reports. He took the short train ride into Lisbon at regular intervals to deliver them at the safe deposit box, and collect his salary. The Abwehr officer reading Juan's reports believed that he was seeing a view of Britain, but the view he was getting was manufactured, and much closer to his eyepiece.

Juan appears to have followed two principles in his fictitious reporting. One was simply intelligent guess-work. He would observe from his map and railway guide that a particular stretch of line seemed to be militarily important, and say that it was now guarded by barbed wire and pillboxes. His reports on bomb damage were extrapolations of what he read in the newspapers. Asked about troop movements, he would think up plausible replies. Sir John Masterman writes in *The Double Cross System*: 'Some of his guesses were startlingly near the truth.' The other principle was to tell the Germans what he thought they wanted to hear. So he would report that the British public were demoralised by the bombing and defeatism was rife. When Germany invaded Russia, he said most British people seemed to want to see Bolshevism defeated.

His German spymaster in Madrid was appreciative and

encouraging, so Juan appointed three sub-agents, in Glasgow, Liverpool and Southampton. He asked for, and received, payments for all three. The Germans swallowed it all.

This is all the more surprising since Juan had some wild misconceptions about life in Britain that showed up in his reporting. He was stronger on imagination than homework. After a visit to Liverpool, he described the dockers there as a demoralised, drunken lot who would tell you anything you wanted to know if you bought them a litre of wine in one of Liverpool's many bodegas. His English pseudonym was Smith-Jones. He did not even master the pounds, shillings and pence currency system, so that his expense accounts were sometimes strange.

One can imagine Juan at Cascais, a slim, youthful-looking figure with luminous eyes, as one of his colleagues described him, reading his British newspapers over a mid-morning glass of coffee at one of the sidewalk cafes overlooking the little harbour, before going back to his room to write his report. Did he make friends among the young idlers from Lisbon's better-off families who used to congregate in Cascais? Did he tell them that he was in business privately, perhaps that he used to go into Lisbon to attend meetings? He was an eligible young man. Did he meet families with marriageable daughters? One certainly did not meet marriageable daughters in Portugal without their families. 'And tell me, Senhor, what is your, er, occupation?'

By late 1941, British Intelligence, intercepting messages passing between Madrid and Berlin, realised that someone they knew nothing about was feeding false information to the Abwehr in Madrid. Then they noted that a report of his about an imaginary convoy was given sufficient credence to send a pack of German submarines on a wild goose chase, and they decided, as Sir John Masterman put it, that this man, whoever he might be, 'was more fitted to be a worthy collaborator than an unconscious competitor'.

They traced the messages to Juan, and got in touch with him through the American Embassy in Madrid, which fortunately, had kept his forwarding address after turning down his services as a spy. They invited him to come to Britain and work for British Intelligence. He might well have refused; after all, he had been rebuffed before, and was leading a comfortable life in Cascais, receiving salaries for himself and his three sub-agents.

But he seemed to like playing the double-spy game, and the idea of being part of a bigger game appealed to him, so he went to England in early 1942.

He worked under the XX Committee as part of the network of double-agents, feeding back the misinformation they wanted. He was the agent code named Garbo. He was no passive instrument, but a valuable and sometimes brilliant addition to the team. He produced some ingenious ideas and would write up his reports in a luxuriant prose.

Once in London and with a firmer grip on life in the wartime capital which he had previously inhabited only in imagination, he produced more inventions and more sources of information. He reported that he was a member of the Brevet Club, which was frequented by Allied officers, and picked up tips there. He had his friend in the Ministry of Information. He knew a secretary in an important Government office, and made her his mistress, an affair he described in lurid detail–he said she was thirtyish, dowdy and passionately responsive. He had expanded his network of sub-agents imaginatively to include pro-Nazi Welsh Nationalists, a Palestinian Arab, and a Gibraltarian working in the canteen at an important army depot.

When the armada for the North African invasion was being assembled in Liverpool in late 1942, it was decided that it would be implausible if Juan's sub-agent in Liverpool did not take note of it, but it was not advisable to tell the Germans about it, so Juan had him suffering from a lingering illness from which he eventually died; the death was reported in the *Liverpool Daily Post*. He sent over some useful and accurate information about the movement of senior military officers which they knew would arrive too late. After this the Germans, as expected, equipped him with a radio transmitter and instructed him on communicating with Madrid radio. As one of the most trusted German agents in Britain, Garbo played a key part in the D-Day deception.

The Abwehr always believed in Juan, and assumed that it was only their interpretation of his information that was faulty. In December 1944, they sent him a message saying that he was being awarded the Iron Cross for his valuable services. He expressed, in return, his profound appreciation, and his gratification at being able to be of service to the Nazi cause. This was just about the time that he received the Medal of the British Empire. He was delighted by the irony.

Sir John Masterman paid tribute to Juan's eloquence, but his last exchange with his Abwehr controller was positively terse, summing up to the point of parody the atmosphere of espionage operations.

In the last weeks of the war, when Allied armies were rolling across Germany and German Intelligence was obviously going out of business, Juan's controller, with commendable concern for the welfare of his agents, sent a radio message asking Juan what he was going to do.

'I'm going away,' replied Juan.

'Where and how?' asked the Abwehr man.

'Clandestinely,' messaged back Juan, and closed down his radio for the last time.

Some Notes on Sources

Most of the episodes told in this book have been checked with several sources, either living or, where the participants are long dead, literary sources. I have left out some good stories that fit into some of the themes because, although they *might* have happened, I can find no firm evidence that they did. Many magazine articles and a few books have been written about hoaxes and frauds which avoid giving names, places and dates, so that one is left wondering whether the ingenious and amazing deceptions recounted actually took place. Or else the same deception—and this is particularly true of practical jokes—is credited to different people in different articles.

Here are the principal sources for the material in this book.

CHAPTER ONE
A Hoaxer For All Seasons

Interviews with Professor R. V. Jones, his family and some of his friends; various articles and monographs by R. V. Jones; *The Second World War* by Winston Churchill. I am grateful to Professor Jones also for pointing out to me the passage in Francis Bacon's writing from which the title of the book is taken.

CHAPTER TWO
Two Jokers

On Horace de Vere Cole, I received generous help from Tristan de Vere Cole, who made available to me many family papers. I also drew on *Beautiful and Beloved: the Life of Mavis Cole*, by Tristan de Vere Cole and Roderick Owen; *The Dreadnought Affair* by Adrian Stephen; an interview about him with Mrs. Madden in a B.B.C. radio programme in 1955; and all the London newspapers for contemporary accounts of the *Dreadnought* hoax in 1912 and its repercussions. (Most articles about Cole published later turn out to be unreliable.)

On Alan Abel: interviews with Abel, American newspaper files, and Abel's own books, particularly *Yours for Decency* and *Confessions of a Hoaxer*.

CHAPTER THREE
Just for Fun

George Edinger himself told me the story of his Emil Busch lecture on psychoanlysis at Oxford; it was originally told in an article in *The Leader* some time in 1952.

The stories of Sothern come from *A Memoir of Edward Askew Sothern* by T. E. Pemberton, published in 1899, and *The Melancholy Tale of Me*, the reminiscences of E. H. Sothern (his son) published in 1916. Graham Greene recalled the founding of the Anglo-Texan Society in *Remembering*, in the *Weekend Telegraph* in 1974, and present officers of the society added to it for me. For Hugh Troy's career, I drew on stories in the *Washington Post* and *New York Herald-Tribune*, particularly articles by Tom Wolfe, and private information.

For the Piltdown man story, I went to *The Times* and other newspapers for the original find in 1912 and the exposure in 1953, and two books, *The Piltdown Fraud* by J. S. Wiener and *The Piltdown Men* by Ronald Millar.

CHAPTER FOUR
Fit To Print: Hoaxing and the Media

Most of these stories were taken directly from the relevant newspapers or broadcasting scripts. The hoax filler items were reprinted in Curtis McDougall's *Hoax*, the improbable but true ones taken from the True Stories column of the magazine *Private Eye*. A full account of Hearst's waywardness with the truth is contained in *Imperial Hearst* by William Swanberg, and *The Career of a Journalist* by William Salisbury. The principal source of the Reichenbach stories is his own autobiography, *Phantom Fame*; others have attested to his exploits.

The story of Rutherford Aris's encounter with *Who's Who In America* was told to me in correspondence by Professor Aris, confirming stories in newspapers and the account by the *Who's Who* editors. The H. L. Mencken article on bathtubs is reprinted and its consequences discussed in Mencken's *Shouts and Murmurs*.

CHAPTER FIVE
Nom de Plume

In most cases of literary fakery, as of journalistic ones, I have gone to the work itself for the material. A general source is *Literary Forgeries* by J. A. Farrar. The main sources for my account of William Ireland's fake Shakespeariana are *The Great Shakespeare Forgery* by Bernard Grebanier, and *This Solemn Mockery* by Thomas Whitehead, his confession, and the text of *Vortigern and Rowena*, which exists only in the 1799 edition.

For Jack Bilbo's invention of a gangster life, I drew on his autobiography and newspaper reports and reviews; for the fantasies of *The Man Who Wouldn't Talk*, on Quentin Reynolds' autobiography, *By Quentin Reynolds*, and the *New York Times*; for Clifford Irving's Howard Hughes literary venture, on his own account, *What Really Happened*, *Fake*, by the three *Sunday Times* authors cited in the text, plus some private information.

The Boris Vian story is told fully in *Dossier Sur L'Affaire 'J'Irai Cracher Sur Vos Tombes'* by Noel Arnaud; I also bumped into Vian during a winter spent mostly on the Left Bank in the 1950s, and heard the story back then from a friend of his, albeit an inaccurate account.

I talked to Mike McGrady for the fake sex-novel story, and drew additionally on his own hilarious account of it, *Stranger Than Naked or How to Write Dirty Books for Fun and Profit*, and also on newspaper files. The Lobsang Rampa story comes from the Rampa books, newspapers, particularly the *Daily Mail*, which first exposed Rampa, and some useful private information.

CHAPTER SIX
Strictly for Money

On the Portuguese money swindle, I went to newspaper files, House of Lords records and received help from an official of the Portuguese Embassy in London, but found nothing of substance not contained in Murray Teigh Bloom's book about it, *The Man Who Stole Portugal*. The facts on the Musica brothers are taken mostly from the files of the *New York Times* and *Herald-Tribune* of 1938–40.

CHAPTER SEVEN
The Mask and the Face: the Hoaxer as Imposter

I cannot remember where I saw the remark attributed to John Barrymore quoted at the head of the chapter, and would be grateful if any reader could tell me. It was not in *Goodnight, Sweet Prince*, the biography of Barrymore by Gene Fowler.

The story of Azov and other double-agents with role-problems is told best in *Three Who Made A Revolution* by Bernard Wolfe.

There are many published accounts of the Tichborne case. I drew principally on *The Tichborne Case* by Lord Maugham, *The Tichborne Affair* by Douglas Woodruff, and *Famous Imposters* by Bram Stoker. For Stanley Weyman's story, I drew on his obituary in the *New York Times*, and the accounts by Alan Hynd, and by Irwin Ross in the *American Mercury* in 1951. Joseph Demara's story has been told most fully by Joseph McCarthy in an article in *Life* magazine, and in a Canadian Broadcasting Corporation television programme. Sources on Grey Owl are *Wilderness Man* by Lovat Dickson, all Grey Owl's own books, newspaper stories both during his hey-day and after his exposure, particularly in the London *Times, Daily Express* and *News Chronicle*, and the *Ottowa Citizen* and *Toronto Star*.

Chapter Eight
Since the Trojan Horse

The Tetuan revolt invention and the exchanges about it are recounted in Claud Cockburn's autobiographical *Crossing the Line*; the episode is also referred to in *The Spanish Civil War* by Hugh Thomas. The principal sources on the D-Day deception and several others are *The Double-Cross System* by Sir John Masterman; *The Counterfeit Spy* by Sefton Delmer, and *The Longest Day* by Cornelius Ryan; I am grateful for information on Second World War deception operations from Col. John Beavan and Dennis Wheatley, both formerly members of the London Controlling Section, and Sir John Masterman, who ran the network of double agents.

On Operation North Pole, research was done for me in Holland in Dutch newspaper files and in the Dutch Parliamentary Commission report on the subject in 1946. I used this material and the book *Operation North Pole* by H. J. Giskes. On British black radio operations, I drew on interviews with Sefton Delmer, Clifton Child and Ellic Howe, all of whom worked in black radio, and on *Black Boomerang* by Delmer and *The Truth Benders* by Ronald Seth. Sources on the oss black operations are interviews with Professor Fred Zuckerman of the University of Texas and James Withrow Jr., both formerly in the oss, and *The OSS* by Harrison Smith. *Psychological Warfare* by Paul Lineberger has useful material on this general subject. For contemporary black propaganda shenanigans, I drew on private information and *The Game of Nations* by Miles Copeland, *Inside the Company: My CIA Diary* by Philip Agee, and *The KGB* by John Barron.

Index